TILLY FLEISCHMANN

TRADITION AND CRAFT
IN PIANO-PLAYING

TILLY FLEISCHMANN-SWERTZ (1882-1967)
MUNICH 1910

TRADITION AND CRAFT
IN
PIANO-PLAYING

BY
TILLY FLEISCHMANN

with the collaboration of

ALOYS FLEISCHMANN

Professor of Music, University College, Cork

Edited by Ruth Fleischmann and John Buckley
Introduced by Patrick Zuk
DVD Musical Examples Played by Gabriela Mayer

To
Sir Arnold Bax

A Carysfort Press Book

Tradition and Craft in Piano-Playing
By Tilly Fleischmann
Edited by Ruth Fleischmann and John Buckley

First published in Ireland in 2014 as a paperback original by

Carysfort Press, 58 Woodfield, Scholarstown Road

Dublin 16, Ireland

ISBN PAPERBACK: 978-1-909325-52-4

Typeset by Ruth Fleischmann and John Buckley
Digital photography by Max Fleischmann

Cover design by Max Fleischmann
Printed and bound by eprint limited
Unit 35
Coolmine Industrial Estate
Dublin 15
Ireland

CONTENTS

ILLUSTRATIONS

Digital photography by Max Fleischmann

Images from the Tilly Fleischmann Papers
Fleischmann Collection, Archives, University College Cork

Ruth Fleischmann
Preface to the 2014 Edition

Tradition and Craft in Piano-Playing is now published for the first time in its original unabridged form, sixty-two years after it was written.

The author, Tilly Fleischmann *née* Swertz, was born in Cork in 1882 to German parents. Her father sent her at the age of nineteen to study at the Royal Academy of Music in Munich with the pianists Bernhard Stavenhagen and Berthold Kellermann, both pupils and close associates of Franz Liszt; she graduated there in 1905. Her years in that great centre of continental culture left an indelible impression, her experiences constituting the foundation for her long career as performer and pedagogue.

It was the composer and folk music collector Herbert Hughes who suggested she ought to write a book documenting what she had learnt in Munich about the Liszt tradition of piano-playing. After Hughes's unexpected death in 1937, she resolved to follow his advice; by 1940 she had started the work, and completed it before the death of Arnold Bax in 1953, to whom the book is dedicated. That year her son began a long and unsuccessful quest for a publisher. Ireland was at that time an impoverished country in which the arts generally and music in particular were deplorably neglected. The Arts Council had only just been founded, with a budget of a mere £10,000 per annum, and there was no prospect of securing funding for such a book. The London literary agent Curtis Brown failed to find a publisher in Britain and the USA, as did Aloys Fleischmann's musician friends and contacts. It was a cause of grief to him and to his mother that the many years of work on the book had been in vain. Shortly before her death in 1967, she remarked sadly to one of her students that perhaps in a hundred years' time somebody might come across the manuscript in a drawer somewhere and might then be able to find a publisher for it.

But partial publication, at least, was to come very much sooner. Four years after Tilly Fleischmann's death, her student Michael O'Neill decided to try again. As before, the publishers to whom the typescript was sent were impressed by the content but dismayed by its size and by the number of costly music illustrations. O'Neill then abridged it, but still to no avail. So in the early 1980s, he began organising a private publication of the edited version entitled *Aspects of the Liszt Tradition*. He wrote to hundreds of people; undertook the music engraving himself and had 350 copies printed in 1986, the centenary of Liszt's death. In 1991 the Wendover music publisher, Kenneth Roberton, reissued the book together with the Theodore Presser Company of Pennsylvania.

A decade later, while doing research for an exhibition in Dachau, the Bavarian town whence the Fleischmanns had come to Cork, the music historian Josef Focht and the director of the District Museum, Ursula Nauderer, discovered the family.[1] *Aspects of the Liszt Tradition* had been presented to the director of the Bavarian State Library in 1986 and included in its exhibition of

---

[1] The exhibition 'Musik in Dachau', held at the town's District Museum, served as a pilot study for Josef Focht's major project, *Bavarian Musicians Lexicon Online* (BMLO) undertaken for the University of Munich in cooperation with the Bavarian State Library. See: http://www.bmlo.lmu.de/

that year *Music in Munich 1890-1918*. In 2009 Josef Focht began negotiations with the Library about the publication of a digital edition of the whole book, provided the family could deliver one, in its Virtual Library of Musicology.

Whereas typing, editing, checking of references and reproduction of images could be looked after by the Fleischmanns (all of us non-musicians), two essentials lay outside our competence: the digitising of the music examples and the playing and recording of these illustrations. While progress in computer technology had by now impacted on the typesetting of music, it remains a field reserved for musicians familiar with the complex software programmes and is slow and tedious work. At a reception in Dublin during the Aloys Fleischmann centenary celebrations of 2010, Fleischmann's friend, the composer John Buckley, most generously offered to typeset the 311 musical examples of the book. Similar generosity was shown by Gabriela Mayer, head of the Department of Keyboard Studies at CIT Cork School of Music, who played and recorded the musical examples. She knew of Tilly Fleischmann before ever setting foot in Ireland, having come across *Aspects of the Liszt Tradition* during her research for her doctoral thesis at the University of Maryland. It so happens that she now occupies the position to which Tilly Fleischmann was appointed in 1919 by the School of Music committee whose members included Terence MacSwiney, Daniel Corkery and Father Christie O'Flynn. Finally, in December 2013, Dan Farrelly of Carysfort Press, Dublin, took up John Buckley's proposal that he produce a print edition of the book, together with a DVD of the video-recordings. St Patrick's College, Drumcondra grant-aided the publication; Gabriela Mayer's department at CIT Cork School of Music funded the DVD.

And so it has come to pass that this year sees a twofold publication of Tilly Fleischmann's book: one in Ireland where she performed for decades and taught hundreds of students, and the second – in a form which she could never have imagined – in that Bavarian city where she studied over a hundred years ago and accumulated the knowledge recorded in the book.

Acknowledgements

The Fleischmann family is greatly obliged to all those who have made the publication of *Tradition and Craft in Piano-Playing* possible. We are deeply grateful to Dr John Buckley for undertaking the major task of digitising and formatting the 311 musical examples of the book, to his colleague Seán Mac Liam for his proof-reading; to Dr Gabriela Mayer for taking on the exacting task of playing and video-recording the music illustrations; Dr Dan Farrelly of Carysfort Press Dublin for publishing the print edition; St Patrick's College Drumcondra for grant-aiding the Carysfort publication, the Department of Keyboard Studies of CIT Cork School of Music for funding the DVD with the recordings of the musical examples. We thank Dr Josef Focht of the Music Department of the University of Munich for the idea of the electronic edition and his support for its realisation, Jürgen Diet of the Bavarian State Library for its publication. We thank the Beethoven Haus, Bonn for help in locating the painting by Wenzel Ulrik Tornøe, 'Beethoven playing to a blind girl', and the Bornholms Kunstmuseum of Denmark for granting permission to reproduce it. We thank Hugh McCarthy of the IT staff of the CIT Cork School of Music for his advice. To Dr Séamas de Barra and Dr Patrick Zuk we extend our thanks for twenty-two years of support in all matters concerning the legacy of the Fleischmann musicians.

John Buckley
Preface to the Musical Examples

The musical examples in this publication are typeset directly from the original manuscript of Tilly Fleischmann and also draw on the published editions to which she referred. Fleischmann's examples are meticulously notated on small pieces of music manuscript paper, which are pasted at intervals into the typescript of the book.

Interestingly, these examples are notated by a number of different hands. Comparison with manuscripts of known provenance reveal the two principal copyists to be Aloys Fleischmann senior and Aloys Fleischmann junior, the author's husband and son respectively. A small number of examples are in another hand, which can be shown to be that of the author herself. Regrettably, no identifiable samples of Tilly Fleischmann's music manuscript exist, but the labelling of some of the music examples is clearly in her handwriting and it can safely be assumed that the music notation in these examples is also by her.

Totalling over three hundred in number, the examples fall into two broad categories. The first and by far the most numerous consists of excerpts drawn from the standard piano repertoire, in particular the works of Beethoven, Chopin and Liszt. The works of contemporaneous composers are also included; amongst them are Bax, Moeran, Khachaturian, and Ó Rónáin, the pseudonym of none other than the author's son Aloys Fleischmann, professor of music at University College Cork and one of the leading composers and cultural figures of the twentieth century in Ireland. The second category of musical examples is comprised of technical exercises devised by the author and suggestions for the interpretation of technical elements such as phrasing, pedalling, fingering, dynamics, articulation and so forth.

Fleischmann's musical examples are unnumbered in her typescript. This causes no great problem as they are always pasted next to the appropriate text which refers to them. In this publication however, all examples are numbered following the author's sequence. Where little or no text exists between musical examples, I have labelled them a, b, c, etc. While Fleischmann's examples are labelled extremely accurately, the labelling is not always entirely consistent; individual movements for example are sometimes referred to by number and at other times simply by tempo indication. All examples are here standardised by movement number.

Though there are occasional references to bar numbers in Fleischmann's text, the musical examples themselves include no such indications. In keeping with contemporary academic conventions, it seemed to me essential that accurate bar numbering should form part of the captions for the musical examples. I am extremely grateful to the author's granddaughter Ruth Fleischmann for her assistance in the laborious task of counting and checking bar numbers, which are now included in the example captions.

Bar numbers are counted according to standard convention i.e. beginning with the first full bar and always including the final bar, even if it consists of just a downbeat. There are however, some exceptions to this general rule, particularly in relation to very short musical examples across two bars. In excerpt 125, Bax *What the Minstrel Told Us* for example, it would make little sense just to give the second downbeat bar. The first bar, while incomplete, constitutes most of the example, and consequently both bar numbers are given.

Tempo indications are generally included in Fleischmann's examples drawn from the repertoire. Where she does not include them, I have taken them from the published sources. Tempo markings in lower case and brackets indicate that the tempo has been established earlier in the passage. Fleischmann included time signatures only where they occur in the original score, but for ease of reading, they are included in all examples in this publication, with the exception of the technical examples of the author. These need neither time signatures nor tempo marks.

It has been a great privilege to work on these musical examples over a period of more than a year. The examples are vital to an understanding of the text; taken together they offer extraordinary insights into the great tradition of piano playing and teaching established by Liszt.

While I never knew Tilly Fleischmann, I consider myself very fortunate to have had her son Aloys Fleischmann as a friend. His warm friendship is fondly remembered by all who knew him, not least myself, who benefited greatly from his wonderful support and encouragement in the early stages of my career. The typesetting of the musical examples in this publication is a small attempt to repay some of that debt to the Fleischmann family.

I am extremely grateful to the College Research Committee, St Patrick's College, Drumcondra, a college of Dublin City University for its generous financial support of this publication. I gratefully acknowledge the help of my colleague Seán Mac Liam in St Patrick's College. Mac Liam was a student of Aloys Fleischmann junior at University College Cork and familiar with the genesis of *Tradition and Craft in Piano-Playing*. His meticulous proofreading of the musical examples and his insightful and practical suggestions have been invaluable. Any remaining errors are entirely mine.

GABRIELA MAYER

PREFACE TO THE RECORDINGS
OF THE MUSICAL EXAMPLES

Tilly Fleischmann's book presents a fascinating insight to the great golden era of Liszt and to his pedagogical tradition handed down through his students. The multiplicity of Tilly's own roles, first as a student of Stavenhagen and Kellermann, and later as a practitioner in this tradition, as performer, teacher and scholar, determines a modern approach and results in a truly unique reference book for pianists and teachers.

This is a living, practical compendium of examples that illustrate stylistic interpretation and pianistic solutions which help to illuminate the musical text and make intelligent choices in interpretation. It is committed to the poetry of music, to sound and image, and ultimately to the magic of music making.

Tilly decided to undertake this project at the suggestion of Herbert Hughes because she realized that this tradition could become lost or forgotten. Her dedication to this project means that we now have access to a record of an oral tradition as close to the primary source as possible.

The book brings together the poetical search for the 'hidden' musical essence behind the notational blueprint, with scholarly documentation of solutions passed down from Liszt to his students. Practical suggestions are supplemented with contextual consideration of a composer's style as well as historical material that had influenced interpretation in the past.

Pedagogically, this book is a treasure trove of advice and an invaluable reference book for pianists. It contains advice ranging from technique development, pedalling and phrasing to the skill of score study. It advocates textual accuracy and identifies common pitfalls in interpretation. Texture, articulation, *rubato* and dynamic shaping are some of the aspects dealt with through specific examples, and extensive chapters are dedicated to individual composers and their works (Beethoven, Schumann, Chopin and Liszt).

The idea of recording musical examples to illustrate the book came from Tilly's granddaughters, Ruth, Anne and Maeve, and together we decided that video rather than audio examples would work best. The examples are intended to bring to life her suggestions, and I have striven to faithfully illustrate the instructions given in the book. I recorded the examples using a video recorder, which had the advantage of high quality built-in microphones, and the slight disadvantage of a fixed lens. This meant that I was somewhat limited in terms of adjusting the visual span, which results in only a partial view of the piano keyboard. The examples were recorded in the CIT Cork School of Music, in a teaching studio, on a Steinway Model B grand piano.

The recording process was very interesting, although at times challenging because of the brevity of the examples, and the lack of surrounding context. Nonetheless, it was a rich learning experience for me, and I hope that it will enhance the usefulness and relevance of this gem of a book, which was a joy to discover. It was a privilege to be involved in this new edition, and I am grateful to Ruth Fleischmann and John Buckley for their enthusiasm and support and for making this recording project a reality.

The CIT Cork School of Music was founded in 1878 as the first municipal school of music to be established in the British Isles. Tilly Fleischmann taught here from 1919-1937, during which time the School began the expansion which eventually led to its becoming the largest music school in the Republic of Ireland. In 1956, the Cork School of Music entered a new purpose-built facility, which it shared for over 50 years with RTÉ, the national broadcaster. In 1993, the Cork School of Music became a constituent college of Cork Regional Technical College, renamed in 1998 as the Cork Institute of Technology. Today the school is known as the CIT Cork School of Music.

The school delivers conservatoire model education to over 3000 students, including specialist third level education in music and drama. At postgraduate level, it offers highly successful MA degrees in performance, conducting, composition and music technology as well as research MA and PhD. In 2007, an award-winning building, designed specifically for the 21st century needs of a music conservatoire was opened, and has become a hive of activity and the cultural heart of the city.

PATRICK ZUK

AN IRISH TREATISE ON THE
LISZTIAN TRADITION OF PIANISM

Tradition and Craft in Piano Playing is a treatise on the Lisztian tradition of piano pedagogy written by the Irish pianist, Tilly Fleischmann, who studied in Germany at the turn of the last century with two eminent students of Liszt, Bernhard Stavenhagen and Berthold Kellermann. In her book, Fleischmann records much fascinating lore imparted to her by her teachers about interpretative traditions deriving from Liszt's own performances, as well as his suggested practice methods for overcoming various technical difficulties. As a consequence, it represents an unusually rich source of information on this important pianistic tradition.

As her surname might suggest, Tilly Fleischmann was of German extraction. Her father, Hans Conrad Swertz, had come to Ireland from Bavaria in 1879 to take up an appointment as choirmaster and organist in Cork, from 1890-1906 at the Cathedral of St Mary and St Anne; from 1883 he was also on the staff of the newly established Cork Municipal School of Music. His daughter Tilly was born in Cork in 1882. She received organ and music theory lessons from her father, playing from about the age of 15 for major church services at the cathedral. We know little about her piano training, but she may have been a pupil of W. H. Hannaford at the School of Music. She evidently displayed considerable promise, because Swertz was prepared to countenance her embarking on a career as a professional pianist. Musical life in Ireland at this period was comparatively restricted, however, and music students with aspirations of this nature had little choice but to go abroad in order to receive training at an appropriately advanced level. In 1901, Tilly's father decided to send her to the Royal Academy of Music in Munich, where she remained until 1905, studying the piano initially with Stavenhagen, later with Kellermann and her second subject, the organ, with Joseph Becht. From her second semester, she was invited to perform at all the Academy's public concerts, in her final year giving a performance of the Schumann *Piano Concerto* under the baton of Felix Mottl and of the Weber *Konzertstück* under the direction of Stavenhagen himself. This led to an invitation to play for the royal family at Nymphenburg Palace.[2]

In 1905, she married a former fellow student at the Academy, Aloys Fleischmann of Dachau, who had studied composition under Joseph Rheinberger and had begun to make a name for himself as a composer in his native Bavaria.[3] The following year, the couple decided to move to Ireland: Tilly's father had resigned from his cathedral post in Cork and her husband was

---

[2] See Aloys Fleischmann (Ed.), *Music in Ireland: A Symposium*, Cork, Oxford 1952, p. 272. See also Josef Focht, 'München leuchtete – Das Münchner Musikleben der Prinzregentenzeit', Ursula K. Nauderer, Ed., *Aloys Georg Fleischmann: Von Bayern nach Irland – Ein Musikerleben zwischen Inspiration und Sehnsucht*, Catalogue for the Fleischmann exhibition, District Museum, Dachau, 2010, pp. 9-22.

[3] See Ursula K. Nauderer, 'Die Dachauer Weihnachtsspiele (1903-1906) und ihr Schöpfer Alois Georg Fleischmann', *Auf Weihnachten zu: Altdachauer Weihnachtszeit*, District Museum Dachau, 2003, pp. 69-86.

successful in applying for the vacant position. Tilly and Aloys Fleischmann both became intensely involved in the musical life of the city. Tilly was much sought after as a teacher and continued to perform as frequently as circumstances in Ireland at the period allowed, giving solo recitals and participating in chamber music. She was also the first Irish pianist to broadcast on the BBC. Her concerts were notable for their enterprising choice of repertoire: apart from giving recitals entirely devoted to the music of Liszt, for example, she was the first pianist to introduce the music of Arnold Bax to Irish audiences and even presented an all-Bax programme in Cork in 1929.[4] Bax was one of several distinguished foreign musicians with whom the Fleischmanns developed a warm friendship and the composer stayed with them annually on his visits to Ireland for about twenty-five years.[5] The Northern Irish composer Herbert Hughes, who is now chiefly remembered for his sensitive Irish folk song arrangements, became a good friend, as did the English composer E. J. Moeran. Tilly Fleischmann tells us in her Foreword to the treatise that the idea of the book originated with Hughes and that he strongly encouraged her to preserve an account of the remarkable training she had received in Munich. She commenced work on the project around 1940 and completed it by about 1950, having weekly editorial sessions with her son during the final year. This substantial manuscript of over 300 pages is now housed with the Fleischmann Papers in the Archives of University College Cork.

Fleischmann had indeed been particularly fortunate in her teachers at the Munich Academy. In the first place, both of them were musicians of a quite exceptional order. Bernhard Stavenhagen was regarded as one of the greatest virtuosi of his generation, combining the highest poetic and imaginative qualities with an incomparable technique. Berthold Kellermann, who had been appointed Professor at the Academy in 1881, had acted as secretary to Wagner and music master to Wagner's children during his youth. He too was a pianist of remarkable gifts, particularly admired for his control of pedalling, a subject on which he wrote a comprehensive treatise. Liszt thought very highly of Kellermann's performances of his compositions, saying 'If you want to know how to play my works go to Kellermann – he understands me'.[6] By the time Fleischmann came to study with him, Kellermann had largely ceased playing in public, but he continued to make appearances as a conductor. He was a tireless propagandist for Liszt's music up to the time of his death in 1926 and was widely considered to be the living embodiment of the Liszt tradition of performance.

Both Stavenhagen and Kellermann had enjoyed an unusually close relationship with Liszt, who clearly held their abilities in especially high regard. As a consequence, both of them were particularly well-placed to transmit authoritative accounts of the great virtuoso's teaching, far more so, in fact, than most of Liszt's other students – a fact which must be borne in mind when we attempt to assess the wider significance of Fleischmann's treatise. As is well known, Liszt taught extensively in later life, incorporating regular, fairly lengthy series of master-classes given in Weimar, Budapest and Rome into the restless routine of what he called his *vie trifurquée*, his trifurcated life, which he spent in incessant travel backwards and forwards between these three

---

[4] See Séamas de Barra, *Aloys Fleischmann*, Dublin 2006, pp. 1-10, and Joseph Cunningham, Ruth Fleischmann, Séamas de Barra, *Aloys Fleischmann (1880-1964) Immigrant Musician in Ireland*, Cork 2010, chapters 2 and 4.

[5] See Tilly Fleischmann, 'Some Reminiscences of Arnold Bax', *British Music Society Newsletter*, June 2000; also on the Arnold Bax website, and on the Aloys Fleischmann website hosted by Cork City Libraries.

[6] Berthold Kellermann, *Erinnerungen: Ein Künstlerleben*, Zürich and Leipzig 1932, pp. 20-21.

cities.[7] These master-classes undoubtedly exerted a profound influence in shaping the musical and technical ideals of a younger generation of performers.[8] Many of the most eminent pianists of the late nineteenth and early twentieth centuries came from all over the world to study with the legendary virtuoso, including Sophie Menter, Moritz Rosenthal, Alexander Siloti, Giovanni Sgambati, Frederic Lamond, Arthur Friedheim, Emil Sauer and Eugen d'Albert, to mention only a few familiar names from what is commonly regarded as a golden age of pianism.[9]

In view of Liszt's central importance as a pedagogue, responsible for transmitting an entire tradition of pianism which he had created virtually single-handed, it is somewhat disappointing to discover that most of the contemporary accounts of Liszt's teaching contain so little specific information about his teaching. A few of the participants at his master-classes, such as Friedheim, Lamond and Siloti wrote memoirs, in which they describe their periods of study with Liszt,[10] but for the most part, the authors largely confine themselves to recounting various colourful anecdotes about the great man and there is little, if any, detailed discussion of what transpired in their lessons. These accounts are interesting up to a point, but they are comparatively uninformative. Furthermore, they are mostly eulogistic and entirely uncritical, and it must be said that a few of them, such as Amy Fay's autobiography *Music-Study in Germany*,[11] lapse into hero-worship of a particularly unfortunate kind.

Perhaps this comparative dearth of detailed information about Liszt's teaching is not as inexplicable as it might initially seem, when one considers how his master-classes were organised and structured. It appears that Liszt preferred to teach his students in groups, in classes which were open to an invited audience, rather than in private. In general, he would make himself available on two afternoons every week for these sessions, which generally lasted for about two hours. In the course of each session, up to six students might have the opportunity to play pieces they had prepared. Naturally, these works were often quite long, sometimes entire concertos or sonatas. Liszt mostly allowed the students to play them through without stopping. Sometimes, if he felt in the mood, he might sit at the piano himself and demonstrate. Otherwise, he confined himself to making a few remarks at the end of the performance, generally, it seems, of an approbatory nature.[12] In view of the comparatively short length of these sessions, there simply would not have been time for him to say a great deal, let alone discuss interpretative or technical points in any detail. Consequently, it is difficult not to form the impression that Liszt's engagement with his students at these master-classes took place on a comparatively superficial level.

This impression is confirmed by a few perceptive eye-witnesses who expressed a certain measure of scepticism about the ultimate value of this aspect of Liszt's teaching activities. Felix

---

[7] See Oliver Hilmes, *Franz Liszt: Biographie eines Superstars*, Munich 2011, p. 282.

[8] See Paul Rehberg, *Liszt: Die Geschichte seines Lebens, Schaffens und Wirkens*, Zürich 1961, pp. 255-6.

[9] Alan Walker provides a full list of Liszt pupils in *Franz Liszt, The Final Years 1861-1886*, London 1997, pp. 249-252.

[10] Arthur Friedheim, *Life and Liszt* in *Remembering Franz Liszt*, New York 1987; Frederic Lamond, *The Memoirs of Frederic Lamond*, Glasgow 1949; Alexander Siloti, 'Meine Erinnerungen an Franz Liszt' in *Zeitschrift für der Internationalen Musikgesellschaft* 12, 1912/1913.

[11] Amy Fay, *Music-Study in Germany*, Chicago 1880.

[12] See Lina Ramann, *Franz Liszt als Künstler und Mensch*, Vol. 2 Section 7, Leipzig 1894, pp. 102-6.

Weingartner, for example, points out that while these master-classes undoubtedly attracted some students of real ability, a significant proportion of the participants were not perhaps quite so deserving of Liszt's attention. Liszt, with characteristic generosity of spirit, never accepted fees from any of his students, preferring to give of his services for nothing.[13] It seems incontestable that this generosity was abused in some cases, as students attempted to exploit their association with Liszt in various ways, whether for the purposes of furthering their own careers or from other unattractive motives.[14] Weingartner and others wondered why Liszt allowed himself to suffer impositions of this kind, continuing to waste his time and dissipate his energies to no profitable end. For the most part, however, Liszt seldom expressed negative criticisms of either his students' playing, or of their behaviour, even when they were amply justified, concealing his feelings beneath his polished courtier's manner, perhaps out of a self-imposed discipline of Franciscan humility.[15]

It is important to emphasise that the relationships of Stavenhagen and Kellermann to Liszt were of a very different order to those that Liszt formed with by far the greater majority of students with whom he came into professional contact. His initial professional relationship with both men deepened with time into a genuine friendship and he seems to have taken a keen interest in their artistic development, no doubt recognising the unusual nature of their talents. Kellermann studied with Liszt at Weimar from 1873 to 1878 and knew Liszt as teacher and friend for sixteen years, working for him as an assistant for a period. He emerges from the pages of his autobiography as a most attractive personality, entirely free of affectation or pretentiousness, whose attachment to the older man was undoubtedly wholly sincere. Stavenhagen's closeness to Liszt is also well attested. He was the last pianist to work consistently under Liszt's guidance and took over his master-class at Weimar after his death.[16]

In the case of both men, Liszt took the unusual step of teaching them privately, rather than offering them tuition at the usual forum of his public master-classes. From Kellermann's autobiography, it seems clear that Liszt took considerable pains over these lessons, offering far more detailed instruction than was his wont. Kellermann, however, does not dwell on this aspect of his relationship with Liszt in his book, and Stavenhagen never wrote anything at all.[17] It seems entirely reasonable to conjecture that Liszt would have sought to impart to these young men some particularly detailed guidance not only on questions of interpretation, but also on questions of pianistic technique, assisting them to achieve something of the extraordinary physical control over the instrument of which he himself was capable. Liszt, of course, was renowned not only for his astonishing dexterity in rapid figurations and facility in chord and octave playing, but also for his remarkable refinement of sound production and subtleties of tone colour.[18] Although in his case these accomplishments were undoubtedly at least in part the result of an exceptionally favourable

---

[13] Felix Weingartner, *Lebenserinnerungen*, Zürich 1929 pp. 221-2, 223-4..

[14] See Emil Sauer, *Meine Welt: Bilder aus dem Geheimfache meiner Kunst und meines Lebens*, Stuttgart 1901, pp. 164-174.

[15] Berthold Kellermann, *Erinnerungen: Ein Künstlerleben*, 1932, pp. 25-27.

[16] Elgin Strub-Ronayne, 'Bernhard Stavenhagen: Pianist, Dirigent, Komponist und letzter Schüler von Franz Liszt' in *Das Orchester*, No. 3, 1987.

[17] Elgin Strub-Ronayne, *Skizze einer Künstlerfamilie in Weimar*, London 1999, p. 28.

[18] See Robert Stockhammer, *Franz Liszt: Im Triumphzug durch Europa*, Vienna 1986, Chapter XIV Klaviersatz und Spieltechnik pp. 149-155.

physical endowment, it is also incontestable that Liszt worked extremely hard as a younger man in order to perfect his natural gifts.[19]

The first section of Fleischmann's account of her studies with Stavenhagen and Kellermann presents us with an unusually detailed account of what Liszt taught his most interested and gifted students about the manner in which he himself had worked on technical challenges. To judge from her treatise, the regime of practice that Stavenhagen imposed on himself and expected from his students was rigorous in the extreme, so much so as to seem dauntingly exacting to the neophyte. The overriding aim of this technical study was to achieve complete control of sound production so that the most complex music could be played with crystalline textural clarity. This tonal control was built up in the early stages through an intense concentration on improving finger technique. Stavenhagen taught his students a set of exercises which had been devised by Liszt with the aim of strengthening the fingers and making them independent of each other, eliminating unwanted sympathetic movement. The basic exercise was what Fleischmann describes as a *Klopfübung*, a German term which one might translate as a tapping or drumming exercise. For this, the student had to place the fingers of the hand on adjacent keys, initially just the white keys, but later in other combinations of white and black notes. Keeping the hand, wrist and arm as relaxed as possible, the student had to raise and drop each finger repeatedly in turn, gradually accelerating the rapidity of attack, but taking care that no finger adjacent to the finger in action should move to the slightest degree. Each finger in both hands was to be exercised in this way. Later, a similar method was to be employed in practising scales, passages in thirds, arpeggios and trills. Stavenhagen also provided her with further series of exercises for the study of octave and chord playing, which aimed to build up dexterity and rapidity in a comparable fashion.

A considerable proportion of Fleischmann's treatise is devoted to describing Stavenhagen's suggestions on how best to approach the study of new works and assimilate their expressive content. Needless to say, Stavenhagen and Kellermann expected that their students would attempt to become rounded musicians, with a thorough knowledge of harmony, counterpoint and form, as well as being well-versed in music history. Stavenhagen advocated a preliminary study of the work during which the student would analyse the piece carefully, determining its overall structure as well as examining local details of harmony and phrase structure to assist in formulating an interpretation. The best methods of fingering complex passages would also be worked out at this stage. Only when these tasks were completed would physical practise commence. Stavenhagen advocated practising extremely slowly at first, at a tempo in which one could proceed fluently and confidently from note to note and chord to chord without the slightest hesitation. The student was to listen with minute attention to the quality of tone produced, ensuring absolute evenness and control of line and voice-leading. Stavenhagen held that this form of disciplined practice was the surest way of learning a work thoroughly and accurately, believing it also to assist the student in memorisation. As the student became more familiar with the music, the speed of execution could be gradually quickened until the desired tempo was attained, but never until the technical challenges had been thoroughly mastered at the previous slower tempi.

---

[19] See Auguste Boissier, *Franz Liszt als Lehrer*, Vienna 1930 (translated from the French edition of 1832) pp. 28, 66 and Lina Ramann, *Franz Liszt als Künstler und Mensch*, Vol. 1 Leipzig 1880, pp. 165-6.

As Fleischmann discovered to her surprise, Stavenhagen employed this systematic working method himself, as thoroughly, if not more so, than any of his students. In one place in her book, she tells us:

> I remember hearing the sound of piano-playing in the Munich home of Stavenhagen one day, and so hard did I find it to believe that the slowly-played scale passages and the long pauses between each successive chord could have been the handiwork of the master himself that I finally entered the room with an apology for disturbing his teaching, at the same time looking around in astonishment for the person of his pupil. "Perhaps you would look under the piano?" said Stavenhagen, smiling. "It seems you do not yet know what practice means; you think one only has to play – is that not so?" [...] But like many other enthusiasts, not yet emancipated from dilettantism, I imagined expression and interpretation to be more important than practise, until the drudgery undergone by Stavenhagen and others taught me what real work means.[20]

The second main section of Tilly Fleischmann's treatise is of much value, being concerned with descriptions of Liszt's interpretative approaches to various works from the standard repertoire as well as his own music, as recorded by Stavenhagen and Kellermann. Some of these discussions are quite extended, recording much interesting lore transmitted to her by her teachers about Liszt's performances of his own works. In some cases, such as in the section on the *Second Ballade* in B minor, she discusses a number of fascinating alterations in which Liszt reorganised the textures of the original for heightened dramatic or colouristic effect and which Kellermann recorded in written form.[21]

Tilly Fleischmann's treatise is a document of considerable historical importance, offering as it does an authoritative account of Liszt's teaching methods and interpretations of piano music as imparted by two of his former students to whom he was particularly close, having taught them regularly over a number of years. It contains much valuable information of a kind that is unavailable elsewhere: none of the reminiscences of Liszt which were published by his students discuss technical matters or the finer points of interpretation in comparable detail.

Unfortunately, Fleischmann was unable to find a publisher for the book during her lifetime. The publishing houses to which it was submitted recognised its uniqueness and quality but – perhaps partly because Liszt's critical stock was rather low at the period – it was regretfully declined on commercial grounds. This was a cause of sadness to Fleischmann in her last years. She did not live to see an extract privately published on a subscription basis in 1986 by her former pupil, Michael O'Neill, with a subsequent edition in 1991 by Roberton Publications in Britain and Theodore Presser in the United States. That the complete work is now being published in Ireland for the first time is a most welcome development.

---

[20] Tilly Fleischmann, *Tradition and Craft in Piano-Playing*, p. 26. Stavenhagen often gave his master classes at home in the Franz-Josef Strasse – see Elgin Strub (Stavenhagen's grandniece), *Skizze einer Künstlerfamilie in Weimar*, London 1999, p. 27.
[21] See Chapter 20: Liszt, pp. 254-9.

BERTHOLD KELLERMANN (1853-1926)

PROFESSOR OF PIANO AT THE ROYAL ACADEMY OF MUSIC, MUNICH 1882-1919

Photograph: Hilsdorf, Munich 1924

TILLY FLEISCHMANN
FOREWORD

As long ago as 1937 Herbert Hughes suggested that I should write a book on the traditions of piano-playing which were current a generation ago, chiefly among the students and disciples of Franz Liszt, and which are now in danger of becoming lost or forgotten. Herbert Hughes himself volunteered to edit the book, but his intention was never realised due to his untimely death in the same year.[22]

In producing this book now I have attempted to record what I learnt in Munich at the start of this century from my teachers Bernhard Stavenhagen and Berthold Kellermann as regards piano-playing in general, and the interpretation of Beethoven, Schumann, Chopin and of Liszt in particular.

During my student days, which came at the close of one of the greatest epochs of artistic and creative activity in Germany, the influence of Liszt was still paramount. Most of the famous pianists then active had been students or associates of Liszt in his later years – Stavenhagen and Kellermann themselves, Sophie Menter, Moritz Rosenthal, Alexander Siloti, Giovanni Sgambati, Alfred Reisenauer, Frederic Lamond, Konrad Ansorge, Arthur Friedheim, Emil Sauer, Eugen d'Albert. Bernhard Stavenhagen, with whom I studied at the Royal Academy of Music in Munich from 1901 to 1904, was as a young man the last pianist to work consistently under Liszt's guidance, in Weimar, Budapest and Rome. Stavenhagen succeeded Liszt at Weimar, in as much as he took over Liszt's *Meisterklasse* on the death of his master, and kept the tradition alive by continuing to teach at Weimar during the summer months of each year. In 1890 he became court pianist at Weimar and in 1895 court conductor. In 1898 he was appointed court conductor at Munich, and in 1901 director of the Royal Academy of Music. As a pianist Stavenhagen was one of those rare phenomena who combine the highest poetic and imaginative qualities with incomparable technique; his performances were for me the most memorable of all those which I heard abroad. As a teacher he was somewhat aloof and incommunicative, but he possessed the ability to impart a sense of style and an understanding of what interpretation really means. His *Meisterklasse* at the Academy consisted of sixteen students of many nationalities, including Miss Grace O'Brien[23] and myself from Ireland.

On Stavenhagen's retirement from the directorship of the Academy in 1904 I studied for a year with his colleague, Berthold Kellermann, who had been professor of piano-playing at the Academy since 1882. In his youth Kellermann had acted as secretary to Wagner and music master

---

[22] Herbert Hughes (1882-1937) was born in Belfast, and studied at the Royal College of Music in London. He was a composer, collector of Irish folk music, one of the founders of the Irish Folk Song Society, music critic to the *Daily Telegraph* for twenty years. He was a friend of W.B. Yeats, of Padraic Colm and Joseph Campbell. In the mid 1930s he took a house in Kerry with his family to study the folk music of the county. It was during that time that Arnold Bax introduced him to the Fleischmanns.

[23] Grace O'Brien was a daughter of the Fenian leader J. F. X. O'Brien; she was music critic of *The Irish Press* for many years, and author of the book *The Golden Age of German Music*.

to his children, and had been a member of the *Parsifalkanzlei*.[24] He studied with Liszt at Weimar from 1873 to 1878, and knew Liszt intimately as master and friend for sixteen years. Liszt thought highly of Kellermann's playing, and often said: 'If you want to know how to play my works, go to Kellermann – he understands me.' By 1904 Kellermann had ceased to be a concert virtuoso, but as a teacher he had more humanity and deeper psychological insight than Stavenhagen, together with a far greater capacity for imparting detailed instruction. In 1910 he told me that he intended re-editing Liszt's piano works, but never seems to have done so. As a conductor and as a propagandist for Liszt's works, however, Kellermann was active up to his death in 1926, and was frequently acclaimed as the living embodiment of the Liszt tradition. His *Memoirs*[25] give an interesting picture of Liszt's personality, but little about his music or its interpretation.

In stressing the extent of Liszt's influence and the indebtedness to Liszt of the pianists and teachers of a generation ago, the question arises as to what the Liszt tradition has to do with piano-playing today. First of all, in matters of technique Liszt did for piano-playing what Paganini had done for violin-playing, with the difference that Liszt, to a far greater extent than Paganini, used technical virtuosity as a means to an end, namely, the enrichment of the means of expression. It is often said that there could be no Liszt method of piano-playing since he actually never taught technique. This may be partly true, but he frequently gave technical hints to his pupils and from his playing for them they were able to deduce much valuable information. Kellermann's mastery of pedalling, for instance, on which subject he wrote a comprehensive treatise, was largely derived from the practice of his master. Both Kellermann and Stavenhagen were in an altogether different category from the 'one-day' pupils who cashed in so lamentably in later years on Liszt's name, for both lived for years on intimate terms with him and had detailed information as to how he practised and worked. The methods of a pianist who was probably the greatest virtuoso of all time could not be without significance, even after the lapse of so many years.

But apart from questions of technique, it is in the field of interpretation that Liszt's influence can still be of value. Even Liszt's enemies had to acknowledge his powers as an interpreter of contemporary (i.e. romantic) as well as of classical music. Wagner said of Liszt's interpretation of the Beethoven Sonatas Op. 106 ('Hammerclavier') and Op. 111 that those who had not heard him play these sonatas among a circle of friends could never hope to know their real meaning. His was not a reproduction; it was a re-creation. Wagner's opinion is borne out by Berlioz, who wrote of a performance Liszt gave of the Sonata Op. 106 that if the composer could have heard it in his grave, a thrill of joy and pride would have come over him – it was the ideal execution of a work which had been regarded as unplayable.

Again, Schumann said that Liszt played Chopin incomparably, with the deepest sympathy, and that outside Chopin himself he knew of no one who played with such magical tenderness. Through his friendship with Chopin Liszt must have secured an insight into the Polish composer's mind and music which was denied to most of the other famous pianists of the day. On one occasion Chopin expressed the wish that he could steal from Liszt his way of playing his own *Études*. At the end of his book on Chopin Liszt says that as a frequent interpreter of Chopin's

---

[24] Literally: The *Parsifal* office; the group of friends and pupils who assisted Wagner in preparing scores and parts for the performance of his opera, *Parsifal*.

[25] Berthold Kellermann, *Erinnerungen: Ein Künstlerleben*, Eds. Sebastian Hausmann and Hellmut Kellermann (Zürich and Leipzig 1932).

works he was favoured by Chopin himself, that more often than others he had heard the principles of his methods from Chopin's lips, and that Chopin had identified Liszt with his own views on art as they had come to life in his works, more or less in the relationship of author to translator.

The denigration and the defence of Liszt as artist, composer and as man has given rise to a literature in itself. As a typical example of the misrepresentation to which he has been subjected one might quote the statement frequently made that Liszt himself said he always played for the gallery. This is merely a perversion of a statement ascribed to Liszt, for Kellermann often told us, if our *pianissimo* tone was too thin and feeble and lacked carrying power, that Liszt on such occasions used to say: 'The man in the gallery must have something for his sixpence too.' It was from such remarks that we derived a knowledge of Liszt, not as a spectacular virtuoso but as an artist and craftsman.

In the pages which follow I have tried to incorporate some of this tradition, though it has not always been feasible to distinguish between opinions and precepts derived from my own experience and those derived from my Munich masters. Above all, I have tried to revive some of the lore associated with a number of well-known works, especially those of Schumann, Chopin and Liszt. Even where this has not been authenticated, or is not capable of being authenticated, it may help to give the works perspective and to stimulate the pianist's imagination.

Today the pendulum has swung in the opposite direction, in avoidance of the danger of a false pictorial basis being given to music which is intended to be abstract and absolute. One must, however, guard against proceeding from one extreme to the other – from an insistence that a certain work means such-and-such, to an insistence that it means nothing in particular.

Obviously a piece of music can mean many and different things to different people within certain limits, limits which are prescribed by the general mood and structure of the piece. For instance when Czerny relates that the theme of the Finale of Beethoven's D minor Sonata, Op. 31 was prompted by seeing a horseman gallop past his window, whether the story be true or not it is clear that it could have no direct bearing on the interpretation of this graceful theme and of the movement as a whole. But if the source of the composer's inspiration happens to be known beyond reasonable doubt, or if his work is traditionally interpreted in terms of a certain subject, no ill results can possibly ensue provided it be understood that the player or listener is free to accept or reject whatever in this interpretation seems natural or unnatural to his intuition. That such-and-such an interpretation has been accredited can be a matter of factual information which should be at least of interest and which might on occasion greatly stimulate the player's or listener's imagination. Just as in the interpretation of abstract or non-representational painting one man's guess may be as good as another, but a hint from the artist himself will go a long way, so too in music. If Beethoven had carried out his intention of writing a commentary for a complete edition of his works to explain the imagery which lay behind his music, it can scarcely be denied that such a commentary would have been of absorbing interest. It might not always have been decisive as a guide, for composers may be fallible or even misleading with regard to their own works. But one might expect that much of it would have been useful to the executant in deciding broad principles of interpretation. The artist is usually chary of expressing his ideas in terms of concrete imagery, since the written word is so inadequate for this purpose; again, many or even most composers are not motivated in their musical thinking by any concrete images whatever. But a stray remark of a composer to a pupil, a hint transmitted through a generation of pianists can sometime suggest a new line of approach and new features of interpretation even in the case of well-known works.

This book has been written in the hope that some such hints or clues scattered throughout its pages may help the pianist on his way.

TECHNIQUE AND PRACTICE

CHAPTER ONE
TECHNICAL EXERCISES

It seems strange that after some two centuries of piano-playing pianists should still dispute questions of technique, tone and colour, still indulge in altercations regarding percussive and non-percussive touch, rigidity and relaxation, whole-arm and forearm action. Treatises are written on the anatomical and physiological processes involved in piano-playing, and the deductions are used to propound new technical methods, often with the expressed or implied opinion that preceding generations of pianists followed false paths. It would indeed be foolish to decry investigations into the scientific basis of technique, or to suppose that the advances made in anatomy or physiology should not be availed of and applied in such investigations. Yet even if the latter should occasionally help to correct an erroneous idea, the main results will be analytical rather than constructive. The technique of any of the great pianists of yesterday or to-day such as Busoni, Petri or Gieseking has not been based on the conscious application of anatomical or physiological principles, and it seems unlikely that the application of these sciences to piano technique will produce a generation of pianists of superior calibre to those who never heard of muscle viscosity or rotary relaxation. It is generally admitted that the mere technical achievements of Franz Liszt are still unsurpassed, a phenomenon which would scarcely be possible if the mechanics of piano-playing had made any remarkable advances within the past sixty years.

The first section of this book, then, does not touch on the mechanical foundations of piano technique, but aims at giving a practical course based chiefly on the Liszt style of piano-playing, on the assumption that the technical practice of the greatest masters will not appreciably vary in essentials from one generation to another. It is true that in his piano classes Liszt did not insist on a specific type of technical foundation, and for the simple reason that his students were all advanced performers, many of them artists of European fame. He concentrated on interpretation, but always illustrated how he achieved this or that effect. His octave playing was unique, and so too was his tone and colour largely owing to the remarkable way in which he used the two pedals.

The main technical studies and devices practised by Liszt and transmitted orally to their pupils by Stavenhagen and Kellermann will now be dealt with, each under its own heading.

KLOPFÜBUNG (DRUMMING EXERCISE)

(N.B. Throughout this book, the five fingers will be termed thumb, second, third, fourth and fifth fingers respectively, to bring the terminology into line with the numerals of continental fingering.)

The *Klopfübung* is a foundation-exercise which has become a tradition among some of Liszt's pupils. It is the best possible exercise for strengthening the fingers and making them independent of one another.

The thumb of the right-hand, slightly curved, and the fingers, well curved so that they lie vertically, are placed on the edges of the notes C, D, E, F and G, without depressing the keys. The knuckles must be kept in a horizontal line, not sloping towards the little finger. The wrist must be fully relaxed, and the hand, wrist-joint and forearm should roughly form a straight line, neither sagging nor mounting at the wrist-joint.

The thumb is then raised about one and a half inches above the keyboard and allowed to fall quickly on C, with just enough force to depress the key. This process is repeated, a slow three, then two, then one being successively counted between each repetition, followed by a gradual *accelerando* to maximum speed. According as the repetitions become quicker, the height to which the thumb is raised becomes less, until at last it scarcely loses contact with the keys at all. At the same time the action must be only thumb-action, and must not involve movement of the wrist or arm. Each successive finger is then exercised in this way, and the same procedure followed for the left hand. Above all, care must be taken that no finger adjacent to the finger in action moves in the slightest degree. If the knuckles of the fourth and fifth fingers tend to slope downwards they should be raised by placing the second (index) finger of the other hand under the knuckle of the fifth finger. Such support should continue to be given until both knuckles are capable of remaining in line with the others.

Sometimes the beginner's fingers are inclined to give at the joints. To counteract this tendency they should be curved to a somewhat greater extent than would normally be necessary, so that they will always strike the keys with the firmness of a hammer.

Later, when the fingers have become strong and more independent of one another, the *Klopfübung* may be practised in thirds in the same way, on C and E, D and F, E and G.

SCALES

Scales should at first be practised with each hand separately, and in slow practice the same procedure should be adopted as in the case of the *Klopfübung* i.e. each finger in turn should be raised above the keyboard and then dropped, the height diminishing as the tempo quickens. In slow practice it is most important that the thumb, when out of action, be immediately swivelled under the fingers in order to be in readiness for its next position, without any movement, rotary or otherwise, of the wrist or arm. Similarly, when a change of position is necessary after the thumb has been placed, the next finger to come into action should move into position as swiftly as possible while the thumb is depressing the key. For instance in the scale of D major, immediately the thumb has released D, and while the second finger is depressing E, the thumb should be swivelled underneath and placed in readiness on G. Again after the third finger has released F sharp, and while the thumb is depressing G, the second finger should be swiftly moved into position on A. This type of preparation of thumb and fingers ensures an even motion, and the avoidance of any jerking or unnecessary wrist or arm movement.

While the scale is being played the hand must be kept perfectly still and the wrist relaxed, the fingers doing all the work. Stavenhagen was wont to place a sixpenny piece on the back of each of his hands when playing scales, to show how even the action should be. Even in the quickest tempo the coins never fell off. When his pupils attempted to do likewise the coins almost invariably fell and rolled under the piano, amidst general amusement. 'No churning!' he would say, and indeed when he played scales the notes rippled along under an effortless and apparently motionless hand.

It is interesting to note that Liszt in his essay on John Field[26] relates how Field was accustomed to practice technical exercises for a few hours daily, even in his old age, with a large coin on the back of his hand to ensure evenness of execution. Liszt adds that this in itself will indicate the quietness which pervaded his style of playing.

Liszt's contemporary, Kalkbrenner, actually invented a *guide-mains*, a bar of wood placed parallel to the keyboard on which the forearm rested just above the wrist, to ensure that the technique was based on finger action only. Even if such methods seem far-fetched and extreme, they are not more so than the methods of those who prescribe rotary movement in the playing of scales, with exaggerated contortions of wrist and elbow. It seems pointless to avail of arm and wrist movements when the main purpose of scales is to strengthen and develop the fingers. Adopted in scales, which lay the foundations of one's technique, such movements lead to a cumbersome and unsightly style of playing.

When a scale has been practised with each hand separately, beginning in the slowest tempo and quickening to *presto* (see section on Practice, p. 21) it should then be played with both hands together, an octave apart and later a third or sixth apart, beginning *moderato*, as slow practice is unnecessary at this stage. Scales should be played in similar and contrary motion, *staccato* (see pp. 12-13) as well as *legato*, in *piano* and in *forte*. In *forte* playing, the wrists will naturally be somewhat rigid, as a result of the use of pressure from the whole arm which now becomes necessary. Accentuation in groups of three or four notes is to be recommended as an occasional study, but the exclusive use of such rhythmic grouping, such as used to be prescribed in the examination syllabuses of some colleges of music, tends to impair the ability to execute scales with that evenness and smoothness which should always be kept in view as the main objective.

An excellent study must also be mentioned which may be regarded as the final test of scale-playing, namely, to use the five fingers successively throughout the course of a scale in two or three octaves, whether major or minor, beginning with the thumb and allowing the fingering to take its course mechanically in the order 1, 2, 3, 4, 5, 1, etc. This may prove an excruciating exercise, but the effort of overcoming the awkward finger-manipulations involved will be amply repaid.

In conclusion it may be mentioned that some teachers advise the abolition of scales and arpeggios. This is a profound mistake. Scale-playing is the best mode of achieving finger control, velocity of movement and melodic *legato*. Perhaps the following story will be a consolation to the

---

[26] Franz Liszt, *Aus den Annalen des Fortschritts*, ed. Lina Ramann (Leipzig 1882), Vol. 4, p. 266.

young student who finds it difficult to reconcile himself to the practice of scales. On one occasion Edward Martyn[27] told me that he and a friend had made their way to the Villa d'Este outside Rome, where Liszt was staying as a guest of Cardinal Hohenlohe. Having discovered the hour at which Liszt usually practised they crept stealthily to the window of the room in which they knew him to be at work, and eavesdropped outside. To their intense disappointment, stay as long as they could, they heard nothing but scales. And if Liszt still practised scales in his old age, how much more need for the young beginner whose fingers are undeveloped and weak.

SCALES IN THIRDS, EACH HAND SEPARATELY (For advanced players only)

Of all the systems of fingering thirds which have been advocated from time to time, Liszt's system still seems the simplest and the easiest to master. The essential point is to discover the position which will allow the most comfortable transition, in the right hand from the third and fifth fingers upwards to the thumb and third finger, in the left hand from the third finger and thumb upwards to the fifth and third fingers. For instance in the key of D flat major, right hand, it will be found that when the third and fifth fingers are placed on E flat and G flat respectively, the transition to thumb on F and third finger on A flat can be most easily made. Consequently one will commence with the second and fourth fingers, while the third and fifth fingers will not again come into action until they reach a corresponding position in the octave above.

Ex. 1: Scales in thirds

The following table gives the fingering for the first third of each major and minor scale, as well as the placing for third and fifth fingers, in each hand:

Right Hand. Major Keys:-

---

[27] Edward Martyn (1859-1923) was a writer, musician, founder and endower of the Irish Literary Theatre (later Abbey Theatre) together with Yeats and Lady Gregory, founder and endower of the Dublin Pro-Cathedral Palestrina Choir. He was a most generous patron of the arts, an Irish nationalist and first president of the pro-independence party Sinn Féin. He came to Cork on several occasions to hear Fleischmann senior's choir at the Cathedral of St Mary and St Anne.

Ex. 2a: Scales – right hand, major keys

Right Hand. Minor Keys:-

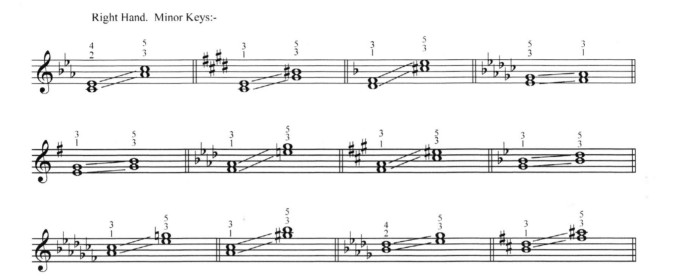

Ex. 2b: Scales – right hand, minor keys

Left Hand. Major Keys:-

Ex. 3a: Scales – left hand, major keys

Left Hand. Minor Keys:-

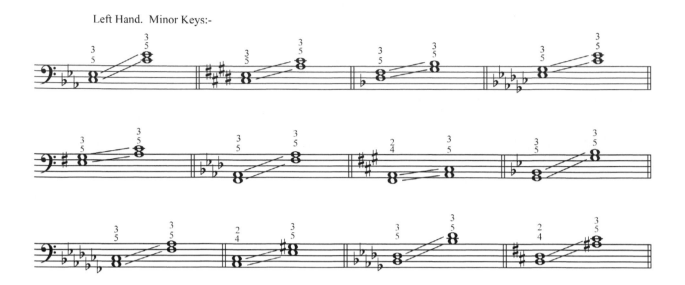

Ex. 3b: Scales – left hand, minor keys

In some cases it is, of course, easier to start in the right hand with thumb and second finger, and next slip to thumb and third finger, e.g.

Ex. 4: Right hand, alternative fingering

Again, when the top of the scale is reached the scheme is not adhered to for the topmost third, if easier fingering can be adopted, e.g.

Right hand

Left hand

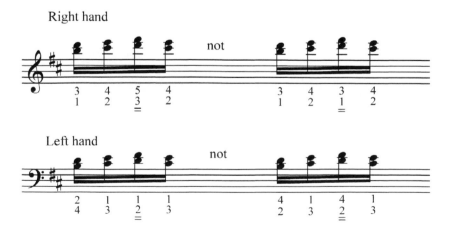

Ex. 5: Topmost third, right hand, left hand

In slow practice two points should be observed, namely (1) when the fingering $\frac{3}{1}$ and $\frac{4}{2}$ is alternated, ascending in the right hand and descending in the left, the thumb and third finger, as soon as they are released, should immediately stretch towards the next notes to be played; and (2) the transition from third and fifth fingers upwards to first and third fingers in the right hand, and the corresponding movement in the left hand, should be made as quickly and evenly as possible, with a minimum of movement.

The above system of fingering is easily memorised, in fact after some practice the fingering will suggest itself automatically, and brilliant passages in thirds such as frequently occur in the piano music of Chopin and Liszt can be executed without undue difficulty.

ARPEGGIOS

In the slow practice of arpeggios, as of scales, anticipatory movement of the thumb is important, and needs careful attention. Thus in the C major arpeggio, while the second finger plays E, the thumb is quickly passed underneath as far as it will stretch, and is held suspended until the third finger depresses G. As soon as G is depressed, the thumb is stretched further forward to reach C, every effort being made to achieve this with a minimum of wrist movement and without any movement whatever of the elbow. Similarly in descending, as soon as the thumb depresses C the third finger must stretch immediately over to G with the same economy of movement. According as the tempo quickens the lateral movement of hand and wrist will actually become less, since in the ascending arpeggio, for instance, the third finger will have released G as soon as the thumb reaches C. In *presto*, the arpeggio playing will be quite effortless if a proper degree of thumb flexibility has been achieved through the stretching process practised in the slower tempos.

Arpeggios, like scales, should be first practised in all tempos with each hand separately, and then with both hands together, beginning *moderato*.

THUMB-STRETCHING EXERCISE

The following exercise is recommended to pianists who find difficulty in thumb-stretching, as prescribed in the foregoing section:

Right hand:

Ex. 6a: Right hand thumb-stretching exercise

Left hand: *etc.*

1 2 1 2 1 2 1 2 1 2 1 2 1 2 1 2

Ex. 6b: Left hand thumb-stretching exercise

With each finger in turn as pivot note the exercise is practised slowly at first, then with a gradual increase in speed.

FINGER-STRETCHING EXERCISE

Students who possess small hands, or webbed fingers, will find the following exercise useful for extending their stretch. Arpeggios in all keys are played upwards as far as the tenth and back again with fingering in the order one to five, first of all in root position, then in the first and finally in the second inversion. In the root position the major stretch takes place between the third and fourth fingers, in the first inversion between the second and third fingers, in the second inversion between the fourth and fifth fingers.

1 2 3 - 4 5 4 3 2 1   1 2 - 3 4 5 4 3 2 1   1 2 3 4 - 5 4 3 2 1

Ex. 7: Finger-stretching exercise

WRIST, ARM AND FINGER *STACCATO*

Staccato scales and arpeggios should be practised with wrist action. Beginning *moderato*, before each note is played the hand is lifted from the wrist so that the fingers rise some inches above the keyboard, and is then dropped again, falling by its own weight. The finger concerned, having lightly touched the key, releases it immediately so that the tone is clipped short. All the fingers remain curved as in scale-playing. As the tempo increases the height to which the hand is raised from the wrist is correspondingly reduced, until in *presto* the wrist movement is barely perceptible.

This type of wrist *staccato* is especially suited for *piano* and *pianissimo* passages. With Leschetizky and some of the earlier pedagogues it was the sole type of *staccato* employed. Liszt, however, advised his pupils to play *staccato* passages as a rule with the whole-arm, since whole-arm action, strange to say, allows a lighter *staccato*, is more accurate and produces a crisper result generally. Whole-arm *staccato* should however be reserved for advanced playing, and it is sufficient to practise it when one meets *staccato* passages in the particular work one is studying. Such passages should first be played *legato*, so as to ensure familiarity with the notes before the *staccato* action is applied. The method of practice is the same as that suggested for wrist *staccato*, except that the hand is raised with the whole arm, from the shoulder, and not from the wrist only.

For *staccato* scale passages, played *presto*, there is a further species of *staccato*, namely finger *staccato*, in which finger action alone is employed. Here the fingers scarcely touch the keys before they are released, or in Hummel's words: 'The fingers are hurried away from the keys, very lightly and in an inward direction' (i.e. with a slight scooping movement).[28]

WRIST OCTAVES

As a technical study, octaves should be practised from the wrist. In slow practice, with thumb and fifth finger outstretched to the necessary extent, the hand should be raised from the wrist as far as it will naturally go, and then dropped quickly on the keys, falling solely by its own weight. The wrist should be allowed to drop somewhat below the level of the keys after each descent, in order to ensure complete relaxation. When the thumb and fifth fingers strike the octave the other fingers barely touch the keys between, and continue to lie lightly on them. The second finger should be curved to greater or lesser extent according as the hand is large or small, and the other fingers should fall into line with it. This curving of the fingers prevents them hitting the keyboard lid when the black keys are involved, and at the same time ensures better hand-balance and control. In the case of a small hand the strain of stretching is so much greater that the fingers can only be curved slightly, if at all.

According as the practice tempo quickens the height to which the hand is raised each time gradually decreases, and the amount of relaxation becomes also proportionately less. In *presto* the fingers barely leave the keys, while the wrist and forearm become taut and firm.

Young students who cannot stretch an octave should practise sixths instead in the same way, until their hands have grown sufficiently to allow the octave stretch.

ARM-OCTAVES

When the student has achieved adequate finger control and loose wrist action the following more advanced method may be adopted for any particular octave passage which occurs in the work he is studying. The whole arm is lifted more than a foot above the keyboard, and is then allowed to drop on the first of the octaves suddenly and loosely, but without any relaxation of the wrist. This process is repeated for each octave of the group, and the whole passage is then played at ever quicker speed, and with a correspondent lessening of the height to which the arm is raised above the keyboard, until finally, the arm movement is reduced to a minimum, remaining so even when maximum tone is being reduced. Facility in this species of octave-playing is essential for the brilliant execution not only of *bravura* octave passages, but also of quick successions of chords. It is the crowning point of the virtuoso's technique.

---

[28] Hummel, Johann Nepomuk, *A Complete Theoretical and Practical Course of Instruction on the Art of Playing the Pianoforte* (London 1828), p. 65.

SKIPPING OCTAVES AND CHORDS

As a further study in octave-playing the following exercise can be recommended, consisting of a series of skips on each degree of the scale from the lower to the adjacent upper octave, e.g.

Ex. 8: Octave playing

This study makes for facility in lateral movement. The method of practice is similar to that described above for octaves with whole-arm action. Later the skip may be extended to two octaves, e.g.

Ex. 9: Skipping in two octaves

By making a pivot of the first octave, useful chromatic variants of this study may be practised as follows:

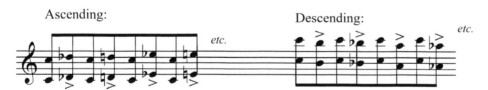

Ex. 10a: Chromatic variant 1

10b: Chromatic variant 2

Skipping chords, similarly involving swift lateral movement, are a prominent feature of modern piano music, and passages such as that for the left hand in the following extract can be singled out and practised in the same manner as skipping octaves:

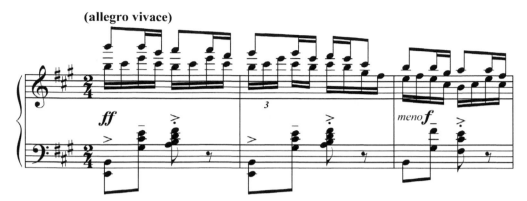

Ex. 11: Moeran *Toccata*, bars 36–38

Apart from their technical value the above studies will help to develop proficiency in sight-reading, since the skipping movement entailed is so rapid that the eye alone cannot ensure accuracy. The player accordingly learns to acquire that unseeing familiarity with the keyboard which is so essential in sight-reading, whereby the eye can follow the score without deviation or interruption.

REPEATED OCTAVES

The following study will help to give the student facility in the playing of repeated octaves. This study should be transposed into all keys:

Ex. 12: Schumann *Toccata*, Op. 7, bars 116–132

The following is a useful rhythmical variant:

Ex. 13: Rhythmical variant

BROKEN OCTAVES

Though it is unnecessary to make a regular study of broken octaves, according as they occur in any particular work which the student happens to be studying, they should be practised as follows. When the upper note of the octave has been played in the right hand, the hand should be turned completely over with the fifth finger held as pivot, until it rests on the keys in reversed position. The hand is then turned backwards again to the normal position, and after the lower note of the octave has been played, a similar turning movement is carried out to the left with the thumb held as pivot, though in the latter case only a slight amount of rotation will be possible, owing to the greater difficulty of flexion. In both cases lateral movement of the elbow must be avoided, so that the rotary movement of the forearm is alone involved. The exercise is at first practised in very slow tempo. As the speed quickens, the rotary movement of the hand and forearm is correspondingly reduced, until in *presto* only the normal amount of movement is involved. But it will be found that both flexibility and evenness of action have been gained from the use of the wide rotary circuit in the slower tempos.

Broken chords such as the following may be practised in similar fashion:

Ex. 14: Liszt *Hungarian Rhapsody No. 2*, bars 219–220

GLISSANDO SCALES AND OCTAVES

Glissando scales, ascending in the right hand, are played with the nail of the third finger held flat on the keys, the hand being turned over so as to lie in line with the keyboard; and descending, with the nail of the thumb curved under the hand, which is now held in normal position. In the case of the left hand the thumb is used in similar fashion for the ascending, the third finger for the descending scale.

For glissando sixths and octaves the thumb of the left hand and the third finger of the right hand are used jointly in the ascending scale, as in the following:

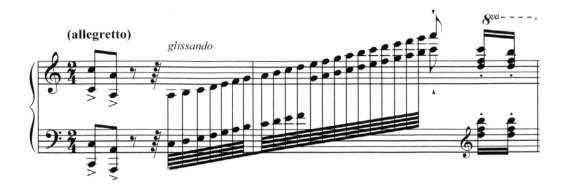

Ex. 15: Liszt *Grandes études de Paganini*, No. 5 in E, bars 70–71

Here the glissando will have a more delicate, rippling effect if taken at a moderate speed.

Sometimes, however, the left hand has to supply the bass at the apex of an octave glissando, in which case the left hand cannot participate in the glissando without omitting a few of the last notes if the leap to the bass is to be taken in time, as in the following example:

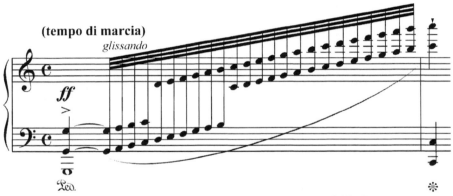

Ex. 16: Weber *Konzertstück* in F minor, Op. 79, bars 260–261

In such cases the glissando must be executed by the right hand alone. The thumb and fifth finger are placed firmly on the first octave and then with rigid arm the hand is moved swiftly up the scale, the fifth finger curving so that its nail is drawn along the keys.

Practice of this type of glissando, however, results in soreness of the thumb and finger concerned. I remember asking Stavenhagen about this in 1903, a few days before a performance at which I was to play the Weber *Konzertstück* under his baton. His advice was to try the glissando once or twice a few days before the performance (on no account even on the day before) and to trust to luck to bring it off. As the event proved, his advice was sound.

TRILLS

Few students know how to practise trills. The best method is to play the trill against a moving bass, and to treat the notes constituting the trill first as quavers, then as semiquavers, then as demisemiquavers and finally to accelerate until as many notes as possible are played against each note of the bass. The fingers should lie quietly on the keys, with wrist relaxed as in the *Klopfübung*:

Ex. 17: Trills

The following exercise in two-hand trills may also be found useful. The thumb and second finger of both hands are used to execute simultaneous trills in contrary motion, the initial notes of which are a fourth apart. Accenting the first notes rather heavily, a gradual *accelerando* is made from *sostenuto* to *prestissimo*, the accentuation becoming less marked according as the tempo becomes faster. The notes are next played in reverse order, and subsequently the other fingers are taken in pairs and similarly exercised. The following examples, which should be played in all keys, will make this clear:

Ex. 18: Two-hand trills

Finally, the trills may be practised in thirds:

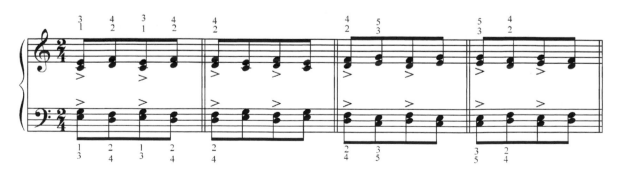

Ex. 19: Trills in thirds

CHAPTER TWO
TOUCH AND TONE

Liszt's tone production was undoubtedly of the non-percussive kind. Neither he nor any of his disciples such as Tausig, Stavenhagen, Kellermann, D'Albert, Sophie Menter, 'hit' the keys in the manner advocated by some of our present-day pedagogues, and yet both he and they had magnificent tone, rich, full and sonorous. Percussive action may indeed be used for special effects – take for example the opening chord of *Isoldens Liebestod* in Liszt's transcription, where the context demands a hardness, even harshness of expression:

Ex. 20: Liszt *Isoldens Liebestod* from Wagner's *Tristan und Isolde*, bars 1–2

But such instances are comparatively rare.

Stavenhagen was wont to quote Liszt as saying that 'no matter how loud the chords, they must always sound rich and beautiful in tone; not noisy and hard. Noise is not music.' Even the loudest tone can be produced without any preliminary lifting of the fingers from the keys, the necessary force being achieved through pressure with the whole arm from the shoulder, exerted accumulatively, while the full weight of the body is used to support and buttress the pressure from the arms. This method of production ensures that the tone, however loud, will always remain musical, for the degree of pressure applied, and consequently the degree of loudness that results, is more surely controlled when the player calculates from the actual position of leverage. Even in the case of notes and chords leaped to, and of *staccato* passages, the pressure only begins to be exerted when the fingers have reached the keys. The player will then remain sensitive to the instrument's every response, and will never force the tone to a degree which is beyond its proper capacity.

Advocates of the percussive touch already mentioned, however, direct that the hands be actually raised above the keys before striking each successive chord in *fortissimo* passages. The resultant tone must then tend to be harsh and strident. In the first place the percussive sound made by the fingers hitting the keys is an unmusical one, which may indeed be used for special effects as already stated, but which becomes both ugly and monotonous when habitually used. In the second place there is less possibility of controlling or, in the last split-second, of checking the degree of force used than when the action is effected through cumulative arm pressure, since in the case of percussive action the energy for the 'hit' is largely generated in the air while the hands are in process of descending. As a result insensitive jarring tone is produced, characteristic of so much present day piano-playing on the part of pianists who do not realise, in Kellermann's words, that tone must be coaxed, not thrashed from the piano.

The position of the left foot is of some importance in the achievement of *fortissimo* tone. Normally the right foot rests on or over the sustaining pedal, while the left foot is placed close to the *una corda* pedal. For *fortissimo* playing some strange alterations of this position are adopted from time to time by eminent pianists. Georg Liebig (who seemingly had long limbs) was accustomed to press his knees firmly against the under-structure of the keyboard for the purpose of securing greater firmness and grip. Others such as Alfred Cortot have been know to curl the left foot around the left leg of the piano-chair with the same end in view. But such positions are eccentric and not always effectual. The best means of allowing a maximum amount of support from the body in *fortissimo* playing is to withdraw the left foot some ten inches from the *una corda* pedal and nearer to the chair for the time being. This secures better equipoise, and by leaning somewhat on the left foot, greater power of arm-movement can be gained.

So much for *forte*-playing. Softness of touch is helped by the development of 'cushions' under the finger-tips. The larger the cushions the softer the touch, since the extra 'give' afforded by the cushions allows more sensitiveness and variety in the mode of depression of the keys, as against the hard and uniform touch which is inevitable when the finger-tips are thin or meagre. Even students with slender, delicate fingers develop 'cushions' after they have spent some years in strenuous practice, thereby allowing the production of soft, velvety tone. Such cushions also serve the more immediate purpose of preventing the tips of the nails from reaching and rattling on the keys. Long nails, are, of course, out of the question in piano-playing. Women pianists must here sacrifice their vanity on the altar of the Euterpean Muse and file their nails short, since no noise can be allowed to emanate from the nails or even from the finger-tips on the keyboard.

Touch is ultimately dictated by the personality and character of the player, and more important than all the mechanical aspects of touch dealt with above is the player's predominant disposition, whether robust and vigorous, coarse and insensitive, gentle and persuasive, or timid and irresolute. This is where character-training becomes part of the curriculum and where the teacher with personality can exert a wholesome influence in moulding the student's disposition, if his particular type of touch indicates traits requiring either to be strengthened or subdued.

When the student has matured, one of the indispensable assets he must possess is that singing *cantabile* tone which is the life and soul of piano-playing. Coupled with the art of producing a rich resonant tone must be the ability to devote one's whole conscious being to the simple and sincere utterance of the music one is engaged in playing. One must listen to and feel every note. This absorption will then be reflected in one's bearing. All the really great pianists I remember hearing sat at the piano quietly on low stools or chairs, their arms horizontal with the keys. There was no melodramatic lifting of arms in the air, or swaying about with the body; no wriggling of shoulders or awkward movement of the elbows common to so many pianists who naively think that these affectations heighten the effect of their playing. One saw fingers and hands moving quietly, energetically when the music demanded it, but always with an outer demeanour of restraint and dignity.

CHAPTER THREE
PRACTICE

GENERAL METHOD

A sound method of practice is the pianist's most essential requisite, yet it is rarely to be found owing to the amount of discipline and labour involved. To the great majority of students practice consists of playing through the music they are studying at that particular speed at which they can just manage to master its difficulties, and having worked perhaps somewhat more cautiously at the difficult passages they continue to play the work over and over again as close as possible to the required speed. When this can be done with any degree of assurance, the work is regarded as 'finished', and added to the repertoire.

Now this type of practice can only lead to careless and uneven playing. Sometimes it results in steady deterioration of the work practised, so much so that it is better played after the first few attempts than after it has been played dozens of times. The reason is that a series of minute muscular movements are involved in every bar of music one is studying. When the brain prescribes this series of movements for the first few times in which the music is played through, concentration is at a maximum because one is dealing with fresh material, and every detail must be watched if it is to be realised in execution. When the same order of movements has been repeated a great many times, however, some of these movements or movement-groups become so familiar as to be executed by an automatic response, just as in walking down a familiar street, landmarks are registered subconsciously. According as one continues to play at top speed, concentration becomes unevenly distributed, conflict arises between conscious and subconscious response, defects begin to creep in without correction, and the mind, instead of concentrating on the activity of the moment, will tend to anticipate some difficulty which is lurking ahead, with consequent loss of control. The more one practises in this fashion the more one's chances are lessened of ever gaining a grip. Moreover, ceaseless repetition of the same music at a quick tempo soon begins to try the nerves.

It is essential then that a method of practice be adopted which will ensure a gradual and steady progress towards technical mastery. When commencing a new work it is advisable to read it through first several times to the best of one's ability, in order to gain an idea of the work as a whole, its character and form. Next, all those passages which present any technical difficulty should be carefully fingered (see next chapter), since if awkward fingering is adopted through lack of proper attention at this stage, hours of practice may be spent in vain. Then the real work of practice begins. The first phrase is taken by itself (or, if the work is especially difficult, even less than a complete phrase) and played so slowly that approximately three seconds might be counted between each successive note or chord. Both rhythm and dynamics are eliminated and one's entire concentration is devoted to the progression of parts alone. Students who have the necessary knowledge should reflect on the tonality and harmonic structure of the passage, noting modulations or characteristic features. Students who have not had an all-round musical education and lack knowledge of harmony (unfortunately many students of piano-playing belong to this category) can reflect on the chords and progressions even if they are not able to analyse their nature. At the same time one should watch every movement involved, correcting any tendency of the hands to slope by keeping the knuckles of the fourth and fifth fingers at the level of the others, and seeing that the wrist is adequately relaxed after each contraction.

Having played the phrase or portion of a phrase at this first slow tempo, it is then repeated at a slightly faster tempo, so that about two seconds might be counted between each note or chord. In the second tempo, rhythm and dynamics are still left out of account, and each progression is alone the subject of concentration. The third tempo, while neglecting dynamics, now takes time and rhythm into account, so that values are proportionately true, but played at an exceedingly slow pace. If the rhythm should be of a complicated kind, and especially if minute sub-divisions of the beat should occur, it is advisable in a bar of common time, for instance, to count eight quavers, or if necessary, even sixteen semiquavers, in order to ensure accuracy.[29]

From now on at each repetition the tempo is quickened, dynamics, phrasing and even mode of interpretation are all considered, until the phrase finally takes shape at the correct speed without defect of any kind. If this should not be the case, and some difficulty which has arisen remains insuperable, the tempo should be kept below that at which the difficulty tends to arise, until some improvement manifests itself.

The succeeding phrases are then practised in the same manner. When the end of the first period has been reached, one commences practice on it as a whole, beginning *moderato* and working gradually up to maximum speed. The remaining periods are then similarly dealt with, and the entire work (or a movement of it, if it is a sonata) is finally played through, at first cautiously, and then at the correct tempo.

The most trying but at the same time the most important part of this method of practice lies in the first three slow tempos. The drudgery here entailed will not be found easy by those who are accustomed to quick and haphazard practice, or accustomed to give full vent to their emotions by enjoying the music they are playing and evading the real issue, namely that of coming to grips with its technical realities and difficulties. But it is by concentrating properly in these slow tempos that one can lay a sure foundation for ultimate technical mastery. The mind has time to take in the order of the progressions and the muscular movements and the significance of each, as if one were following and studying a slow motion picture, and the repetition of this close analysis at all times, even when the work is already mastered, will preserve and consolidate one's technique.

Sometimes it is objected that the ability or inability to endure slow practice is a matter of temperament. Actually it is not a matter of temperament, but a test of one's capacity for hard work and of one's power to concentrate.

---

[29] The Air (*Lento non troppo*) of Handel's *Third Suite* is a case in point. For students who have a poor sense of time this movement, as well as the *Adagio* of the *Second Suite*, makes an excellent study. [*Inserted in Tilly Fleischmann's hand*: Examples from Bach's *Partitas* might be better: more widely known.]

USE OF EMPHASIS

If in playing up to time there should be a tendency to miss any particular note in a difficult passage, it is often helpful to emphasise this note strongly so that it sounds out clearly above the others. When one reverts to normal accentuation again, it will be found that the note now takes its rightful place among its neighbours. If a group of notes should cause trouble, one should practise accentuating each note in turn, and having concentrated on the notes individually in this manner, the group as a whole will then become clear.

A similar plan may be adopted with whole passages which have not been properly mastered or which – as often happens – have become increasingly uncertain, though in the beginning they may have presented no difficulty. Commencing at some point well ahead of the passage in question one should approach it at top speed, as if about to take it in one's stride. As soon as it has been reached, however, the tempo should be abruptly reduced to a slow *moderato*, while every individual note should be strongly accentuated. This process should be repeated several times with a lesser reduction of the tempo each time, until finally the passage is approached and played at its true speed. It will be found that this method of studying and emphasising difficult passages will have a most reassuring effect, psychologically as well as technically. It will also help to check that most frequent of bad habits – the tendency to rush passages which are especially difficult.

Conversely it is sometimes useful to plunge into a difficult passage at full speed as a test as to whether one has mastered it or not. Then, reversing the procedure already described, one should repeat the passage several times, each time somewhat more slowly, and with greater use of emphasis. Both the foregoing methods can be applied to a difficult passage, the first (i.e. slowing down on its approach) to gain a surer control, the second to gain confidence in what one might call the unanticipated attack. According to Liszt, when a difficult passage can be played faultlessly five or six times in succession, it has then been mastered.

As a final point it should be mentioned that when a pianist has difficulty in reaching a remote note, or the extreme notes of skipping passages, it is well to practise the skips with the involved hand alone, heavily accentuating the extreme note, and doing so moreover without looking at the keyboard. This device is especially useful for such left-hand patterns as occur in Chopin waltzes, since it accustoms the hand to reach the low bass notes accurately without the help of the eyes.

RHYTHMIC PROBLEMS

Students often ask how they should play or practise passages in which such different rhythms are combined as groups of three notes against groups of two, e.g.:

Ex. 21: Chopin *Trois nouvelles études,* Op. posth., No. 2, bar 1

Here the student should first be told that the second note in the left hand comes immediately after the second chord of the triplet group in the right hand. By counting six semiquavers (the lowest common multiple of the two groups) for the first half of the bar, the second chord in the right hand will fall on the third semiquaver, while the second note in the left hand will fall on the fourth semiquaver:

Ex. 22: Chopin *Trois nouvelles études,* Op. posth., No. 2, bar 1, coordination of hands

The student should not be further encouraged, however, to work out the problem mathematically, since he can achieve the required result more easily by ear alone. Taking the right hand by itself he should play the triplet groups allotted to that hand in strict time, counting two in the bar. Then he should take the left hand by itself, counting the same two beats at exactly the same tempo. Having played each part alternately in this manner, so that one hand follows the other continuously without a break, he should then, without pausing to think, play both hands together. If he has a good rhythmic instinct the passage will be correct even at this first attempt, for his fingers will continue to run on in semi-mechanical fashion, keeping to the rhythm of each part as played individually, while his ear is in process of accustoming itself to the joint rhythmic result.

Untalented students, however, experience great difficulty in alternating the hands at the same tempo before ultimately combining them. Unless the tempo of the right hand agrees exactly with that of the left hand, so that the counting is identical in each case, when both hands are combined the balance will be thrown out of joint. The only remedy is to insist that the student count aloud while playing with each hand separately, clearly tapping out the beats at the same time with his foot. When this has been practised sufficiently often, even the most unrhythmical of students must succeed.

Let us take another example, in which two groups of three quavers are pitted against one group of three crotchets:

Ex. 23: Chopin *Études*, No. 14 in F minor, Op. 25, No. 2, bar 1

In slow practice this works out quite evenly, since every second note of the right hand agrees with each successive crotchet in the left. But in quick tempo it is impossible to get the accentuation right by attempting to think of the coincidence of the notes in this way. Once slow practice has been dispensed with, the method already described should be adopted, counting two beats in the bar for each hand.

So also for the grouping of four notes against three which will be found in Chopin's *Fantasie-Impromptu* in C sharp minor, Op. 66, or indeed for any of the complicated counter-groupings so often found in the works of Liszt, Debussy, Scriabin, and more especially modern writers such as Arnold Bax. By counting the lowest common multiple of the two groups involved one can obtain a slow-motion picture of the actual relative position of the notes, e.g. four notes against five:

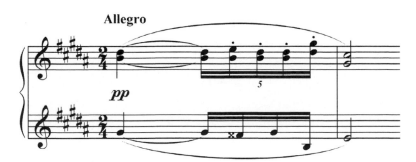

Ex. 24a: Scriabin *Five Preludes*, No. 2, Op. 16, bars 1–2

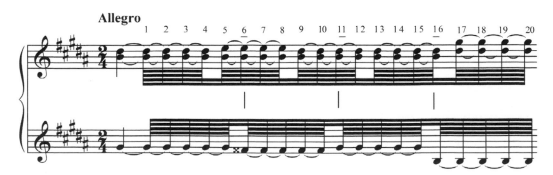

Ex. 24b: Scriabin *Five Preludes*, No. 2, Op. 16, bars 1–2, coordination of hands

But this method is too complicated in such cases to be used for anything but reference.

An excellent study for practice in this connection is Czerny's *Study* in A major, Op. 299, No. 26, from which Czerny's pupil, Liszt, seems to have derived his well-known study in F minor, *La Leggerezza*.

DAILY ROUTINE

Devotion to systematic work is a characteristic of the true virtuoso. Without routine and without a sound method of practice no worth-while achievement is possible. Paderewski reveals in his memoirs that he spent his early years playing instead of working, and when at the age of twenty-four he came to study with Leschetizky the latter discouraged him positively from becoming a pianist, saying that it was too late! Paderewski persisted, and was obliged to start from the beginning again – with finger exercises.[30]

To take another example, after sixty years of piano-playing Pachmann discovered a new method by which he declares he saved three-fourths of the energy which his work had previously demanded of him. This method consisted merely of keeping the hands horizontal and in an almost straight line from the wrists, whereas previously he seems to have played with his hands making an angle with his wrists. Though the new method would seem to be nothing else than the adoption of the most natural position for the hands, the change from his previous cramped style of playing allowed him to reduce his daily practice from ten hours to six, part of which was still devoted to finger exercises according to his 'new method'.[31]

Both the neophyte and the concert public are unaware of the drudgery associated with genuine practice. I remember hearing the sound of piano-playing in the Munich home of Stavenhagen one day, and so hard did I find it to believe that the slowly-played scale passages and the long pauses between each successive chord could have been the handiwork of the master himself that I finally entered the room with an apology for disturbing his teaching, at the same time looking around in astonishment for the person of his pupil. 'Perhaps you would look under the piano?' said Stavenhagen, smiling. 'It seems you do not yet know what practice means; you think one only has to play – is that not so?' Hard words to one who had practised from three to four hours each day from the age of twelve, and thought to know something about it. But like many other enthusiasts, not yet emancipated from dilettantism, I imagined expression and interpretation to be more important than practice, until the drudgery undergone by Stavenhagen and others taught me what real work means.

Stavenhagen, quoting Liszt, used to say that three hours a day would be sufficient for any pianist who practised regularly, not spasmodically once or twice a week. Chopin used to go so far as to forbid his pupils to practise more than three hours.[32] This was Liszt's practice period even when he was over sixty years of age, and had played with triumph in every capital in Europe. Moreover, he was one of those naturally gifted geniuses, who had only to glance at a score to be able to play it.

[30] Ignace Jan Paderewski and Mary Lawton, *The Paderewski Memoirs* (London 1939), p. 99.

[31] Vladimir de Pachmann, 'My New Method of Piano-Playing', *The Music Lovers' Portfolio*, Ed. Landon Ronald (London 1922), Vol. IV, pp.77-78.

[32] Frederick Niecks, *Frederick Chopin* (3rd edition, London 1902), Vol. II, pp. 183-184.

Before a recital, however, it is essential to practise at least five hours a day, since it would be impossible to work through a programme lasting an hour and a half or so in three hours. We have seen that Pachmann worked for ten hours, and some pianists say that they can work consistently up to seven hours a day, but for most this would entail too great a physical and mental strain. If we are to choose between extremes, however, it is a preferable attitude to adopt to one's art than the attitude of those who think that necessity for hard work connotes lack of ability. I can recall a pianist who worked secretly before a recital, lest it get around that he had to labour at his art, and his reputation might suffer thereby! It was his proudest boast that he had performed such and such a work without an opportunity of adequate practice. Contrast the honesty of Cortot, always ready to admit that the least phrase would cost him infinite trouble. So it is with all great artists, their greatness being chiefly due – to use Emerson's phrase – to their 'infinite capacity for taking pains'.

Whatever the period – three hours or five – which the pianist is accustomed to devote to practice per day, regularity is essential. Hans von Bülow, when court pianist to Ludwig II of Bavaria, once said to a friend that when he missed practice for one day he noticed it himself, when he missed practice for two days his friends noticed it, and when he missed practice for three days everyone noticed it. If a concert pianist's playing reacts so sensitively to any deviation from the routine of practice, it follows that those who do not practise regularly or only when a concert is imminent, can never achieve real virtuosity. One so often hears pianists bewailing their lack of technique because they teach and have no time to practise. But one cannot have it both ways – teaching must either yield to concert work, or vice versa. Undoubtedly, nothing absorbs one's nervous energy as much as excessive teaching, provided of course it be conscientious teaching, and concert pianists who must earn their daily bread by this means find it difficult to give recitals and retain a high standard of playing. The lucky ones are those teach, not for a livelihood, but to train disciples who will carry on their tradition. They can pick and choose their pupils, and reduce their hours of teaching to a minimum so as not to interfere with concert work.

Some pianists continue with technical studies long after their need for these studies has ceased, and to an extent which limits their repertoires. Once a correct and fluent technique has been acquired – I speak of course of mature players – studies such as those of Czerny, Clementi and Cramer can be dispensed with, and if needs be, studies by Chopin, Liszt or Henselt chosen in their stead, since these can always be included in one's concert repertoire. Moreover all the masters, both old and modern, provide sufficient opportunities in their works for technical development of every type. On the other hand different groups of exercises chosen from among those recommended in the first chapter should be played for some fifteen minutes every day at the commencement of one's practice. The remainder of the time should then be entirely devoted to the works one is studying – preferably two or three together, since by confining study to a single work over a long period monotony results, one's sensibilities in relation to the work become blunted, and practice becomes too laboured.

At first the attention must be devoted to the purely technical aspect of the work. Interpretation in the ultimate sense does not begin until one has overcome the technical difficulties, and can play the work creditably up to time. Phrasing, dynamics, pedalling – already tentatively considered in preliminary practice – are then reconsidered in the light of the work as a whole, and adjustments made until improvement is no longer possible. The work may then be relegated to one's repertoire. To neglect it wholly for a period, however, may mean to forget it to an extent which will involve a renewal of all one's previous labour at some later stage, whereas to keep a number of works on repertoire, it is merely necessary to play them through *moderato* a few times each week. By doing this they will never be forgotten, and can always be brought up to performance standard in a short time.

When a long stretch of practice has induced weariness and more remains to be done, or when one is not in practice mood, it is often beneficial to turn to a digitorium, or dumb piano. Silent practice is refreshing to the sound-weary musician, and allows difficult passages to be played again and again without the tonal irritation which would ordinarily arise therefrom. Such practice can actually help one's concentration, since it calls for the mental realisation of sound. It is also technically helpful to practise with the different degrees of action-weight available on most digitoriums. For instance one may begin practising a particular exercise or passage with the indicator at two ounces – the lightest action available – and then gradually increase the weight up to a maximum of twelve ounces. This helps to strengthen the fingers. It also helps the pianist to adjust himself to pianos of every type of action, whether heavy or light. One might go so far as to say that every mature pianist should possess a digitorium. Apart from the advantages already mentioned it allows one to practise at all times, and in all places, and under circumstances in which the sound of piano-playing would not be allowable. For children or immature players, however, the digitorium cannot be recommended, since without hearing the actual sound they are unable to detect their mistakes, and silent playing leaves them insensitive to touch and tone.

BEFORE PERFORMANCE

In choosing a piano for a performance Stavenhagen used to advise that for solo work the Blüthner piano, with its soft, mellow tone, should be preferred, while for performance with orchestra the more strident, penetrating tone of the Bechstein gives the pianist a better opportunity of being heard above the orchestral background, and also affords a better contrast to orchestral tone. A similar comparison might be made between the Schiedmayer and the Steinway piano, the former as a solo instrument, the latter for concertos.

Strenuous practice should be avoided on the day of performance itself. Nor is it wise to pick out difficult passages and to concentrate on these, since the psychological result is only to fix them more firmly in one's mind as danger zones, and if anything to arouse a dread of them as they approach in actual performance. I remember a scene in the Green Room at an Academy concert in Munich when a student pianist, against all our advice, insisted on repeatedly playing a difficult passage with much swagger before leaving for the stage. He played faultlessly each time, but when the supreme moment came in performance, his nerves seemed to forsake him, and he muffed it abominably – I regret to say, much to the malicious amusement of his fellow-students.

From experience I have found that on the morning of a concert it is best to engage for half an hour or so in technical exercises such as *Klopfübungen*, scales, arpeggios and octaves, and not to risk wearying oneself with work on the actual programme. Stavenhagen made it an inviolable rule never to practise on the day of the recital, except for technical exercises in the morning and five minutes' finger-work before leaving for the hall. Some eminent pianists go still further and make a habit of busying themselves with totally different work for two or three days before a recital, so that they can approach their programme on the night of the performance with a fresh mind. At any rate, for those who can afford it, relaxation of one kind or another is advisable for at least the greater part of the day on which the performance takes place.

For the final exercises with which to animate one's fingers for a few minutes before leaving for the hall Stavenhagen used to recommend *Klopfübungen*, together with the following five-finger exercise, adapted by Liszt from *Studies No. 16* and *17* in Clementi's *Gradus ad Parnassum*. The exercise should be played up to time with each hand separately:

Ex. 25: Liszt Five-finger exercise, adapted from Clementi's *Gradus ad Parnassum*

Concert players have various idiosyncrasies as to the best beverage which will give them heart before appearing on the platform. A cup of hot milk or tea is a safe stimulant (with a dash of whiskey for those who can withstand it). Just before commencing to play, one should pause a while, gathering one's powers of concentration, so as to start with calmness and resolution.

The non-musician is sometimes inclined to think that practice for the artist must be drudgery, whereas performance must be a sheer delight. Actually, the reverse is the case. Amidst the hard work of practice there are many moments when the player can abandon himself to the inspiration of the music he is interpreting, experiencing that elation which arises when the inner beauty of a work is suddenly revealed in all its glowing intensity. But in performance it is otherwise. The audience is there to be mastered and overcome. The player must arm himself for a stern struggle, one which requires a clear, cool head and indomitable will. For now it is not the player who must react to the experiences which his playing embodies, it is his audience who must be swayed into reaction. To achieve this the player must remain cold as ice, no matter how moved his audience may become. Like a medium in a spiritualist trance he must leave the consciousness of his own personality behind, and without any outward display of emotion or enthusiasm so grip himself and his hearers that he seems to become the living embodiment of the composer's mind.

CHAPTER FOUR

FINGERING

Fingering is ultimately a matter for the individual, since the most suitable position for the fingers must depend on the size and the peculiarities of the hand. When the pianist begins to study a work in which the fingering is unmarked, or in which he finds that the editor's fingering is unsuited to his particular needs, he will do well to mark in his own fingering of all the difficult passages at the outset.

In testing the fingering for a passage it is essential to make the test at the actual speed at which the passage should be played, since fingering which is suitable for a passage when played slowly is often impracticable at the full speed because of the altered tensions involved. Scale passages should usually be fingered as they are played in scale practice, since the student will then know instinctively where to place the thumb, from which the position of the other fingers is then determined. To give an instance, the following scale passage is usually fingered according to the upper row of numerals in the following illustration:

Ex. 26: Beethoven *Piano Sonata No. 14* in C sharp minor, Op. 27, No. 2, 3rd movement, bars 40–41, right hand

At first sight this would seem the simplest and most logical fingering. But since in playing the scale of A major, the thumb is placed on D, it will be found that to finger in accordance with the lower row of numerals is in fact easier and more natural, while the repetition of the fifth finger for the top E merely gives extra zest to the accent.

Again, in the following example it seems simpler to adopt the lower rather than the upper fingering given, since the same fingering can then be adopted for each bar, and the repetition of the fifth finger at the end of one phrase and the beginning of the next merely ensure proper phrasing:

Ex. 27: Mozart *Piano Sonata No. 16* in C, K.545, 1st movement, bars 50–52, left hand

Comparing the upper and lower fingerings for the following passage it will be seen that the upper fingering involves some awkward wrist movements, whereas the lower more readily facilitates the light, rippling *legato* at top speed which is so essential here:

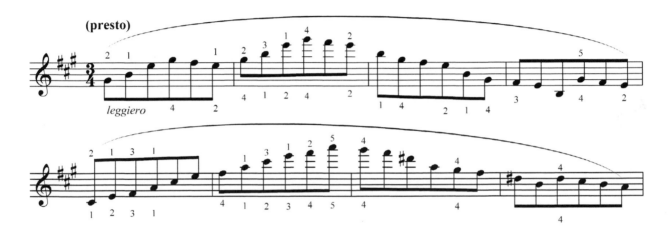

Ex. 28: Chopin *Scherzo No. 2* in B flat minor, Op. 31, bars 329–336, right hand

For chromatic runs, the smoothest and readiest fingering to adopt is to alternate thumb and third finger on consecutive white and black notes, with thumb and second finger for two consecutive white notes:

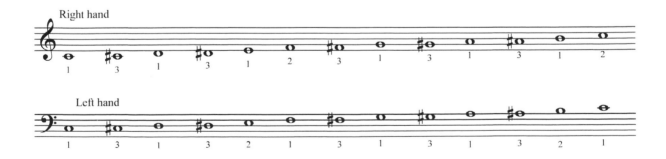

Ex. 29: Chromatic runs, right hand and left hand

Difficult passages can often be simplified by dividing up the note-groups between the two hands, e.g.

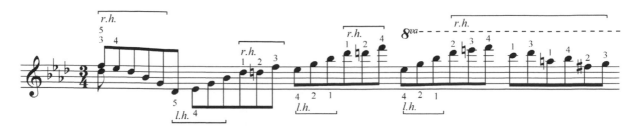

Ex. 30: Liszt *Liebesträume, Nocturne No. 3* in A flat, bar 60

Sometimes this may be done even when not intended by the composer, provided that the effect remains unaltered. For instance the following difficult passage can be made comparatively easy by taking the crotchet at the top of each chord in the lower stave with the thumb of the right hand. The *arpeggiata* effect can still be got between the two hands, and it will be found that the skip from the lower-stave crotchet note to the first octave in the right hand is an easier matter, and that the crotchet will sound out more clearly than if the left hand were to attempt all four notes of each chord *arpeggiata*:

Ex. 31: Brahms *Rhapsody* in B minor, Op 79, No. 1, bars 81–82

When the composer inverts the natural position of the hands for the sake of the visual pattern, he need not always be literally followed. As fingered in most editions, this passage presents no small difficulty because of the skips involved in the crossing of hands:

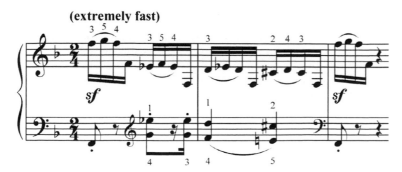

Ex. 32: Schumann *Phantasiestücke,* Op. 12, *Traumes Wirren,* bars 19-21

With the following lay-out, however, by which the crossing of hands is eliminated, all difficulty disappears and greater clarity is ensured:

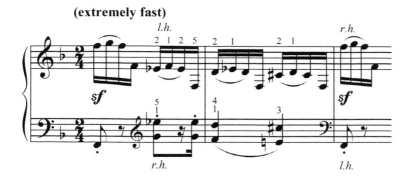

Ex. 33: Schumann *Phantasiestücke*, Op. 12, *Traumes Wirren*, bars 19–21, alternative layout

In the case of a single, wide-spaced chord, played *arpeggiata*, the notes should be distributed between the two hands so as to secure maximum smoothness and ease of movement, e.g.

Ex. 34: Liszt *Valse impromptu* in A flat, final chord (bar 314)

For octave passages in which *legato* playing is not essential the thumb and fifth finger only should be used. In the case of *legato* octave-melodies, however, the fourth and even the third fingers should also be used where practicable, to ensure a smoother continuity of tone, e.g.

Ex. 35: Legato octave playing

Ex. 36: Albéniz *Chants d'Espagne*, *Seguidillos*, Op. 232, No. 5, bars 15–16

When melodies or chord successions need to be played *legato*, and when adjacent fingers cannot be used for adjacent notes, or when the most convenient fingering would involve at any point the lifting of a finger momentarily from its key before the next key is depressed, a method of fingering by substitution should be employed, whereby a change of fingers is effected on the one key while it is still depressed. This substitution will release a vital finger for further action, and so allow maximum smoothness. Sometimes the same finger can even be released twice successively, as in the fourth and fifth chords of the following passage:

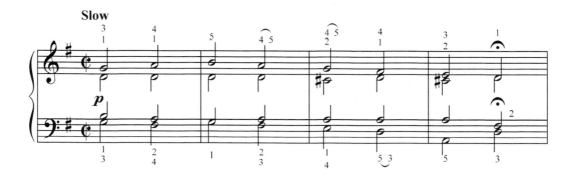

Ex. 37: Schumann *Album für die Jugend*, Op. 68, No. 4, *Ein Choral*, bars 1–4

Such substitution is common on the organ, and should be used in piano-playing, even in relatively quick tempos, wherever the context demands an unbroken *legato*. Further reference to this type of fingering, in conjunction with pedalling, will be found below (see p. 40).

In quick passages involving wide stretching of the fingers, these will tend to lie almost flat on the keys, since their stretch becomes thereby slightly increased. This is the explanation of Kleczynski's statement that Chopin, according to several of his pupils, sometimes held his hands absolutely flat. Madame Dubois' contradiction, and Niecks' suggestion[33] that such a procedure may have been due to physical exhaustion are both invalid, since in such passages as the following it is merely natural to spread the fingers flat, the stretches being too wide to allow the fingers to curve. In slow practice one should then place the fingers as flatly on the keys as will be found natural at the full tempo.

---

[33] Frederick Niecks, *Frederick Chopin* (London 1890), Vol. II, p. 182, footnote.

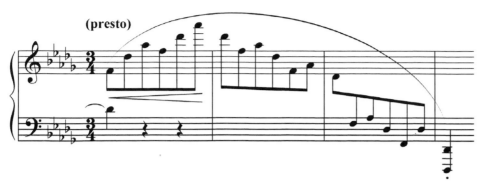

Ex. 38: Chopin *Scherzo No. 2* in B flat minor, Op. 31, bars 126–129

Ex. 39: Chopin *Études*, No. 5 in G flat, Op. 10, bars 33–36

When a single note demands a maximum amount of emphasis in performance, especially when it is approached by leap, it is sometimes advisable to strike it with a combination of two fingers and thumb. The third finger, being the longest, actually depresses the key, but supported by the second finger, which presses closely against it, and by the thumb, which is placed firmly under and between the two fingers so that all three form one compact unit, with the third finger projecting slightly beyond the others. This device may be used in either hand in contexts such as the following:

Ex. 40: Brahms *Piano Sonata No. 3* in F minor, Op. 5, 1st movement, bars 1–2

Ex. 41: Bridge *Three Sketches,* No. 2, *Rosemary*, H.68, bars 32–35

Further instances where it may be used with advantage are the Beethoven *Sonata* in F sharp, Op. 78, *Allegro vivace*, bars 57 and 61 etc.; Chopin's B flat minor *Scherzo*, Op. 31, bar 5, 13, etc.; Liszt's *St. François de Paule,* seventh and sixth last bars (upper notes of lower stave); Liszt's *Ballade* in B minor, bars 206–207, and his *Concert Study Waldesrauschen*, bars 55–58; Dohnanyi's *Rhapsody* in C, Op. 11, No. 3, bars 38–39; Rachmaninov's *Polichinelle*, Op. 3, No. 4, bars 1 and 4, etc.

CHAPTER FIVE
PEDALLING: TECHNICAL ASPECT

The sustaining pedal has three main functions, namely (1) to increase and beautify the tone, (2) to effect or facilitate *legato*, (3) to fuse successive sound groups. The latter function is an important element in interpretation, and will be discussed in Chapter 12. In this chapter we shall deal primarily with the mechanical aspects of pedalling.

POSITION AND MOVEMENT OF THE FEET

When the sustaining pedal is in use the ball of the right foot rests on the pedal-lever, while the heel is placed firmly on the floor. The action of pedalling is then effected through movement of the ankle joint only, not of the entire leg, an ungainly habit sometimes found with beginners. The foot should never lose contact with the pedal, just as on the key-board the fingers do not unnecessarily leave and then hit the keys.

When the pedal is not in use the position of the heel should not be changed, so that the foot is always ready for instantaneous action. Some pianists swivel the foot slightly to the right, or keep it suspended half an inch or so above the pedal, others again never lose contact with the pedal at all. It is, however, definitely culpable to shift or slide the entire leg backwards or forwards, since this is both irritating to see, and a waste of physical energy.

The left foot is not kept in contact with the *una corda* pedal, because this is used so much less frequently than the sustaining pedal. It is normally placed parallel to the right foot, at the same distance from the pedal-lyre, and an inch or two to the left of the *una corda* pedal, so that when this pedal comes to be used no other movement is necessary than a slight swivelling of the foot to the right on to the pedal lever, with the heel as pivot. This position of the two feet, which are then some four inches apart, is the most natural, affords the best balance, and gives access to the two pedals with a minimum of movement. The left foot is only withdrawn some distance from the *una corda* pedal for passages involving *fortissimo* tone.

EFFECT ON TONE-QUALITY AND VOLUME

The sustaining pedal enriches the tone quality of any note or chord which is sounded by lifting all the dampers from the strings, and allowing the other strings which are related to those that have actually been struck to vibrate in sympathy. From its use for this purpose the sustaining pedal is sometimes, if inaptly, termed 'the loud pedal'.

To avail of the added colour one normally pedals individual chords, or even the individual notes of a single melodic line, if it be relatively slow-moving. In the following fugue subject every note might be pedalled (except the fourth and seventh, to allow clearer phrasing):

Ex. 42: Mendelssohn *Fugue* in A flat, Op. 35, No. 4, bars 1–6

When the speed of a melody or series of chords which are not to be fused exceeds that of quavers in moderate time, two alternatives are possible. Either 'half-pedalling' is used, i.e. the pedal is only partially depressed for each note or chord, owing to the speed involved, as for instance in the following:

Ex. 43: Schumann *Piano Sonata No. 2* in G minor, Op. 22, 1st movement, bars 22–23

or the pedal is depressed and released for every alternate note or chord, e.g.:

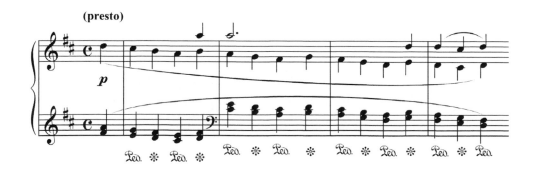

Ex. 44: Beethoven *Piano Sonata No. 7* in D, Op. 10, No. 3, 1st movement, bars 5–8

In the extract from the Schumann *Sonata* above, the *sforzando* chord should be left unpedalled to allow a crisper ending to the phrase, and to give the chord a more clearly percussive and drier quality such as arises when the pedal is not used.

Theoretically it is possible to obtain a *crescendo* after a chord has been actually played by depressing the sustaining pedal, and thereby allowing an increase of volume through sympathetic vibration. This increase, however, is relatively slight, and represents an increase in tone-quality rather than tone-quantity, added richness and depth rather than a greater degree of loudness. Conversely it is possible to achieve a certain amount of *diminuendo* after a chord has been loudly played with the sustaining pedal depressed, by releasing the pedal and so damping sympathetic vibration. This *diminuendo* can be still more effectively obtained on a grand piano by alternately releasing and depressing the pedal a few times in quick succession, as if executing a species of tremolo with the foot, for the repeated action of the dampers on the strings, especially on the lower strings, seems to blanket the tone and reduce it by a process of diffusion. The *forte-piano* which marks the opening chord of Beethoven's *Sonata* 'Pathétique' can best be achieved by this means. After the brief pedal tremolo by which the tone has been reduced, the pedal can finally be allowed to remain depressed in order to bridge the transition to the second chord:

Ex. 45: Beethoven *Piano Sonata No. 8* in C minor, Op. 13, 1ˢᵗ movement, bar 1

In the same way a sonorous *ff* chord occurring at the conclusion of a work can become gradually veiled by means of the pedal tremolo. If a complete *diminuendo* is then desired, this can be obtained by releasing one note after the other, until only the foundation-note remains, as in the case of the final chord of Liszt's *St François de Paule marchant sur les flots* is traditionally played in this manner (the pedal is taken again on the final note, to give a luminous quality to the last vestige of sound):

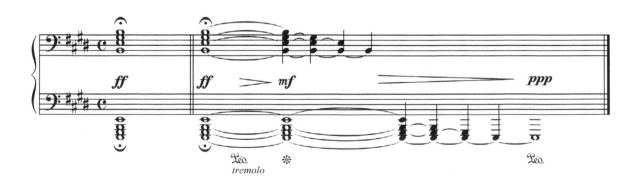

Ex. 46: Liszt *Deux légendes,* No. 2 *St François de Paule marchant sur les flots*, final bar, pedalling technique

USE IN *LEGATO*-PLAYING

One of the functions of the sustaining pedal is to retain the tone when the fingers are obliged to leave the keys in order to reach notes lying outside their immediate scope, and by retaining the tone to bridge the transition in such cases between successive positions of the fingers. If the pedal were not used in the following example, even with the most skilful manipulation of the skips there would be a slight hiatus between the first and second chords in each bar, and between the last chord of the first bar and the first chord of the next. By using the pedal all transitions can be smoothly bridged and the tone of the E major chord can still be retained while the hands are in process of reaching to the D flat major chord:

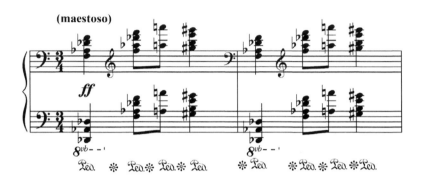

Ex. 47: Khachaturian *Piano Concerto* in D flat, Op. 38, bars 348–349

The above, however, is an extreme example, and the pedal will often be used to facilitate transitions where the change of position is relatively slight. On the other hand it is too often used merely to secure a *legato* which should properly be obtained by the fingers alone. Many young pianists play in a jerky, *staccato* fashion, and use the pedal to give their playing a semblance of smoothness, but unsuccessfully, for the latter can only be a veneer. Stavenhagen once said that every pianist should take a course in harmonium or organ playing to acquire the necessary instinct for *legato*. If this be impracticable it is at least wise to make a definite study of *legato* playing by taking, for instance, the Schumann *Choral* quoted on p. 34 above, and playing it at first without using the pedal. Through fingering by substitution the change from chord to chord should be made without the slightest break until the *Choral* finally moves as smoothly as it if were being played on a harmonium. Then for the first time the sustaining pedal should be used, as it normally would be to enrich the tone.

In the case of beginners every detail of the pedalling process must be carefully watched. For the first chord the pedal is depressed. At the instant at which the keys sounding the next chord are being depressed the pedal is released, and a minute fraction of a second after the chord has sounded it is depressed again. If the pedal is released just before or during the release of the keys of the first chord, and depressed again at the very instant that the keys of the second chord are depressed, the notes of the first chord will continue to sound and a discordant fusion will result, since the fingers will not have left the keys of the first chord in time, and their dampers will still remain lifted, counteracting the previous release of the pedal. At any rate the pedal should only be depressed again a split-second after a new chord has been sounded. Even beginners who have inherent musicianship will do this instinctively, but if a player develops a tendency to muddy pedalling the fault will probably lie in the habit of pedalling a fraction too soon. Normal pedalling is in continuous syncopation with the action of the fingers, the depression of the pedal following that of the keys after the slightest time-lag. Another cause of defective pedalling, however, may lie in the failure to release the pedal fully, in which case the dampers will not come into full contact with the strings, and only partial damping will occur.

THE *UNA CORDA* PEDAL

While the sustaining pedal, as we have seen, can be put to various uses, the *una corda* pedal is solely used for the purpose of lessening the volume, and producing a soft, veiled tone-quality. This it effects on the grand piano by shifting the action about one-sixteenth of an inch to the right, so that the hammers miss one string in striking the three and two-string groups, and in the case of the lowest (one-string) octave, as well as in the case of the other string-groups, the hammer hits the string or strings not along the hard-worn groove, which is its usual striking position, but along the adjoining ridge where the felt is less worn and softer. On upright pianos various mechanisms are employed whereby the *una corda* pedal either interposes a strip of felt between hammer and strings, or brings the hammers closer to the strings, thus allowing them less leverage and ensuring a lesser degree of volume. The former method produces a tone so muffled that the transition from normal to *una corda* tone is disconcertingly abrupt, while the latter method produces a change in volume only, not in tone-quality, so that neither method is ideal.

On the grand piano the veiled quality effected by the *una corda* pedal is more mysterious when the latter is used alone without the sustaining pedal, as for instance throughout the last movement of Chopin's *Sonata* in B flat minor, Op. 35, where an eerie, scurrying effect can be produced in this way. The sustaining pedal, used in combination with the *una corda* pedal, adds richness and colour, but in either case the *una corda* pedal should not be too frequently employed, since it reduces the range of dynamic nuance available, and easily leads to monotony.

Chapter Six

Memorising

Some pianists hold that memorising is waste of time and that the result is not worth the labour involved. It is true that memorising is a slow and tedious process, and if one makes it a principle to play in public only from memory one's repertoire must necessarily be curtailed. On the other hand it is only when a work can be played from memory that one knows it sufficiently to justify a public performance. Not until then has it been fully absorbed, so that it can be reproduced as the expression of an intimate personal experience to which one holds all the clues. When playing from music the mechanical process of reading in itself diverts a part of one's concentration, and prevents one from becoming completely absorbed in the spirit as well as the mechanics of performance. There are movements of the head and eyes not vital to the playing itself; and the attention is more easily distracted, since one is following the printed direction rather than intently working out the argument from one's inner consciousness. In the same way a speaker who reads a speech can never himself become so immersed in what he has to say, nor so influence his hearers, as the speaker who speaks directly, without the aid of a script. In short, the hackneyed phrase 'playing by heart' is peculiarly apt.

The best way to memorise is to practise according to the method outlined on pages 21–2 of Chapter 3. When one is familiar with the content of the music and its technical difficulties have been mastered it is then merely necessary to cover the same ground again, without the music, beginning in slow tempo and gradually working up to the requisite speed. In a surprisingly short time the music can be memorised even by pianists who otherwise have no particular aptitude for this kind of work because by dint of concentration in the slow tempos the details of the music can soak into the mind. Each progression is visualised separately, not as part of a fleeting series of progressions, but merely in relation to the previous progression, and to that which follows. As a result the organic logic of the texture is clearly impressed on the mind before even the mechanical aid of frequent repetition is brought into play, and finally the picture will become so vivid that the pianist could write out from memory the entire piece.

Those who memorise 'by ear', by repeated playing at the full tempo, may be compared to children who learn poetry pit-pat at school – by the sound rather than by thinking about the sense. This parrot-like method of memorising is apt to lead to stumbling and indecision. Again, those who memorise by the inductive slow-practice method are not likely to be affected by self-consciousness or nervousness, since they learn to become completely immersed in their work, and so equip themselves to withstand any ordeal. In a teaching experience of over thirty years the writer has never witnessed a breakdown in performance by a pupil who studied according to this method.

Miss Harriet Cohen, in her book *Music's Handmaid*[34], refers to people who are only able to play from memory with the greatest difficulty, and who have to rely on 'finger memory' – on a

---

[34] Harriet Cohen, *Music's Handmaid* (London 1936), pp. 54 seq.

kind of automatic placing and spacing of the fingers on the keyboard. Such finger-memory may indeed provide a certain mechanical aid, but it seems unwise to focus the attention on the technical and physical aspect of one's playing rather than on the shape and growth of the music itself.

Gieseking[35] adopts a visual method of memorising which involves concentrated reflection on the texture of the music, but by preliminary reading away from the piano. The advantage of this method lies in the fact that concentration is made easier when the mind can work unhampered by physical activity of any kind. But there are two manifest drawbacks. In the first place one foregoes the help which the physical impress of sound gives to the memory. In the second place, the fundamental thing in performance is to co-ordinate the mental concept with its physical execution. Mere mental study neglects such co-ordination, with the result that one may have committed to memory a perfectly clear picture of the music, but when one comes to execute it the new effort of expressing the concept through the medium of physical action disturbs the memory and may necessitate starting the work of memorising all over again. Those who memorise by the 'tactile' method, relying primarily on muscular sensation, and those who rely primarily on the visual image accordingly represent two extremes, the one purely physical, the other purely mental. It seems clear that the suggested method of slow and concentrated reflection on each detail of the music, but at the piano, combines the advantages of both, and will give the best results. Even children can be taught in this way to play short pieces, and later whole Mozart sonatas, from memory without the slightest hesitation or strain.

In fact, this method of memory study is a valuable mental discipline. I have known it to produce a stabilising effect on students inclined to be giddy or unbalanced, once they could be brought to adopt it consistently in practice. In one particular case, of an elderly lady who was suffering from neurosis, this kind of study wrought a surprising change in her mental outlook. So much so that a London specialist whom she had been consulting was moved to enquire into the cause of her improvement. When she had demonstrated her new method of memorising he confessed that in six months it had achieved more for her than several years of his treatment had been able to achieve.

When a work has been memorised one has only reached the beginning of the final stage of study – a stage never reached at all by the majority of pianists, who start new work before the old is chiselled, not to mind polished. In this final stage subtleties of light and shade are worked out and all the finer adjustments are made, such as pedalling effects, nuances of tempo, and so on. If the work is to be kept on repertoire, as already suggested, it is merely necessary to play it through *moderato*, but from memory, once or twice each week.

In the case of modern music, however, it will be found that its complicated harmonic texture and intricate rhythms are quickly forgotten, and a more frequent, perhaps even daily repetition of a modern work is necessary if it is to remain imprinted on the memory. But with the method recommended above even the most difficult type of composition can be assimilated. Within a period of six weeks I have myself learnt and memorised Arnold Bax's *Second Sonata* in G, one of the finest as well as the most complex examples of contemporary writing for the piano.

---

[35] Karl Leimer, *Modernes Klavierspiel nach Leimer-Gieseking* (Mainz 1931), p. 12.

CHAPTER SEVEN
SIGHT-READING

Students often ask how sight-reading should be practised. Song accompaniments, as a rule, are the most suitable for this purpose. Having looked at the key and time signatures, one should take a quick glance at the whole accompaniment, noting its general character, estimating the tempo at which it should be played, and possibly scrutinising any particular passage which appears more formidable than the rest. Having done this one should play the accompaniment right through at the correct tempo without hesitation of any kind, always when necessary sacrificing notes to rhythm, retaining the proper time and flow even if complete misplacing of the fingers on the keys should result. This latter may sometimes happen when attempting to take a difficult passage in one's stride in an accompaniment which is otherwise relatively easy, but it is unwise to attempt to read music which in its general lay-out is quite beyond one's powers. Careful grading is essential, so that the simplest music is chosen at first, and later music which is progressively more difficult.

In sight-reading the movement of the eyes is not continuous or regular, but consists of a series of jumps from point to point, the resting-points being called 'fixations'.[36] Speed depends on the reduction of the time spent in each fixation, and is achieved chiefly through the recognition of patterns, so that whole groups of notes can be read in a single fixation, and the general outline alone is looked at, not the individual notes. The sight-reader must then aim at making himself increasingly familiar with the conventional scale, arpeggio and chordal patterns, so that when there are deviations from these only the deviations need be specially noted. A knowledge or understanding of composition and a vivid imagination are other factors which undoubtedly help sight-reading, since they enable one to follow the composer's line of argument without effort, or even to anticipate his thought. As the period of composition draws nearer to our time, however, the difficulties of sight-reading become greater and in the case of contemporary music, such as that of Bartok or Schönberg, since the idiom is entirely strange to the average pianist and the patterns unfamiliar, each note in a chord or melodic group must be scanned individually, and the pace will be proportionately slowed down.

At first one should cultivate the habit of reading from below upwards. This ensures a correct foundation in the case of chords, and it accustoms the eye to follow a certain routine, especially in homophonic music. Later, with more experience, the eye can begin to rove more freely, up or down according as it follows the most vital line of the texture. This ability to recognise what is vital and what is merely subsidiary is as important in sight-reading as the ability to recognise individual patterns. It will enable one, if hard pressed, to reproduce the main outline of the music convincingly, even though numerous details have to be omitted.

The worst fault in sight-reading is a regressive movement of the eyes, which is liable to occur when one has doubts as to the accuracy of the note-images formed, resulting in hesitation,

---

[36] See Harry Lowery, 'On Reading Music', *The Dioptric Review and The British Journal of Physiological Optics*, New Series, Vol. 1, No. 2 (July 1940), pp. 78 seq.

repetition and stumbling. To wean the student from this habit the teacher should choose an easy song accompaniment, and play or sing the vocal part in strict time, compelling the student to follow unswervingly. Or again, the reading of piano duets is excellent for this purpose since any loss of time through hesitation or repetition on the part of one player will lead to disruption for both, and the annoyance at having to make a new start will soon prove a sufficient deterrent.

In sight-reading one should aim as much as possible at finding the notes on the key-board without the help of the eyes. Every time the eyes leave the music to guide the fingers on the keys precious time is lost which could be devoted to unravelling the music, and foreseeing what is to come. At first it will be found difficult to move blindly on the keyboard, but by practising with eyes resolutely glued to the music, no matter how dire the results, it will soon be found that familiarity with the key-board will grow to the extent that only the furthest leaps, if any, will require the co-operation of the eyes. Reference has already been made (on pp. 13 and 14) to the value of skipping exercises in this connection.

The fluent sight-reader's eyes will usually be ahead of his fingers by anything from a half-bar to two bars. Kellermann is said to have read some six bars ahead, and Liszt, according to legend, a whole page ahead! A time-lag of even a few bars might merely seem a burden on the memory, for the memory must store up the images formed, and while the eyes are forging ahead the finger movements associated with the images stored are put into execution. But in fact this anticipation of the eyes enables one to keep some valuable time in reserve. In the case of difficult passages the eyes can move more slowly and take in more detail well in advance, and when a difficult passage is past pick up again to regain their customary lead ahead of the fingers, without any deviation whatever in the pace of performance. Readers should then try to read as far ahead as possible, and the interval between seeing and executing will in fact widen as he becomes more experienced.

When reading at sight the pedal should always be used, and the dynamics observed. It is painful to listen to the monotonous type of reading in which so many pianists indulge, rarely employing the pedals and reducing the dynamics to a humdrum *mezzo-forte*. A lively sense of dynamic contrast will often redeem sight-reading which is poor in other respects.

When a piece of music has been read through for the first time at the correct speed, it is well to go over it a second time somewhat more slowly, taking special care with any passages which proved too difficult at first for accurate reproduction. The whole might then be played up to time again to see if better results can now be obtained. This practice will correct the tendency, common to so many able sight-readers, of dashing through music carelessly, without due regard for an accurate and sensitive reproduction of the music itself.

To develop one's power of reading at sight it is necessary to practise reading at least ten minutes each day. The ability to sight-read is not in itself evidence of inherent musicality, for the best sight-readers are sometimes wholly unmusical and inartistic, but it is a most useful accomplishment, essential both for the professional pianist and for the amateur who wishes to gain a knowledge of the literature.

INTERPRETATION

CHAPTER EIGHT
PHRASING

Having dealt so far with matters technical, we now come to the finer problems which confront the pianist in interpreting the music of the masters. Among such problems phrasing is one of the most important, since upon the phrasing will depend the clarity of the melodic line, and even of the structure as a whole. Clear phrasing can make complex music intelligible, while unclear phrasing can make the simplest music sound confused.

When the composer does not build his phrases in clearly-divided rhythmic groups or separate them with rests, he can only indicate his intentions with regard to the phrasing by means of slurs or phrase marks. The slur, however, is variously used to indicate a complete phrase, part of a phrase, or any minute grouping within the phrase. Furthermore, the slur is sometimes used to indicate *legato*, irrespective of phrasing in a structural or rhythmic sense, e.g.:

Ex. 48: Beethoven *Piano Sonata No. 2* in A, Op. 2, No. 2, 4th movement, bars 23–26

so that its meaning is by no means uniform. Again, long stretches are sometimes left without phrase marks of any kind, especially where non-*legato* playing is intended. The method of phrasing must then be largely left to the discretion and artistry of the performer.

In its broadest aspect phrasing means the demarcation between one phrase, or part of a phrase, and another, and is regulated (1) by the amount of change in dynamic level between the end of one phrase and the beginning of the next, (2) by the extent of the break or gap allowed between them, (3) by the extent of the *ritardando*, usually almost imperceptible, made towards the end of a phrase, or, more usually (4) by any two or all three of these methods combined. Just as in speech the voice normally sinks at the end of a sentence and rises again at the beginning of the next, and just as one allows a longer gap between sentences than between phrases, while the tempo tends to slow down more towards the end of a sentence than of a phrase, so too in music, with this difference that in music phrasing is a far more subtle process, with a wider range of resources involved. The following illustrations of the various modes of phrasing may help the pianist to realise more consciously the principles which, if he is an artistic player, he will apply instinctively himself.

(1) **Dynamic change** It is often necessary to indicate the first note of a new phrase by an increase or decrease of tone. Instances of both can be seen in the following example, where the other factors of break or *ritardando* are not availed of, and the phrasing, though clear from the rhythmic shape, is underlined by the dynamic changes in bars four and five (of the example below) which the composer himself prescribes. Note that though Mendelssohn inserts the *forte* sign on the strong beat of the last phrase (bar nine of the example below), the latter actually starts on the preceding upbeat, which must then be raised to a *forte* level, without being as strongly accentuated as the downbeat:

Ex. 49 Mendelssohn *Piano Concerto No. 2* in D minor, Op. 40, bars 267–276

A further example occurs in the following passage, where the best mode of delineating the successive phrases is to make a slight *crescendo* in the second bar, and then to mark the beginning of the next phrase (third bar) with a *subito piano*, without any suggestion of break or *ritardando*. The same procedure can be adopted for the entry of the third phrase which follows in similar manner, this time beginning *subito pianissimo*, and using the *una corda* pedal.

Ex. 50: Chopin *Fantaisie* in F minor, Op. 49, bars 21–25

As a final example, one might take the following swift-moving passage, in which if the player wishes to make the phrasing clearly felt, the only device he can adopt in view of the high speed is to impart a slight accent to the first note of each successive group:

Ex. 51: Chopin *Ballade No. 1*, in G minor, Op. 23, bars 158–161

(2) **Break** Even when the composer has not separated two phrases by means of a rest it is still frequently necessary to allow a break or gap between them for purposes of clarity. As a rule the gap is minute, and merely sufficient to allow clear enunciation of the first note of the succeeding phrase. This mode of differentiating phrases is common in Mozart, and the vivacious, much-indented contour of baroque melody loses much of its charm if it is not aptly pointed by crisp phrase-endings. For instance in the following passage the crotchets C and E in the right hand at

the end of the fourth bar should be played as quavers, and a quaver rest allowed to intervene to mark the end of the four-bar phrase:

Ex. 52: Mozart *Piano Sonata No. 12* in F, K.332, 1st movement, bars 41–45

To take a less obvious instance, the pedal should be released just before the fourth beat of the second bar in the next example, and a barely perceptible gap allowed in the right hand between G sharp and D:

Ex. 53: Mozart *Piano Sonata No. 8* in A minor, K.310, 1st movement, bars 1–3

Where the tempo is relatively fast, or the note duration short, the break will often be equivalent to that produced by *staccato*, as in the following, where it is necessary to play the melody and bass notes on the second beat of the second and fourth bars almost *staccato* and lightly, or the phrase-lengths and their symmetry will not be apparent:

Ex. 54: Beethoven *Piano Sonata No. 14* in C sharp minor, Op. 27, No. 2, 2nd movement, bars 18–22

An equally short break, but without *staccato* involved, must be made between the following clear-cut phrases, which demand that at the end of the second and fourth bars the pedal be lifted, and a clean attack made on the first note of the next phrase, without of course interfering with the continuity of movement:

Ex. 55: Chopin *24 Préludes*, No. 17 in A flat, Op. 28, bars 19–23

(3) **Ritardando** The observance of a slight, sometimes almost imperceptible *ritardando* towards the end of a phrase shapes it as clearly and surely as if one were to change the dynamic level at the start of the next phrase, or to allow a break to intervene between the two. In the next example the first beat of the fourth bar is the end of the first phrase, and the note E natural marks the start of the next. Since Beethoven has expressly slurred the fourth bar into the fifth (here the slurs have no structural significance) the two phrases cannot be separated by a break. Any artistic player, however, will slightly broaden the second half of the third bar, so that the shape of the phrase, rising with quiet intensity towards its close, will be clearly demarcated:

Ex. 56: Beethoven *Piano Sonata No. 8* in C minor, Op. 13, 2nd movement, bars 1–5

Cadential *ritardando* occurs most frequently where two phrases overlap, so that the final note or chord of the first phrase is at the same time the first note or chord of the second phrase. In the following passage Chopin covers two four-bar phrases with the one slur, and even if he had not done so, no break would be permissible between them, since the dominant seventh to tonic progression and the melodic line which links them (bars 4–5) could not be divided. A pliant curve, however, is achieved by a slight *ritardando* at the end of the fourth bar:

Ex. 57: Chopin *24 Préludes*, No. 15 in D flat, Op. 28, bars 1–5

As we shall see later, the use of *ritardando* at cadential points is one of the chief factors in *rubato*-playing. More *ritardando* will naturally be used towards the end of a sentence or period than at the end of a phrase.

(4) **Combinations of the foregoing** In the examples already quoted, only one of the three main factors in phrase-demarcation was involved to any extent. Usually, however, two or all three will be present, in varying proportions. Take the following example, in which the end of the four-bar phrase should be marked by a slight *ritardando* in the left-hand accompaniment, and the first melody-note of the next phrase given added tone. A slight break must of necessity occur in the right hand between F sharp and C sharp, but this is counteracted by the continuity of the left-hand part, the change of pedal at the end of the bar being covered by left-hand *legato* playing:

Ex. 58: Scriabin *Five Preludes*, Op. 16, No. 1, bars 3–7

The following example contains some subtleties of phrasing which call for discussion:

Ex. 59: Stanford *Piano Concerto No. 2*, Op. 126, 2nd movement, bars 1–5

These four bars represent the four phrases of a quadruple sentence, overlapping in such a way that the continuity must be sustained and the possibility of a break between them does not arise. The seventh quaver of the first bar is marked *tenuto*, and since it would be unnecessary and inartistic, having observed the *tenuto*, to make even the slightest *ritardando* immediately afterwards, no further demarcation of the actual phrase-length should be made other than a *diminuendo* towards the end of the bar, and that subtle touch given instinctively to the first chord of the next bar which will raise its dynamic level to that of the first chord of the first bar. The end of the second bar is phrased similarly, but this time without a dynamic nuance on the first quaver of the third bar since this must be sacrificed to the heightening intensity and the forward movement which accompanies the rise of the melody to the apex-note G flat. In the third bar there is no *tenuto*, so that the pace can ease off slightly towards the end of the bar, but now Stanford has indicated different phrasing, for the sake of variety. It would be wrong in this bar to underline the phrasing between the second and third groups of triplets, especially when these groups adjoin on the second of two semiquavers, but as a result of the slur connecting the end of the third bar with the beginning of the fourth, the first quaver of the latter marks not the beginning but the end of a phrase, and must be played more lightly, for instance, than the first quaver of the second bar. In the last bar, quavers 2–4 and 5–9 seem to form the natural grouping, the notes E flat and D flat standing out slightly by virtue of their higher pitch. At the end of the fourth bar a quite appreciable *ritardando* and *diminuendo* can be made to mark the end of the sentence.

Sometimes the phrasing of the two hands does not coincide. This is frequently the case in polyphonic music, and where imitation is involved between both hands the differences in phrasing should, if anything, be exaggerated. In the third bar of the following example, left hand, a break should be made between the two F's, so that the first F is played lightly and *staccato*, with the second F slightly stronger, the same procedure being observed in the right hand in the following bar:

Ex. 60: Beethoven *Piano Sonata No. 28* in A, Op. 101, 2nd movement, bars 65–68

The maximum amount of demarcation between two successive phrases is achieved by means of a full use of break, dynamic change and *ritardando*, all combined, as for instance before the statement or re-statement of a main theme. In such cases the composer usually indicates how the phrasing is to be effected, but in the following instance, in addition to making a *ritardando*, as marked, and starting the new theme *fortissimo*, it would be justifiable to make a clear break before the double bar so as to allow a distinct articulation of the first note of the theme:

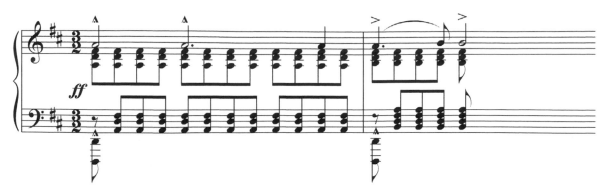

Ex. 61: Liszt *Piano Sonata* in B minor, bars 103–106

Sometimes, however, the texture is such that the ordinary methods of phrasing do not apply. In the following illustration the rhythmic pattern moves so smoothly and continuously through the four-bar phrase-lengths that it would be inartistic to attempt to demarcate them in any way. Yet the shape of the phrases is clearly felt by reason of their harmonic and rhythmic structure:

Ex. 62: Beethoven *Piano Sonata No. 4* in E flat, Op. 7, 3rd movement, bars 96–102

So far we have been dealing with phrasing in its broadest aspect of demarcation between one phrase or part of a phrase and another. In a narrower sense phrasing can mean the demarcation of any of the note-groups which occur within the phrase or sub-phrase. Such demarcation can be effected by two of the methods already described, namely, by dynamic differentiation and by the use of a break. The use of *ritardando* does not arise within the smaller divisions of the phrase. As a general rule, the first note of a slurred group of two or more notes will receive a slight accent. In quick tempo the second note (or the last if there be more than two) will be shortened, so that in effect it is played *staccato*:

Ex. 63a: Mozart *Piano Sonata No. 5* in G, K.283, 1st movement, bar 34

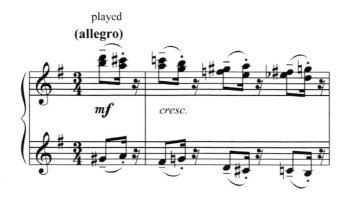

Ex. 63b: Mozart *Piano Sonata No. 5* in G, K.283, 1st movement, bar 34, performance version

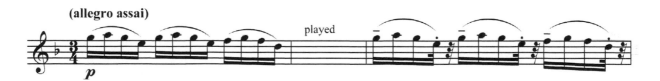

Ex. 63c: Mozart *Piano Sonata No. 2* in F, K.280, 1st movement, bar 28, right hand

In slow tempo the second note (or last of the group) will be played *portamento*, i.e. half-*staccato*, so that a break intervenes before the succeeding note:

Ex. 64: Mozart *Piano Sonata No. 2* in F, K.280, 2nd movement, bars 1–2, right hand

The last note of a group should never be accented, unless the composer so directs. Though Chopin has specifically indicated a *diminuendo* for each of the following phrases, more than one distinguished pianist is accustomed to give a sharp accent to the B double-flat and E flat in the right hand, with a resultant banal effect:

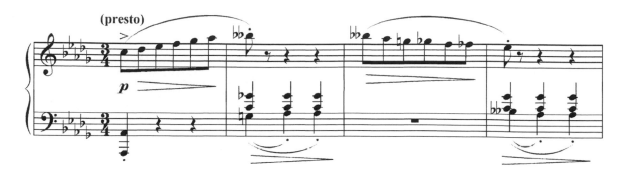

Ex. 65: Chopin *Scherzo No. 2* in B flat minor, Op. 31, bars 53–56

To take a further example, the C sharp in the second bar, right hand, of the following extract is marked *staccato*, and should be played lightly as the last note of a delicate phrase. Yet one often hears this note played with a heavy accent, and even sustained with pedal:

Ex. 66: Chopin *Nocturne No. 5* in F sharp, Op. 15, No. 2, bars 1–3

Upon such apparent trifles will depend that clarity of detail which is so essential if the performance of a work is to be artistic and vivid. From all that has been said it will be obvious that phrasing is a subtle process, and the precise method to be employed, especially where broader phrasing is concerned, can only be determined by the context.

CHAPTER NINE
DYNAMICS

Dynamics are probably more neglected than any other element of interpretation, since the pianist is usually content with a rough and ready fulfilment of the indications prescribed. In classical and to a lesser extent in romantic music such indications are sparse, sometimes even unreliable, yet if the performance of a work is to be really telling the graph of its dynamics must be as clearly defined as that of its formal structure. To take a simple example, one hears Schumann's *Of Strange Lands and People* (the first of his *Scenes of Childhood*) played even by eminent pianists for the most part in *mezzo-piano*, with only the *crescendo* observed in the middle section and with a true *pianissimo* only at the end. But for a really artistic performance the whole piece should present a dynamic form based on a coherent plan such as the following, which has been determined by a consideration of the phrasing and of the melodic contour:

Ex. 67: Schumann *Kinderszenen*, Op. 15, No. 1, *Von fremden Ländern und Menschen*, bars 1–22

Here a considerable liberty has been taken in the middle section, where the *crescendo* which Schumann has indicated in the bar marked with a *fermata* has been transferred to the bars following the double bar, and the *fermata*-bar itself marked *diminuendo* to *pianissimo*. Such a departure from the composer's intentions might indeed seem culpable, but it has only been made because of the conviction that the texture of the *fermata*-bar is too thin to sustain a *crescendo*, and that a *diminuendo* is immeasurably more effective.

Without a general dynamic scheme of this kind there is a danger that the melodic curve of the initial two-bar phrase, which occurs six times in all, will be played more or less alike on each repetition, and will pall as a result of insufficient variety of colour. Note also that the last phrase is marked at a lower dynamic level than on its first occurrence before the double bar, so that the ending fades into the remote distance.

In the absence of any particular dynamic scheme, it is natural for a rising melody to increase and for a falling melody to decrease in intensity. In this way variety of tone will result spontaneously in music which is essentially melodic or polyphonic. A descending line may indeed call for increasing volume, especially if its progressions are sequential – as in the middle section of the Schumann piece dealt with above – or again, an ascending melody may gradually fade into *pianissimo*, achieving a climax by the reverse process of a diminution of tone until the final note is sounded, as it were, in a breathless hush. Frequent as such cases may be, it is nevertheless true that passages which mount in pitch are more likely to acquire a corresponding reinforcement of tone, so that the melodic and dynamic apex will coincide in positive terms. In the case of fugue subjects, for instance, it is often advisable to allow the dynamic shading to rise or fall slightly, according to the melodic curve, e.g.:

Ex. 68a: Bach *Das Wohltemperierte Klavier*, Book I, *Fugue 14* in F sharp minor, BWV 858, bars 1–4

Ex. 68b: Bach *Das Wohltemperierte Klavier*, Book I, *Fugue 21* in B flat, BWV 866, bars 1–5

while the same principle can be applied to entire passages in the course of the fugue (but see p. 84 below).

In dealing with a whole movement or a complete work, not only must the dynamics of individual passages be considered but their comparative levels in relation to each other must also be carefully planned. In music of a lyrical nature, or again in rococo music, the levels will not as a rule be too sharply differentiated, and no outstanding climax may arise. With Mozart, for instance, the intensity is seldom concentrated at one focal point, due to the somewhat formal and decorative style of the period, and the dynamic weight is fairly evenly distributed throughout his movements in sonata form. In music of an epic or rhapsodic type, however, or in polyphonic music such as the Bach fugues, it is usual for the dynamic stress to increase cumulatively over long stretches, producing in shorter works one marked climax as a rule, and in longer works several climaxes, one of which, however, will inevitably stand out above its fellows. In some of Beethoven's finest sonata-movements the main weight of the movement is concentrated in the coda, so that it reaches its peak point of intensity and momentum towards the end. This is the case in the first and last movements of the *Sonata* 'Appassionata', Op. 57, and in the finales of the *Sonata* 'Pathétique', Op. 13, and of the 'Moonlight' *Sonata*, Op. 27, No. 2. A similar shifting of the weight to the close of the movement is often to be found in the sonatas of romantic composers, as in the first and last movements of Schumann's *Sonata* in G minor, Op. 22, and the finale of Brahms' *Sonata* in F minor, Op. 5. In the first movement of the latter work – and this is a fairly common feature also – the main weight occurs towards the end of the development and with the restatement of the principal theme. In the case of slow movements which achieve a depth of passionate expression it is more usual for the climax to occur in the course of the episode or middle section, if the movement be in episodical form. One might take the slow movement of Beethoven's *Sonata* in E flat, Op. 7, as a typical example.

It is essential then for the pianist to recognise the main climax of a movement or work where such exists, and to make it the crowning point by keeping tone in reserve for its arrival. Not every climax of this kind, however, needs to be merely louder than its fellows. Intensity can sometimes be more effectively obtained by tone-quality, by intensity of touch rather than degree of volume. Such intensity is in the last degree indefinable, being a capacity to make the tone tell and ring without forcing it to extremes. But whether the chief climax be marked by a maximum use of tone or by especially telling tone, its intensity should be helped by an almost imperceptible increase in tempo as the climax approaches, or alternatively a slight broadening, according to the context. Subsequently the tempo will then be eased off, or increased again to normal, as the case may be, and provided the adjustment be a subtle, not an obvious one, it will help the hearer to recognise the climax as having a special urgency or special weight which will make it stand out and by its commanding position give a unity to the structure as a whole.

Speaking generally of dynamic levels, with Mozart and Beethoven the contrasts will be more or less solidly juxtaposed, in keeping with the symmetries of classical architecture, while with the romantics, particularly with Chopin, the dynamic outline must be more carefully moulded, the shading more varied and sensuous, and the *una corda* pedal more frequently used. Many of the works of Liszt or of impressionist composers such as Debussy are almost studies in dynamics, relying largely for their effect on the adroitness with which the glittering harmonic texture is worked into a shifting scale of dynamic values.

The problem of balance, i.e. dynamic distinction between different parts simultaneously, are discussed below in Chapter 14. Sometimes a passage can sound ineffective or even meaningless unless from a welter of unessential notes the melody is brought well to the fore, and supplementary shading achieved by underlining secondary melodic strands. The following passage affords a good example:

Ex. 69: Chopin *Impromptu No. 2* in F sharp, Op. 36, bars 73–78

For the first two bars the melody in the right hand must sing out with intense and increasing tone above the left hand accompaniment. At the end of the second bar a sudden *diminuendo* should be made, sufficient to reduce the third bar to a lower dynamic level. The melody, as marked in the Klindworth edition with double stems, is then heard in the third bar on quavers 1, 4–7, 10–12, while quavers 2, 3, 8 and 9 are kept to the subordinate level of the quavers in the left hand. In the fourth bar if only the melody notes marked as such are brought out (i.e. quavers 1, 6, 7, 12 and the first quaver of the fifth bar), the rhythmical effect will be commonplace, and this is where the detail-work of interpretation can manifest itself. By making a *crescendo* on quavers 2–4, and 8–10, and giving a clear secondary accent to quavers 4 and 10, the rhythmical flow of the bar and the melodic curve are considerably improved. Quavers 2–4 are similarly treated in the fifth bar, but for the remainder of this bar and the succeeding bar only the melody notes marked as such should be brought out.

In the next example the upward-moving alto melody must sing out perceptibly in the right hand, and more clearly than the top part, for the first two bars and until the third beat of the third bar, at which point the melodic interest shifts to the top part exclusively:

Ex. 70: Brahms *Sieben Fantasien, Intermezzo* in E, Op. 116, No. 6, bars 1–4

By giving added tone to an inner progression one can often considerably enhance the colour of a particular passage. Compare the effect of playing the following passage with all the lower parts equally subordinate to the melody, and again with a slight emphasis on the line A flat–A natural–B flat in the tenor, and D flat–D natural–E flat in the bass in bars 2–3 and 4–5 respectively, and again on the line B flat–B natural–C in the tenor and E flat–E natural–F in the bass in bars 5–7 and 7–8 respectively:

Ex. 71: Chopin *Waltz No 7* in C sharp minor, Op. 64, No. 2, bars 81–89

It is by devices such as this that one brings out the hidden beauty of the texture. One might, for instance, play a phrase on its first appearance without discriminating between the lower parts, and on its second appearance make such slight distinctions as those referred to above, so that the phrase becomes more intense and telling the second time.

The bringing to the fore of the principal melodic line, whether in an upper, middle or lower part, occurs most frequently and consistently in fugal forms of writing, where a subject in any part has to be underlined. It occurs also in Bach chorale arrangements, such as Dame Myra Hess' arrangement of *Jesu, Joy of Man's Desiring* or Walter Rummel's arrangement of *Mortify Us by Thy Grace*, increased tone being the only means on the piano of demarcating a tune which on the organ, for instance, can be picked out by means of different registration on another manual. Other examples are Chopin's *Study* in A flat, Op. 25, No. 1, in which the melody notes in the right hand and the fundamental bass-notes, each on its first appearance, are printed in larger type and must stand out above the inner swirling accompaniment and – to take a modern instance – E. J. Moeran's *Irish Love Song*, in which a folk tune ('Jimín mo Mhíle Stór') [Jimmy my dearest love] is richly and decoratively treated, the constituent notes of the tune, also printed in larger type, appearing variously as the inner or lower notes of the chordal superstructure. In all such cases the added tone is achieved by pressure from the forearm and the stiffening of each successive finger involved in the playing of the melody-notes, such stiffening being necessary to carry the pressure, and to isolate the finger concerned from its fellows.

Where there is only one melodic line the problem of balance is relatively simple, but where there are two or more melodic lines which require varying degrees of shading, the adjustment involved can be quite a complex matter. In the following passage no less than four parts need to be differentiated:

Ex. 72: Chopin *Scherzo No. 2* in B flat minor, Op. 31, bars 316–323

The two top parts must sing out alternately, the bass part should be kept subsidiary, while the tenor part (dotted minims) should be brought out sufficiently for it to be felt as a constituent melodic part.

Balance becomes a more complex problem when two or more melodic lines are involved. In music of a polyphonic type, then, the pianist must work out the relative intensity of the parts almost with the care with which a conductor will work out the balance of an orchestral score.

CHAPTER TEN

RUBATO

Having dealt with dynamic variation we come now to 'agogic' variation, or variation in the speed of movement, and in particular to that species of agogic variation known as *tempo rubato*, or simply *rubato*. Literally meaning 'robbed' time, the term *rubato* is sometimes used in its widest sense to suggest that flexibility of movement which is always present in an artistic performance, and which redeems time from mere mechanical precision. In this sense *rubato* is called for in the performance of music of every period. But in its more limited and more usual sense the term *rubato* is applied to a more marked type of fluctuation, yet of such a kind that in the long run the time-length covered is much the same as if no fluctuations had taken place, the slight *accelerando* being more or less compensated for by the slight *ritardando* which ensues, or vice versa. In other words, the stolen time is repaid again.

This species of agogic variation, though known already in the eighteenth century, scarcely arises in classical piano music, but is a feature in the music of the romantic composers, and pre-eminently in that of Chopin. According to some of his pupils' testimony Chopin himself seems to have regarded the left hand as the conductor, so that the accompaniment would keep firmly to the beat, while the right hand, the 'singing' hand, would deviate freely, either 'irresolutely lingering, or as in passionate speech eagerly anticipating with a certain impatient vehemence.'[37] This, of course, is an over-statement of the case, for in playing a melody such as that of the *Nocturne* in E flat, Op. 9, No. 2 with *rubato*, both hands must simultaneously share in the minute *accelerandos* and *ritardandos* which will give distinction and delicacy to the melody. It would be nearer the mark to say that the moment the melody becomes quiescent (as in the second half of the fourth bar of the *Nocturne*) the left hand accompaniment should immediately resume strict time, so that the fundamental pace is never changed. In fact it is only pianists possessing a very fine sense of rhythm who can play *rubato* successfully.

Of all the faults committed in the performance of Chopin's music, or of romantic music in general, exaggerated use of *rubato* is the most frequent, and the most fatal. If the hearer becomes conscious of the *rubato*, if the rhythm is distorted rather than gently and imperceptibly swayed, the result is not expressive playing, as the pianist may fondly imagine, but caricature. According to Stavenhagen an excellent illustration of *rubato* was once given by Liszt to a pupil who had been unsuccessfully trying to play his *Nocturne* in A flat. Liszt was living in the Hofgärtnerei in Weimar at the time, and the window of his music room looked out on a park. It was a stormy day. 'Observe that tree,' he said, 'sometimes the wind sways it gently, sometimes violently to and fro, sometimes the whole tree is bent in motion, again it is quite still. Or look at that cornfield in the distance, over which the wind sweeps with an undulating rhythm. That is perfect *rubato*, the tempered movement of the corn, the reluctant yielding of the tree, but when you play *rubato*, your corn, your tree is smitten to the ground!'

---

[37] See Frederick Niecks, *Frederick Chopin* (London 1890), Vol. II, pp. 101 seq.

Chopin himself was outraged by the exaggerated *rubato* with which pianists played his works, and as a result he would often forbid his pupils to use *rubato* at all, forcing them to play in strict time. The exaggerations he suffered from are probably as rampant nowadays as ever, foremost among them being the habit of making such sudden *ritardandos* and *accelerandos* that the actual note-values are altered. Thus one hears the top melody-notes in the following passage:

Ex. 73a: Chopin *Nocturne No.12* in G, Op. 37, No. 2, bars 29–32

played:

Ex. 73b: Chopin *Nocturne No. 12* in G, Op. 37, No. 2, bars 31–32 as sometimes played

Or the following:

Ex. 74a: Chopin *Scherzo No. 2* in B flat minor, Op. 31, bars 259–264

played:

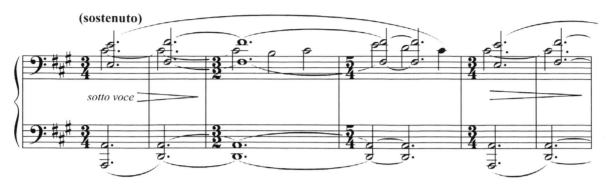

Ex. 74b: Chopin *Scherzo No. 2* in B flat minor, Op. 31, bars 259–264, as sometimes played

Another irritating habit is that of prolonging the first of two equal notes when this note happens to be of special importance, so that instead of two crotchets, a minim-cum-crotchet triplet, or even a dotted crotchet-cum-quaver group results. Again, when a dotted rhythm is prescribed some pianists add an extra dot, so that a final semiquaver becomes a demisemiquaver. Thus one often hears the opening theme of the *Nocturne* in D flat:

Ex. 75a: Chopin *Nocturne No. 8* in D flat, Op. 27, No. 2, bars 2–3

vulgarised as follows:

Ex. 75b: Chopin *Nocturne No. 8* in D flat, Op. 27, No. 2, bars 2–3, vulgarised version

Or the majestic rhythmic line of the C minor *Prélude*:

Ex. 76a: Chopin *24 Préludes*, No. 20 in C minor, Op. 28, bar 1

reduced to:

Ex. 76b: Chopin *24 Préludes*, Op. 28, No. 20 in C minor, bar 1, reduced to

Some of our foremost virtuosi are addicted to the above habits, apparently under the impression that the prolongation of an important melody note to secure added intensity is an essential feature of expressive playing. To any sensitive listener, however, the arbitrary distortion of the rhythm can but seem an affectation, in fact an unpardonable licence. If one's playing is to have the qualities of directness and sincerity one of the first essentials must be to reproduce the rhythmic line as written and intended by the composer. *Rubato* means only a slight modification of the tempo as applied to a whole group of notes, and applied proportionately, nor can such *rubato* modifications be introduced at random.

As has already been pointed out in connection with phrasing, *rubato* is often appropriate at the cadential points. In the following two-bar phrase a rather pronounced *ritardando* is essential from the first to the fourth semiquaver of the second bar if the melodic curve is to be expressively shaped, after which on the fifth semiquaver the accompaniment is resumed in strict time:

Ex. 77: Chopin *Études,* No. 3 in E, Op. 10, bars 1–3

The same procedure is necessary in the case of the semiquaver group in the second bar of the following example:

Ex. 78: Chopin *Nocturne No. 9* in B, Op. 32, No. 1, bars 1–3

Sometimes a sub-phrase can be effectively delineated by means of *rubato*, as in the following phrase in which a barely perceptible lingering on the melody-notes B and C sharp in the second bar will give delicate poise to the two-bar sub-phrase. Without *rubato* the continuous crotchet movement tends to become rigid and monotonous, but it must be emphasised that any agogic variation here should be a matter of subtle implication only:

Ex. 79: Chopin *Impromptu No. 2* in F sharp, Op. 36, bars 7–12

In each of the above instances *rubato* can be used to underline the cadential points. Frequently, however, *rubato* is used quite independently of cadences, and for such a purpose as to give added intensity to any part – even to the opening – of a phrase. For instance the melody-notes which occur at the start of the third four-bar phrase in bar nine of the following passage should be played with a slightly lingering effect if they are to be heard to full advantage:

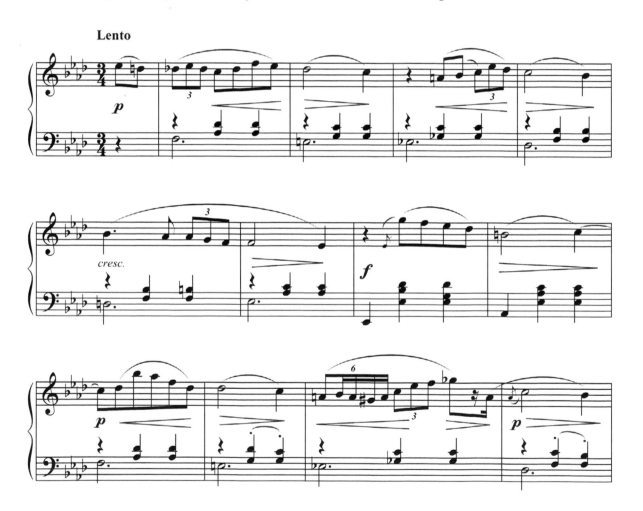

Ex. 80: Chopin *Waltz No. 9* in A flat, Op. 69, No. 1, bars 1–12

while the same applies to the quavers in the second bar of the following example (with a cadential *rubato* in bars 6–7):

Ex. 81: Chopin *Waltz No. 5* in A flat, Op. 42, bars 121–128

Again, *rubato* is often used in the case of embellishments or florid passages, the notes of which need to be given a certain latitude, so that their swifter movement will not fall too suddenly on the ear. For instance it would inartistic to play the sextolets in the second bar of the following passage in strict time. Towards the end of the preceding bar a very slight broadening will allow the melody to sing out, and by retaining this tempo in the next bar the semiquaver groups can be allowed adequate flexibility. In the last group sufficient *ritardando* should be made to round off the whole passage:

Ex. 82: Chopin *Impromptu No. 2* in F sharp, Op. 36, bars 70–72

Where a cadenza-like passage covers a wider stretch it may need to be taken with a gradually increasing and then lessening speed, to give it freedom and shape. In the following cadenza the speed should increase appreciably in the second and third bars, and a marked *ritardando* should be made in the fifth and sixth bars (of Ex. 83):

Ex. 83: Liszt *Valse impromptu*, bars 125–132

Occasionally *rubato* may be used for the purpose of contrasting adjacent phrases, as in the following example, where the poignancy of the second phrase is intensified if – in the course of the chord repetitions (i.e. in approaching the first chord of the last bar) – the relatively brisk tempo which held good for the first phrase be very slightly modified. Here, as ever, one must guard against any tendency to exaggerate, for if a discrepancy in the speed becomes obvious, the phrases remain detached instead of flowing into each other, and the continuity suffers:

Ex. 84: Schubert *Impromptu* in A flat, Op. 90, No 4, bars 3–6

Such variations which arise in miniature within the phrase arise also in terms of a wider perspective in the course of the performance of a work. It has already been suggested that as a climax approaches there may be a tendency for the speed to increase, and after it has passed, or again towards the close of a period or movement, there may be a corresponding tendency towards relaxation of the tempo. To take a relatively small-scale example, in order to achieve the necessary sense of climax towards the end of the middle section of the Schubert *Impromptu* in A flat already referred to, forward movement is necessary for eight bars prior to the apex bar (marked *sff*), with a subsequent easing of the tempo in the course of the next nine bars. Conversely certain types of climax are made still more effective through broadening the tempo and giving full opportunity for weightier tone. Thus in the finale of Grieg's *Piano Sonata* in E minor, Op. 7, the approach to the climax at bar 162 and the climax itself are taken somewhat more broadly, while the final climax on the last page, marked *sempre grandioso*, is similarly approached and taken with a slow-swinging stateliness. Again towards the end of a section or movement leading to a vigorous or tense *dénouement* the tempo may tend to increase, as in the case of the finales of the Schumann *Sonata* in G minor and the Brahms *Sonata* in F minor mentioned on pp. 38 and 35 above, while at the end of Liszt's *Gnomenreigen*, as if to suggest the gnomes dancing off helter-skelter, an increasing tempo is allied with decreasing tone.

For further references to *rubato*, see the description of Chopin's *Study* in E, Op. 10, No. 3 (page 183 below).

CHAPTER ELEVEN
RHYTHMIC SHAPING AND GROUPING

Having dealt with *rubato* in its various aspects, some further problems relating to the shaping of a movement and to the spacing of adjacent movements remain to be discussed.

First of all, should the traditional *ritardando* be made before the entry or re-entry of a subject in sonata form? Such a *ritardando*, provided it is justified by the context, purposes to make the recurrence of the subject clear to the listener and to allow the outlines of the structure stand forth in bolder relief. Some pianists, however, regard the making of such a *ritardando* under almost any circumstances as an unnecessary distortion, holding that the recurrence of a subject should be patent to the intelligent listener without the help of a change in speed. It is true that an exaggerated use of *ritardando* impedes the flow of the movement and is out of keeping with the classical style. But that the composers themselves have felt the need of the emphasis which a *ritardando* imparts, particularly for the lead-back to an earlier idea, is shown by the frequency with which the re-entry of the first subject at the recapitulation, or the re-entry of the main theme in rondo or sonata-rondo form, is preceded by a *fermata*, by a gap, or an inherent rhythmic broadening. Where none of the latter is present, then a *ritardando* is often justified, ranging according to the context from the barest nuance, in which dynamic shading will play a vital part, e.g.:

Ex. 85: Mozart *Piano Sonata No. 18* in D, K.576, 3rd movement, bars 63–66

Ex. 86: Beethoven *Piano Sonata No. 3* in C, Op. 2, No. 3, 1st movement, bars 137–140

to a fairly pronounced *ritardando*, e.g.:

Ex. 87: Mozart *Piano Sonata No. 16* in C, K.545, 1st movement, bars 40–43

Ex. 88: Beethoven *Piano Sonata No. 9* in E, Op. 14, No. 1, 1st movement, bars 87–91

In the first three examples above, no appreciable modification of the tempo should arise until the second half of the bar prior to the re-entry of the theme, though in the last example the *ritardando* should stretch over the whole bar (bar four of Ex. 88). Sir Thomas Beecham is unexcelled in his ability to suggest rather than to actually make a *ritardando* of this kind, and the exquisite poise achieved by this conductor in the delineation of a typical Mozartian curve should be a model to every pianist.

It frequently happens, however, that a *ritardando* is excluded by the nature of the context, as in the first movement of Beethoven's *Sonata* in E minor, Op. 90, where just before the recapitulation a rhythmic broadening is followed by a diminution of the note values, leading directly into the first subject. A *ritardando* here, other than the inherent one already effected by the composer, would be fatal, since the quickening movement must not be interfered with. Again in the following example it would be inartistic to vary the continuous movement into which the rondo theme is dovetailed, the sudden *piano* being sufficient to demarcate its entry:

Ex. 89: Beethoven *Piano Sonata No. 12* in A flat, Op. 26, 4th movement, bars 97–102

Sometimes a slight *ritardando* is called for to mark the entry of the second subject in sonata form, where an obvious lead-in occurs, e.g.:

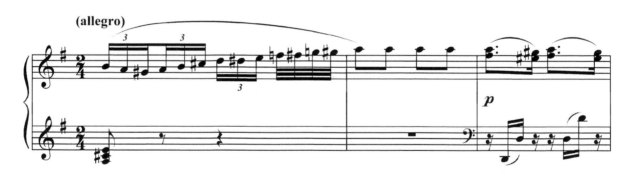

Ex. 90: Beethoven *Piano Sonata No. 10* in G, Op. 14, No. 2, 1st movement, bars 24–26

But the composer, as a rule, demarcates the arrival of a new idea in such a way as to make the emphasis of *ritardando* unnecessary, and recourse to the latter is far more usual in marking the return to an earlier idea.

All that we have been saying so far applies then equally to the return of the first section in ternary, episodical or minuet and trio form. Incidentally, in making such a return any melodic embellishment which serves as an upbeat to the recurring theme should at once be taken in strict time. In the following example the slight broadening in the third bar to emphasise the return of the opening minuet theme ends with the first beat of the fourth bar, and the run on the second and third beats of this bar must then be taken at the full tempo:

Ex. 91: Mozart *Piano Sonata No. 11* in A, K.331, 2nd movement, bars 27–32

In passing from the minuet to the trio, the *ritardando* will be somewhat less marked than it will at the end of the trio leading back to the minuet, for the reason already suggested above, namely, that the return of an idea needs more preparation than does the introduction of an idea not already stated. Moreover, pianists who take the last two beats of the trio (or minuet II) and the upbeat of minuet I in strict time

Ex. 92: Mozart *Piano Sonata No. 4* in E flat, K.282, 2nd movement, bars 39–40 and bars 1–2

blur the outlines, and give an effect of breathlessness which is out of keeping with the easy grace and dignity of this dance-form. A slight hiatus, as if the *ritardando* from first beat to second were prolonged until the start of the upbeat of the minuet, gives just the right sense of poise.

If it is necessary to allow a little ventilation between two adjacent sections, such as the minuet and trio, it is sometimes equally necessary to draw sections or phrases closer together which are separated by rests, since the duration of the rests is often not a matter of precise calculation but is forced upon the composer by the necessity of securing a re-entry at that part of the bar which will give the proper metrical alignment. This is frequently the case with Liszt, whose rhetorical phrases need to be linked and dovetailed to give the proper sense of continuity. In fact, one of the ways in which performers of Liszt most frequently malign the composer is in the literal observation of the rests and pauses which occur so plentifully in his music, whereby the element of interruption and interpolation, instead of being minimised, can be stressed to a point of caricature. For instance, the last fifteen bars of the *Nocturne* in A flat are marked *poco a poco ritenuto*. In bars 8–7 and 6–5 from the end a strict observance of the rests would cause undue suspense, whereas with a slight curtailment, the continuity is more successfully sustained:

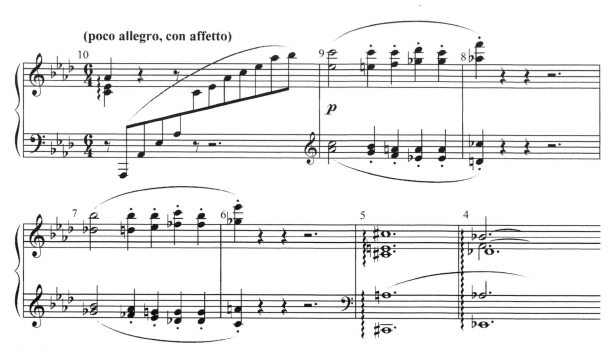

Ex. 93: Liszt *Liebesträume, Nocturne* No. 3 in A flat, bars 77–83

Again at the end of the *Ballade* in B minor an over-long pause also needs to be curtailed:

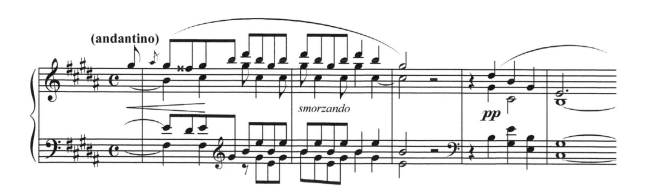

Ex. 94: Liszt *Ballade No. 2* in B minor, bars 308–312

To each of the above cases the maxim might well be applied that if a phrase is rounded off by means of *rubato*, i.e. a certain degree of *ritardando* and rests then intervene, it is often wise to count these rests not at the slightly slower tempo at which the phrase has just ended, but at the basic tempo. If this method be adopted in the two cases quoted, little further curtailment of the pauses will be found necessary.

The artistic player will instinctively make slight adjustments here and there in matters of tempo which are not indicated by the composer, or which many even modify the composer's expressed intentions. At the end of the finale of the 'Moonlight' *Sonata* is the *Adagio* marking to be taken literally?

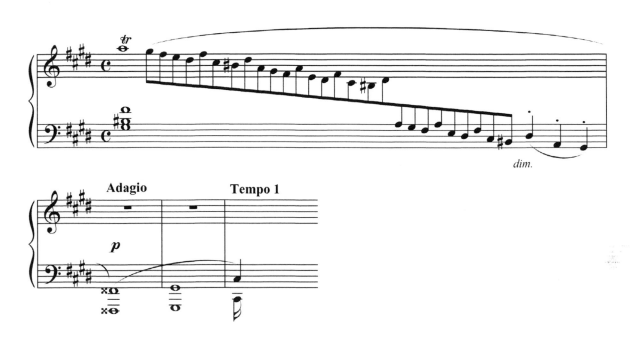

Ex. 95: Beethoven *Piano Sonata No. 14* in C sharp minor, Op. 27, No. 2, 3rd movement, bars 187–190

The two octaves marked *Adagio* belong in fact to the preceding cadenza. If they are played in a strict *adagio* tempo they will tend to separate from the cadenza, instead of forming part of the *rallentando* which should develop continuously from the second half of the cadenza bar up to Tempo 1. Though the marking *Adagio* gives the right psychological impression, by contrast with the main tempo – *presto agitato* – any slower tempo than *andante* would tend to pall. Furthermore, the bars should be differentiated, the second being slightly more sustained than the first if the effect of a broad *rallentando* is to be achieved over the whole passage.

To take a further instance, a slight *stretto* will be made by any sensitive player from bars 6–10 of the passage quoted below. To play these bars strictly at the tempo of the opening sounds dull and laboured, unless a faster tempo be taken than either the opening or the main part of the scherzo would warrant:

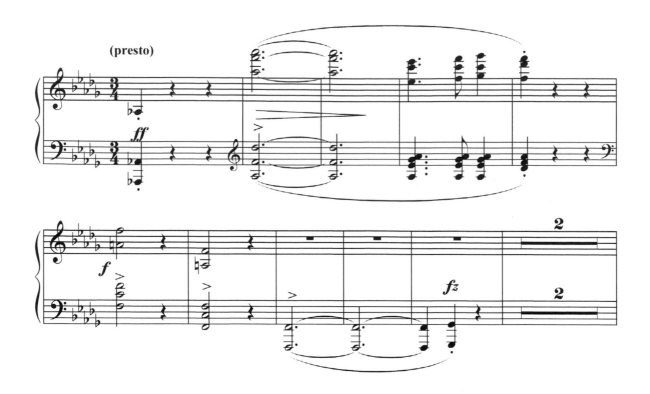

Ex. 96: Chopin *Scherzo No. 2* in B flat minor, Op. 31, bars 13–23

A fault frequently found even with pianists of standing is the inability to end a movement or a work with a sense of finality, a sense of having expressed a sequence of ideas and rounded them off as a whole. The result is as if the movement or work had not ended but merely stopped, as if the cycle of ideas had not moved through their appointed orbit and reached a logical resting-place, but had broken off indeterminately. Again, the impression may be conveyed that the player has remained unmoved by the ideas he has been interpreting, or is at least indifferent as to whether these ideas have reached and moved his audience. Just as the concluding sentence of a good speech will usually have some distinctive quality, will be given greater emphasis or greater intensity, or conversely, when the ending is witty or light-hearted, will be marked by a special deftness and vivacity, so the pianist should impart to the concluding bars of a work a corresponding distinction, so that all that has gone before will be culminated, and the effect of this culmination remain in the mind of his hearers even after the last tones have died away.

To achieve a proper sense of finality it may be necessary, according to the context, to allow the tempo relax very gradually towards the close, or conversely to aim at an increasing tension and acceleration. In many cases, especially with the older masters, a fairly appreciable *rallentando* is necessary and taken for granted by the composer in the last bar or two. The tradition of a concluding *rallentando* is still so strong that it is sometimes assumed, and left unmarked even by modern composers who normally mark every agogic detail. Yet a literal-minded pianist who will not hesitate to make the conventional grandiose *rallentando* in a work of Handel will end a movement of a Mozart sonata, or even a romantic work, without modifying the tempo even by a vestige. Sometimes the composer will so demarcate the concluding bars that no modification is necessary. But as a rule it is incumbent on the performer to effect this modification himself, and to impart to the conclusion a sense of inevitability, so that when he stops it is as if the curtains had been drawn across the stage.

If there be an art in ending a movement or a work, so too there is an art in making the transition from one movement to another in a sonata or suite. Pianists too often fail to realise this, and allow a time-interval to intervene and the interest of their hearers to sag to such an extent that the relationship between the movements is lost, and the atmosphere already created needlessly dispelled. When the last note or chord of a movement has been released, it is fatal for the pianist to relax, look around, hunt for a handkerchief, shift his chair, or indulge in any of the movements which pianists are sometimes wont to cultivate to fill in the few seconds of time which must here elapse. Such movements encourage the audience to fidget, cough, whisper, and generally indicate that the time for the alleviation of physical discomforts has arrived. The effect is much the same as when some of the players in chamber or orchestral music tune between the movements of a quartet or symphony, and with their rude, irrelevant tones shatter the magic web which the music has hitherto been weaving. To prevent this breakdown in the train of thought when a movement has come to an end the pianist should try to increase his own and his audience's concentration during the few seconds' interval by a tense bearing, by making no unnecessary movement, and by retaining the appearance throughout of just being about to continue. No opportunity for distraction will then arise, and the audience will be held in suspense, held by the memory of all that has gone before and by anticipation of what is to come.

The interval between successive movements should as a rule be slightly longer in proceeding from a quick movement to a slow movement, and less long in proceeding from a slow movement to a quick movement, the reason being that the ending of a quick movement is relatively more abrupt than that of a slow movement, and a little more time is then needed to make the transition from *allegro* to *andante* or *adagio*. Movements which are both fast moving, such as scherzo and finale, will need less time between them, while the broader, more tragic or more profound a slow movement happens to be the more space it will require on both sides. In short, just as the shape given to the conclusion of the movement must be in proportion to the movement as a whole, so the time-interval between successive movements must be in proportion to their respective speeds and stresses.

When the transition from one movement to another has been effectively made it will be easier to capture the mood of the new movement from the very first chord. In the critique of a recital by Paderewski, Ernest Newman once singled out as the most impressive achievement of the evening Paderewski's transition from the first movement to the second in the Beethoven *Sonata* in D minor, Op. 31, No. 2. Here the last chord of the first movement prepares the way so effectively for the first chord of the *Adagio* that little else is needed than to impart a sense of perfect poise before the *Adagio* is begun. Even when the composer has not linked the movements together in this way, and the end of one contrasts sharply with the beginning of the next, the 'join' should be all the more carefully thought out and prepared.

Two types of structure need careful treatment if any sense of continuity is to be achieved in their performance, namely works consisting of a number of short pieces, such as Schumann's *Papillons, Carnaval,* or *Davidsbündler,* and secondly, sets of variations or sonata movements in variation form. As regards the former, the interval between the various pieces will be correspondingly less than between the movements of a sonata, because of their shorter proportions. If the intervening intervals are too long, the work will tend both to disintegrate and to drag as a result of excessive pausing and no sense of unity or cohesion will be imparted. Liszt once said of the Schumann works mentioned that they might be regarded as strings of pearls, and it is the pianist's task to avoid isolating the individual pearls in any of these works and to thread them together. So too Chopin's *24 Preludes* should, ideally speaking, be played as one work, in which case it is for the performer to unite the *Preludes* by subtle timing. Played thus the work as a whole assumes a lofty stature, and the individual preludes assume a significance which they lack when played in isolation.

Much of what has been said applies also to sets of variations, which can be drawn even more closely together because of the unity which the common theme imparts. The duration between the variations will again be proportionate to the tempi. Thus it stands to reason that in the variations of the first movement of the Mozart *Sonata* in A (K. 331) a longer pause should be made before and after Variation 5, the *adagio* variation. Again in Beethoven's *Six Variations*, Op. 76, in which the changes of speed from one movement to another are relatively slight, only the least pause, if any, will arise between them.

Having considered the relationship between the sections or movements of a single work, some final words may be said about the relationship between different works forming a group in a piano recital. In choosing a group one should aim primarily at contrast. Unlike works go best together, but the extent to which contrast can be carried and the effectiveness of the contrast can only be tested by experiment and by careful consideration of the atmosphere of each work and of the transition from one to the other. Two contemplative, slow-moving works, two lyrical works, two gay or brilliant works seldom go well together. Within the one work a mood or mood-cycle can be sustained at length, according to the ability of the composer to create on an extended scale. But once the mood-cycle has run its course and the work has come to an end, satiety results if the listener be expected to react anew to a related cycle, a similarity in speed being often sufficient to bring two cycles dangerously close, whereas a complete change of mood will give the necessary respite to one's emotional sensitivities, and infuse freshness and zest.

Groups are sometimes arranged chronologically, the difference in the style of succeeding periods helping to effect the necessary contrast. But a chronological arrangement is by no means necessary, provided one remembers that the transition from a classical, formal and elegant style to a romantic and emotional style is an easier and more natural transition than the other way around. To take an extreme example, one would not play a Scarlatti sonata after a Chopin nocturne, though the former might well precede the latter.

When two keys mutually remote are involved between adjacent works in a group, pianists occasionally indulge in that most obnoxious of practices, namely, the improvisation of a modulation during the pause between the two works. The effect of a series of commonplace progressions or of one or two splashes of arpeggio between the utterances of the masters resembles that of a piece of idle chatter interpolated between the reading of two poems. The hearer is irritatingly aroused from the contemplation of the work he has just heard, and the few moments of silence needed to prepare him for the next work are sacrificed for the sake of the idle theory that an abrupt change of key is distressing to one's sense of tonality. After a short interval, not to mention a quantum of applause between two works, there are no two keys so opposed that will not effectively follow each other, in fact, the greater the distance between them the more dramatic and the more refreshing the change.

In a miscellaneous programme it would be unwise to place two major works in the same form – two sonatas, two sets of variations – beside each other, since the balance of the programme would be impaired by the undue weight of two similarly shaped large-scale works. This does not preclude a programme consisting entirely of sonatas, rare though such a programme may be, just as a chamber music recital will usually consist of two or three string quartets, for all the elements of contrast are contained within a sonata itself, and it is then merely necessary to choose sonatas which as a whole contrast with each other. A generation ago it was the prevailing tendency to place a major work at the end of a programme, so that the interest culminated with the final work. Nowadays it is if anything more usual to place a major work at the beginning of a programme when the audience is still fresh, or to introduce it in the middle after an introductory group of slighter works, and then to end with a group of which technical brilliance is the prevailing characteristic. One might add that the pianist who is prepared to end his recital with something miniature, quiet and subdued has yet to be born.

CHAPTER TWELVE
PEDALLING: INTERPRETATIVE ASPECT

Having dealt with the technical aspect of pedalling in Chapter Five, we come now to deal with its interpretative aspect. Pedalling is one of the most important elements in interpretation, for it is on the mode of pedalling, on the mode of fusion between successive tones or chords, that the coherence of the harmonic texture and consequently the colour of the work depends. In Liszt's words, the pedal is the soul of the piano.

As with *rubato* there are no hard or fast rules, for pedalling is ultimately a matter of individual taste. Broadly speaking less pedal will be used in music of the polyphonic type, so that the utmost clarity will be ensured for each of the combined melodic strands, while more pedal is necessary in homophonic music to blend related tones and chords and allow a maximum amount of colour.

Less pedal will then be used for the older masters such as Byrd, Couperin, Handel, Bach, Scarlatti and their contemporaries, since their music is largely polyphonic and since they wrote for the harpsichord or clavichord, neither of which instruments possessed a sustaining pedal. It would be out of keeping with the style of this period to use the pedal as extensively as in the case of the Viennese masters. On the other hand it is merely pedantic to stipulate that the sustaining pedal should be banned from the present-day performance of seventeenth and eighteenth century music simply because its use was unknown to the composers of the period. No one would have rejoiced more than Bach to hear his clavichord or harpsichord music clothed in the resonant tone of the modern grand piano, or indeed to hear his suites and concertos expressed in terms of the modern orchestra. If the present-day instrument is used at all it should be exploited to the full, not treated apologetically as a substitute for the obsolete. Moreover even though the harpsichord had no sustaining pedal and no effective means of sustaining tone, the instrument had a curious jangling resonance, the general effect being totally unlike that of the unpedalled piano and if anything nearer to that produced on the piano by pedal-fusion.

Hence where *sostenuto* chords are employed, as in the following prelude, there is little excuse for not availing of the richer tone quality which the pedal allows:

Ex. 97: Bach *Das Wohltemperierte Klavier*, Book I, *Prelude No. 8*, in E flat minor, BWV 853, bars 1-2

Again in the following *Preludes* the fusion by the pedal of all notes belonging to the same chord adds a lustre which makes the unpedalled version, by comparison, sound poor indeed:

Ex. 98: Bach *Das Wohltemperierte Klavier*, Book I, *Prelude No. 1* in C, BWV 846, bar 1

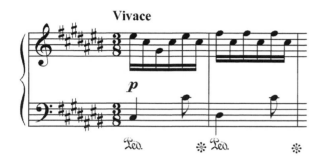

Ex. 99: Bach *Das Wohltemperierte Klavier*, Book I, *Prelude No. 3* in C sharp, BWV 848, bars 1–2

It may be taken as an axiom that arpeggios or broken chords can always be pedalled unless, of course, they happen to accompany some scalic progression the notes of which cannot be fused. In the C sharp major *Prelude* the use of the pedal allows some glowing contrasts between successive pairs of bars, as for instance between the broken chord of the first two bars in the following passage, considerably enriched when pedalled, and the running figure of the next two bars, left unpedalled for clarity's sake:

Ex. 100: Bach *Das Wohltemperierte Klavier*, Book I, *Prelude No. 3* in C sharp, BWV 848, bars 75–82

Even when the texture is mainly contrapuntal harmonic implications can occasionally be brought out by a discreet use of the pedal, without undue injury to the counterpoint. In the following extract from the C sharp major Fugue the pedal may be taken on the first half of each successive beat in the first bar and held for the whole of the first beat of the second bar to give added colour to the melodic climax, while each quaver might be pedalled on the third beat of the second bar, because of the change of harmony involved:

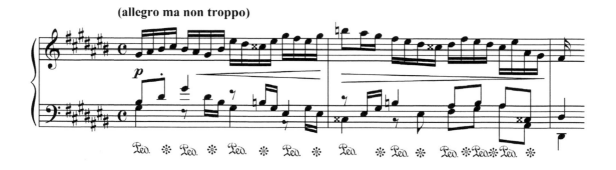

Ex. 101: Bach *Das Wohltemperierte Klavier*, Book I, *Fugue No. 3* in C sharp, BWV 848, bars 12–14

Granted that the sustaining pedal should be employed, there is at least historical justification for treating the music of this period with particular delicacy. Ample use may be made of the *una corda* pedal to secure dynamic contrasts between balanced phrases – just as on some harpsichords such contrasts were achieved by means of a second manual, couplers and swell – while the sustaining pedal should always be discreetly applied, and used rather too little than too much.

According as we move into the nineteenth century the sustaining pedal becomes an increasingly important factor in the welding together of the texture. More pedal is used with Haydn and Mozart than with Bach, and still more with Beethoven. It is true that there have always been pianists and critics who inveigh against the use of the pedal in music of the classical period. Half a century ago the noted Munich pianist Hans Bussmeyer, a pupil of Hans von Bülow, played Bach and Mozart without pedal and pedalled even Beethoven sparsely, and was assailed on the grounds that his playing was dull and colourless as a result. Today the adherents of the no-pedal-for-Bach school are as numerous as ever. Their point of view serves at least to counteract the tendency towards the opposite extreme – too rich a use of pedalling for the earlier masters, with resultant muddiness of effect.

In considering the amount of pedal fusion possible three factors must be taken into consideration, namely phrasing, symmetry and speed. As a rule the pedal should not be sustained beyond the end of a phrase which has to be clearly demarcated as such. In the following extract the end of one phrase and the beginning of the next in the third bar are fused in at least one edition without justification.

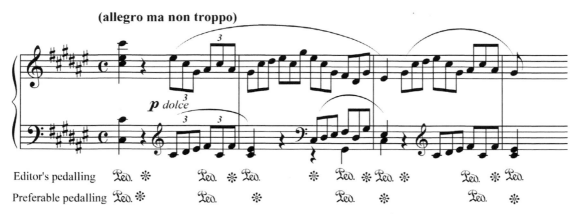

Ex. 102: Beethoven *Piano Sonata No. 24* in F sharp, Op. 78, 1st movement, bars 28–31

Again, a certain symmetry must usually be observed in pedalling so that rhythmic counterparts will be given a corresponding tonal fusion. In the passage quoted below from the same sonata it will be seen that the pedalling, as marked by the editor, is designed so as to cover in each case a corresponding part of the running figure in the left hand. It would, however, be equally symmetrical, and certainly much clearer, to sustain the pedal for the duration of each syncopated chord only:

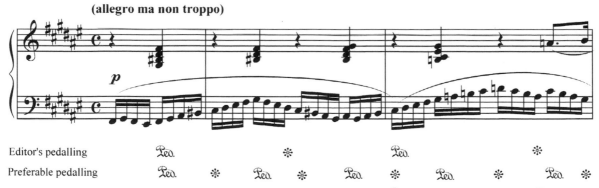

Ex. 103: Beethoven, *Piano Sonata No. 24* in F sharp, Op. 78, 1st movement, bars 37–38[38]

Finally, the consideration of speed is obviously of importance, since an effect which may be quite justifiable for a fleeting moment may jar when prolonged for anything more. In the next extract the editor directs that the pedal be sustained three times for a full bar, though the time values lengthen in each case, until in the second last bar the discordant effect is intolerable. Such pedalling might have been possible on the piano of Beethoven's time, which had far less resonance and less sustaining ability than the grand of to-day, but any sensitive ear must reject the

[38] Beethoven, *Sonata* in F sharp, Op. 78, ed. Giuseppe Buonamici (Augener 1903).

jarring sound involved on a modern instrument. The pedal may indeed be used for the first beat of the first bar, but should be raised on the second beat to allow crisp phrasing in the right hand. In the second bar no pedal at all should be used, to ensure clarity for the imitation, and in the third and fourth bars the notes are sufficiently long to allow pedalling on each for resonance sake:

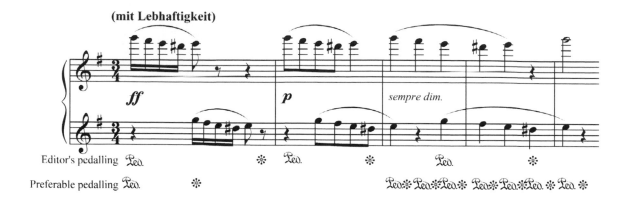

Ex. 104: Beethoven *Piano Sonata No. 27* in E minor, Op. 90, 1st movement, bars 132–136[39]

In piano music of the romantic period a still wider range of colour can be availed of through pedal-fusion. Chopin's piano writing in particular affords opportunities for the most delicate and varied effects. Let us take but one example – the third last bar of the well-known *Nocturne* in E flat, where the full-resounding chord of the dominant ninth is held by the pedal, while a demisemiquaver figure ripples freely above it and then with falling line merges into the chord of the tonic. To heighten the effect the *una corda* pedal may be used immediately after the *fermata*, released for the *crescendo*, and depressed again for the last four note-groups. Pianists sometimes release the sustaining pedal after the *fermata*, thereby robbing the treble of its foundation and impoverishing the whole effect:

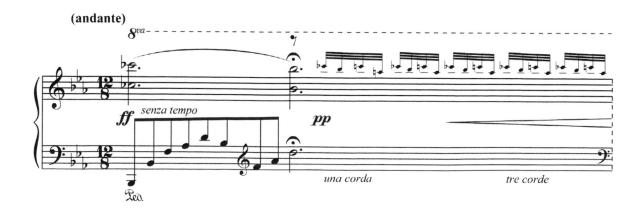

---

[39] Beethoven, *Sonata* in E minor, Op. 90, ed. Giuseppe Buonamici (Augener 1903).

Ex. 105: Chopin *Nocturne No. 2* in E flat, Op. 9, No. 2, bars 32–33.

An interesting problem arises in the pedalling of the chorale section at the end of Mendelssohn's *Fugue* in E minor, where sonorous chords in the right hand are pitted against moving octaves in the left:

Ex. 106: Mendelssohn, *Six Preludes and Fugues*, Op. 35, No. 1, Fugue, bars 105–107

Here there are four possibilities:

(1) **No pedal** Since the left hand is marked *piano e staccato* from the second bar, though the right hand is marked *forte* throughout, it may well have been the composer's intention that no pedal at all be used. On the other hand one misses here the added richness which the use of the pedal would allow.

(2) **Pedal on each quaver** This merely deprives the bass of its *staccato* and does not greatly help the sonority of the right hand.

(3) **Pedal on each alternate quaver** This is preferable to pedalling on each quaver, since it allows more *staccato* in the left hand, but it produces an uneven effect.

(4) **Pedal twice in the bar** This reduces the left hand, when played *piano*, to a smudge, without affording adequate support for the right hand. But if the composer's direction be disregarded and the octaves be consistently played *forte*, a proper balance of volume is achieved between both hands. The confused maze of sound arising from the pedalled octaves helps the sonority of the chords, and the *staccato* effect, however modified, is still discernible above it all. This method, which Stavenhagen was wont to adopt, following Liszt, undoubtedly gives the most impressive results, and makes the close a fitting climax to the whole fugue. But it is at variance with the composer's intentions, and so the pianist must choose according to the dictates of his conscience between a faithful observance of the text and maximum artistic effect.

88

As an extreme instance of the harmonic fusion (or confusion) ventured in the romantic period for the sake of special effect one might take the finale of *Papillons*, in which Schumann sustains the pedal for twenty-six bars before the *fermata* near the close, to illustrate the tumult of the carnival gradually fading into the distance. The tonic note is held in the bass throughout this passage, and forms the foundation on which the conflicting upper harmony rests.

Of all composers of this period, however, it was Liszt who most fully exploited the possibilities of the sustaining pedal. He was one of the few who consistently marked the pedalling himself, thereby showing what an integral part it plays in the texture of his writing. Those scintillating, descriptive passages of which he was so fond rely largely on the blending of sound patterns. Take for example the opening of *St. Francis Preaching to the Birds* with its effect of sunshine and murmurous twittering:

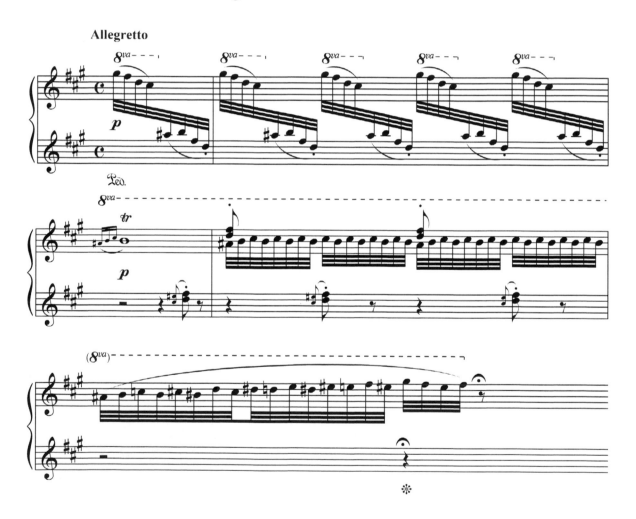

Ex. 107: Liszt *Deux légendes,* No. 1 *St François d'Assise: La prédication aux oiseaux*, bars 1–4

or the sweeping of turbulent water in *St. Francis Walking over the Waves*, where stretches of octaves lasting sometimes for three bars are fused together in a stormy tumult of sound.

Again he uses the pedal for the building up of a colour climax, as in *Les jeux d'eau de la Villa d'Este*, where in the one passage he successively uses the pedal for the first half of the bar:

Ex. 108: Liszt *Les années de pèlerinage* III, No. 4: *Les jeux d'eau de la Villa d'Este*, bar 14.

then twice in the bar:

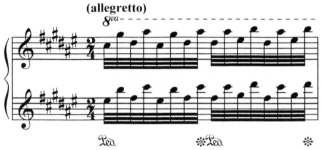

Ex. 109: Liszt *Les années de pèlerinage* III, No. 4: *Les jeux d'eau de la Villa d'Este*, bar 18.

and finally sustains it for the space of two bars to give utmost intensity to his picture of seething jets of spray:

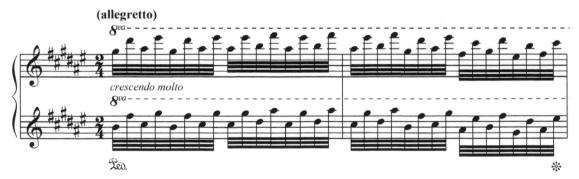

Ex. 110: Liszt *Les années de pèlerinage* III, No. 4: *Les jeux d'eau de la Villa d'Este*, bars 20–21.

By such use of the sustaining pedal, as by his extensive use of the *una corda* pedal for tender and delicate effects, Liszt opened up a new range of colour in his piano music. In fact his usage of colour for its own sake stamps him as the pioneer of impressionism, and much of the iridescent colour of Debussy's nature music is already foreshadowed in that of Liszt.

Unlike Liszt, Debussy seldom marks the pedalling, but the latter is none the less vital to the texture of his piano music. Debussy's use of the whole-tone system gives rise to still further possibilities in the employment of the sustaining pedal, since if the notes of the whole-tone scale be successively played and sustained, a most euphonious sound results, quite unlike the discordant jingle produced by the pedalling of the entire scale in the major or minor mode. Hence it is that the last three bars of *Voiles*, comprising repetitions of the whole-tone scale, can be effectively held by the sustaining pedal (this is the sole indication for the pedalling throughout the prelude which Debussy gives):

Ex. 111: Debussy *Préludes*, Book 1, No. 2: *Voiles*, bars 62–64

Similarly, the pedal should be sustained throughout the following bars from *Reflets dans l'eau*, the low A flat being literally a pedal-bass, and standing for the retention not only of the note A flat but of the whole gamut of harmony involved:

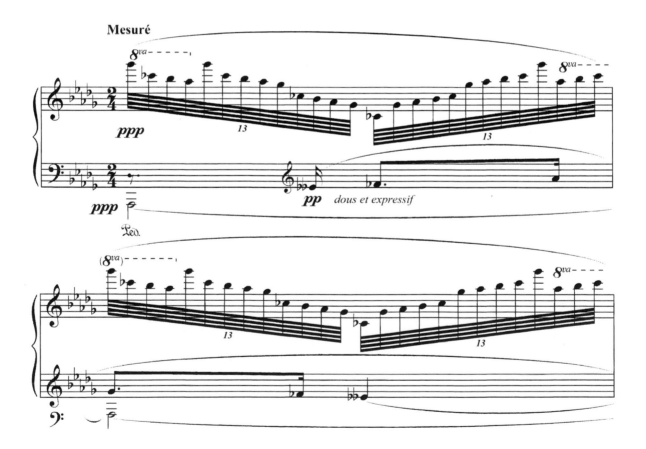

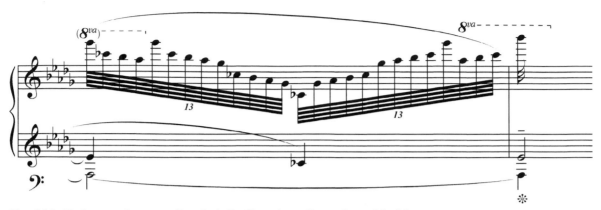

Ex. 112: Debussy, Images, Book 1: Reflets dans l'eau, bars 25–28

By using the third or *sostenuto* pedal of the Steinway Grand (perfected as early as 1874) the low A flat in the above example could be sustained in isolation without the remainder of the texture being affected, but in his piano writing Debussy did not take the possibilities of such a device into consideration. As it is, the sustaining pedal is less successful in damping the vibrations of lower than of higher notes, so that a swift change of pedal, known sometimes as half-pedalling, allows a lower note or notes to sound on virtually undamped, while at the same time damping the upper strings so as to effect a clean change from one harmony to another in the treble. In the following example if the pedal be sustained for the first two beats and a swift change be made on the third beat, it will be found that whereas the octave in the treble will have disappeared, the octave in the bass will continue to sound. However, the context here justifies the somewhat chaotic effect which results from holding the pedal for the whole bar:

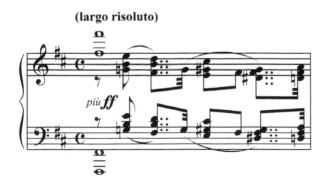

Ex. 113: Ó Rónáin [Aloys Fleischmann], *Sreath do Phiano* [Suite for Piano], 4th movement, bar 17

This simulation of rich orchestral effect is characteristic of a great deal of contemporary music. Take, for example E.J. Moeran's *Windmills*, in which the pedal is sustained for whole stretches at a time to convey the impression of whirling sails:

Ex. 114: Moeran *Windmills*, bars 22–28

Again the first sixteen bars of John Ireland's *The Island Spell* are played without a change of pedal; while in Dohnányi's *Rhapsody* in C the pedal is sustained for the following nine bars, despite the ascending thirds and changes in the harmonic outline:

Ex. 115: Dohnányi *Rhapsody* in C, Op. 11, No. 3, bars 202–211

Even where a tune is intended to come clearly to the fore, the pedal is sometimes retained throughout to achieve a richer harmonic result. A good example is to be found in Bax's *Country Tune*, where a delightful effect is obtained by the retention of held octaves in the centre by means of the pedal, against a lilting *staccato* melody in treble and bass:

Ex. 116: Bax *Country-tune*, bars 28–36

Reference has already been made (see p. 41 above) to the use of the *una corda* pedal alone, without the sustaining pedal. The effect can be sombre and funereal, as for instance in the slow movement of Beethoven's *Sonata* in A flat, where the chords in the fourth and eighth bars, played *staccato* with the *una corda* pedal alone, almost suggest muffled drums:

Ex. 117: Beethoven, *Piano Sonata No. 12* in A flat, Op. 26, 3rd movement, bars 3–4

This procedure can be adopted in similar contexts, such as at the end of each three-bar phrase in Scriabin's *Prelude* in E flat minor, Op. 16, No. 4, where an imaginative player can get just the right drum-like tone.

Such are the devices and problems which confront the pianist in searching for colour and beauty of tone, in striving to adjust the balance between the rival claims of tonal profusion and variety on the one hand, and clarity on the other. As Chopin used to say, pedalling is a lifetime's study, and even the most experienced pianist will still find new possibilities of tonal combination, new effects which will enhance and illuminate the texture. Of the importance of pedalling in piano-playing the average listener has no conception. If he had, and wished to learn, he would watch, not the pianist's fingers – as concert audiences are so naively wont to do – but his feet.

INTERPRETATION AND THE TEXT

CHAPTER THIRTEEN
TEXTUAL ACCURACY

When about to embark on the study of a new work the pianist's first concern should be to procure a trustworthy and helpful edition of the text. For this he must rely on the good faith of an editor whose task it is to furnish an accurate copy of the original, but at the same time to correct obvious errors or omissions which the composer himself or an amanuensis may have made, to collate other versions where these exist, and make appropriate decisions as to the best version to follow, and finally – most important of all – to assist the pianist in interpreting the work by means of pedalling marks, fingering, phrasing and dynamics, metronome marks, and so on.

The editor's work consists then of the readjustment of minute details, yet in spite of the generations of editors through whose hands the classics have passed it is surprising how many errors of detail are still to be found, and how little trouble or care is sometimes expended on the work of revision. New editions are published with all the old errors still enshrined, or even additional ones to boot, and entirely lacking in those hints for the executant which should be the chief asset of any good edition. Blank and unhelpful editions will readily be rejected by the student, but in other respects how is he to assess an edition's value and reliability? The following discussion may help to awaken his critical faculty and make him alive to some of the problems by which he may be confronted.

MISPRINTS

The first consideration, that the notes of the text are correctly reproduced, is a matter for the printer and proof-reader as well as for the editor. Even in the best editions misprints are liable to occur, and it is necessary for the pianist to be on his guard against them. Examiners often test a candidate's intelligence, or his teacher's, by means of misprints, and woe betide both if a misprint should escape their observation, revealing insensitiveness and lack of perception, as well as an undue reverence for the printer's craft. I remember how Stavenhagen and Kellermann chuckled when a world-famous pianist who gave a recital in Munich in 1903 innocently played a number of misprints in a group of Brahms *Intermezzi*. Their sardonic comments were a warning to us students.

Some examples will show the various types of misprint which the pianist may expect. For instance in the following extract it is obvious that Czerny would not write such a discord in the left hand, nor perpetrate such unseemly fifths:

Ex. 118: Czerny, *100 Progressive Études*, Op. 139, No. 19, bars 11–12, Augener edition

and that the left hand should read thus:

Ex. 119: Czerny *100 Progressive Études*, Op. 139, No. 19, bars 11–12, left hand, Augener edition

Again in the next extract it should be clear that the rising left hand progression is based on the chord of B major, and that the notes G sharp and B are a misprint for B and D sharp:

Ex. 120: Beethoven *Piano Concerto No. 3* in C minor, 2nd movement, bar 26, Breitkopf & Härtel edition

Only a pianist without any ear whatever would fail to recognise that something was amiss with the following where, in the second bar, right hand, E flat has been erroneously printed at the beginning of the bar instead of a tied F:

Ex. 121: Schumann *Papillons*, Op. 2, No. 5, bars 15–17, Guildhall edition

Sometimes a misprint which might of itself pass unnoticed can be recognised by a comparison with the corresponding passage in an earlier or later recurrence. The following melodic detail

Ex. 122: Mozart *Piano Sonata No. 11* in A, K.331, 2nd movement, bar 33, right hand

reappears in one edition[40] at the repeat of the minuet as follows:

Ex. 123: Mozart *Piano Sonata No. 11* in A, K.331, 2nd movement, bar 33, right hand, Associated
        Board edition

The pianist should realise that such a change is aesthetically meaningless, and in deciding which version is correct he will see that a melodic progression similar to the first version quoted occurs in the second bar of the minuet, proving the correctness of this version and the incorrectness of the other. Yet one may be certain that scores of young students will continue to reproduce this error unwittingly.

Again, the recognition of a misprint may involve a certain acuteness of observation. In the following passage the final note, C sharp, in the upper stave would only be recognised as a misprint for A if the pianist had observed that Schumann is gradually eliminating the notes of the *Papillons* theme (the process has begun six bars earlier), the last note of the previous group being dropped in each successive bar, so that A is the logical final note.

---

[40] Mozart, *Sonata* in A (K.331) Associated Board of the Royal Schools of Music Edition

Ex. 124: Schumann *Papillons*, Op. 2, No. 12, bars 59–65, Guildhall edition

When we turn to modern music misprints are less easily distinguished according as the texture becomes more complicated. Where each bar is laden with accidentals the most painstaking proof-reader cannot be blamed for an occasional oversight. Sometimes it is difficult to tell whether a given note is a misprint or not. For instance, a glance at the following passage would suggest that the natural sign had been erroneously omitted before D in the left hand on both sides of the bar line, yet D sharp is a pivot note throughout, and at the end of the first bar it is merely a constituent of the dominant discord on F natural:

Ex. 125: Bax *What the Minstrel Told Us*, bars 61–62

Often, however, the idiom is so esoteric that only the composer himself can be expected to decide a doubtful point with certainty, and even he (like Browning on a memorable occasion) may sometimes be at a loss. On the face of things it does seem difficult to understand why misprints should not be disposed of by the composer himself, or by his publisher, within his own lifetime, and one cannot help wondering why in John Ireland's *The Island Spell*, played as it is in countless performances, there should be a quaver rest too many in the fourth bar of the last page, or again why E. J. Moeran's impressive *Toccata* should have been published in a second edition with the seven misprints of the first edition still securely enshrined. But misprints are not only stubborn squatters – they also have a habit of propagating, and subsequent editions or reprints sometimes entail an increase rather than a decrease in their number.

As a final point it might be mentioned that faulty spacing is almost as bad as an actual misprint, since an error in spacing is liable to cause a rhythmical error in sight-reading, which may be unconsciously retained even in subsequent practice. For instance one must observe this bar carefully

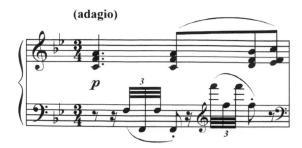

Ex. 126: Beethoven *Piano Sonata No. 17* in D minor, Op. 31, No. 2, 2nd movement, bar 65, d'Albert edition

before one discovers that it should be:

Ex. 127: Beethoven *Piano Sonata No. 17* in D minor, Op. 31, No. 2, 2nd movement, bar 65 amended

Again, the following example speaks for itself:

Ex. 128: Brahms *Vier Klavierstücke*, Op. 119, No. 2, *Intermezzo*, bar 62, Simrock edition

VARIANT READINGS

The pianist will occasionally be confronted with variant readings in different editions, of a note or passage in the text, which are not the result of a printer's error, but of differences of opinion on the part of the editors. This occurs where the composer's real intention is a matter of doubt, through the possibility of an error in the autograph, because of an error or emendation in a copy or early printed edition. As regards autographs, where some doubt exists it is seldom that a solution can be regarded as final and absolute. As Ernest Newman has pointed out,[41] a suspected error in the autograph can only be substantiated by the existence of a proof-sheet in which the error stands corrected by the composer himself, an eventuality which may arise in one case out of a hundred. As regards copyists' errors, or emendations accredited with varying degrees of authenticity, the problems which arise are often extremely complex.

Take for example Bach's *48*. Several MSS of Part I exist in Bach's own hand, together with copies by pupils and others. The most popular of nineteenth century editions of the work, that of Czerny which appeared in 1837, contains numerous emendations for which there is little or no MS authority. The MS material was subsequently sifted by Franz Kroll in Volume XIV (1864) of the Bach Gesellschaft's publications, and in 1884 a further edition by Hans Bischoff followed in which some newly-discovered MSS were collated. In modern editions, based on the work of Kroll and Bischoff and on some MS material more recently made available, Czerny's emendations have been largely eliminated. But where the MSS themselves disagree, the various editors can only choose according to their own varying criteria – and prejudices. In the Preface to his edition of the *48*, speaking about conflicting readings, Tovey admits that an autograph is not always superior on such points to the copy of a pupil or son-in-law, but when he says that the capacity to discriminate between Bach's own alterations and those of a copyist or a pupil-theorist may be based on solid scientific knowledge, one feels that the sentiment, however praiseworthy, may be a trifle self-assured. In fact, in at least one case Tovey's opinion is proved to have been wrong.[42] Ultimate scientific proof is often unattainable even by the specialist, let alone by the average editor, and the latter as well as the player will usually have to resort to reasoning on stylistic grounds, however fallible these may be.

A few instances must suffice for illustration. In the C sharp major *Fugue* all the MSS agree in the following version of counter-subject and answer in the final group of entries (bar 44):

Ex. 129: Bach *Das Wohltemperierte Klavier*, Book I, *Fugue No. 3* in C sharp, BWV 848, bars 3–4

But in the first group of entries (bar 3) and in the inversion at the added entry (bar 10) Kroll, followed by Bischoff, Tovey and others, prints F double sharp at (1) and F sharp at (2). The earliest Peters edition and the Czerny edition print F double sharp both at (1) and (2) in bars 3 and 10. Now Kroll's version follows two out of the three autographs of Book I. The C sharp major *Fugue* is missing in the third autograph, but another MS (No. 8 in Kroll's bibliography) which is a

[41] Ernest Newman, 'Are Autographs Authoritative?', *The Sunday Times*, June 23 1946.

[42] See Walter Emery, 'New Methods in Bach-Editing', *The Musical Times*, August 1950. See also the same writer's articles on 'An Introduction to the Textual History of Bach's *Clavierübung*, Part II', *The Musical Times*, May and June 1951.

faithful copy of this autograph, and probably made before the missing pages were lost, has F sharp both at (1) and (2) in bar 3. It is exceedingly likely then that one of the three autographs contained this reading. Though he does not adopt it, Kroll admits in a note that the reading in question happily overcomes the crudeness which results from the angular F double sharp, so that the modulation to the dominant is not affected immediately on the entry of the answer but arises anon. Tovey declares that most of the autographs show discrepancies in this fugue with regard to F sharp and F double sharp, and that 'Bach evidently does not care for uniformity on this point.' Granted that uniformity cannot be achieved, at least some sort of consistency might be desirable, and from this standpoint the reading of MS No. 8 (i.e. F sharp at (1) and (2) as against both the Czerny and Kroll editions) seems more logical, for since the last group of entries is virtually a recapitulation of the exposition, it follows that the counter-subject should agree in each case. All the autographs agree in introducing F double sharp at (1) in bar 10, but again Kroll follows two of the autographs in contradicting the F double sharp at (2), while MS No. 8 and the Czerny edition leave the F double sharp uncontradicted. The contradiction in Kroll's version causes the tonality to vacillate unduly from the key of G sharp back to C sharp and then to G sharp again at the beginning of the following bar, and one might well decide against adopting it. Bar 10 would then read as follows:

Ex. 130: Bach *Das Wohltemperierte Klavier*, Book I, *Fugue No. 3* in C sharp, BWV 848, bar 10

In the same fugue the autographs and all but two MSS contradict the F double sharp at the end of bar 21:

Ex. 131: Bach *Das Wohltemperierte Klavier*, Book I, *Fugue No. 3* in C sharp, BWV 848, bars 21–22

The two MSS which retain F double sharp at the asterisk, and are followed in this by the Peters and Czerny editions, are not trustworthy sources, so that here the MS evidence is overwhelmingly in favour of the contradiction to F single sharp. Yet the latter note suggests the chord of the augmented sixth in a context wherein it sounds quite alien (transpose enharmonically to the key of F minor, and think of G flat instead of G natural) and one cannot help feeling that an initial slip in the somewhat ambiguous notation of accidentals at this period may well be responsible for so unexpected a progression.

Let us take one more instance, the circumstances of which are much the same as in the first two instances quoted. In the following example from the Prelude in C sharp minor, Kroll, following the main autographs, prints B natural in the bass of the second bar, as against B sharp in MS No. 8 and the Czerny edition:

Ex. 132: Bach *Das Wohltemperierte Klavier*, Book I, *Prelude No. 4* in C sharp minor, BWV 849, bars 25–26

Now the progression C sharp–B in the bass in the second bar of the above quotation agrees with the whole-tone progression F sharp–E of the corresponding melodic figure in the treble in the first bar. Yet the semitonal progression E–D sharp appears in the treble in the second bar, while the progression C sharp–B sharp occurs under similar circumstances in bar 18:

Ex. 133: Bach *Das Wohltemperierte Klavier*, Book I, *Prelude No. 4* in C sharp minor, BWV 849, bar 18, right hand

In view of the strong reiteration of B sharp in the vicinity of the note at issue in the previous quotation above, B natural as an auxiliary note has poor validity, and B sharp seems a more logical and consistent reading.

Other examples abound in which the divergence between the MS sources makes a decision still more difficult for the editor. Such minutiae might seem unimportant, yet to a pianist who has adopted the readings of a particular editor without question the conflicting readings of another edition are peculiarly annoying, and the individual variants sound like wrong notes. If he is gifted with a scrupulous and enquiring mind he can only achieve equanimity again by entering into the pros and cons of the various readings, and deciding the issues for himself.

In the case of the Mozart and Beethoven piano sonatas the sources are relatively uniform, as compared with the sources of the *48*, yet surprising discrepancies occasionally arise. Witness the following passage which in one edition is printed as follows:

Ex. 134: Mozart *Piano Sonata No. 11* in A, K.331, 2nd movement, bars 23–27, Associated Board edition

with C natural given as a variant at each of the points marked with an asterisk. Yet the F natural of the first bar and the C natural of the fifth make it clear that the key of A minor should have been maintained throughout (in juxtaposition to the B minor statement of the same idea, in the four bars preceding those quoted), so that C natural should be regarded as a necessary emendation in each case, not as a variant. This is the customary reading and is undoubtedly correct.

Other types of discrepancy are also to be found. In the notes to his edition of Beethoven's 'Pastoral' *Sonata*, Tovey suggests that bars 135 to 137 of the first movement be played as:

Ex. 135: Beethoven *Piano Sonata No. 15* in D, Op. 28, first movement, bars 136–137

with the explanation that the sign ⁓ was introduced by Cipriani Potter into his edition of the sonata and stands for a repetition of the note produced by the catching of the key a second time before it has finished rising. Tovey says that though this has been identified with the *Bebung* of the clavichord the device is peculiar to the pianoforte, and he terms the sign to be trustworthy evidence of Beethoven's intention, since Potter had intercourse with Beethoven, and the sign could not have been invented. Now in the first place the fact that Potter had intercourse with Beethoven does not necessarily mean that he had Beethoven's sanction for his adoption of a special effect in this context. In the second place the *Bebung* effect achieved on the clavichord was a species of vibrant tremolo, while this particular effect on the piano, however skilfully attempted, merely results in a clear repetition of the note such as here definitely impairs the syncopation. In the other cases mentioned by Tovey (*Cello Sonata* in A, Op. 69, *Piano Sonatas* Op. 106 and 110) where Beethoven specifies a similar effect, this is obtained by the fingering which Beethoven himself marks. It seems reasonable that if he had desired the same effect in the 'Pastoral' *Sonata*, he would also have marked the fingering accordingly. Otherwise it would merely be logical to apply the *Bebung* effect in the trio of the 'Moonlight' *Sonata*, or in the case of any of the numerous recurrences of this virile type of syncopation of which Beethoven was so fond.

In Frederick Corder's edition of the *Sonata* Op. 28 the key signature is changed from that of D major to that of A major from the second page of the first movement to the end of the exposition, with the object of assisting the student, because of the 'abnormal number of G sharps in this section.' Even if Beethoven sometimes changes the key signature in the first movements of his later sonatas, for the editor to do so in a comparatively early work is to destroy the sense of relationship between technique and period. And if students cannot cope with a series of G sharps when they meet them, then they should not attempt this sonata at all. Again towards the end of the development section of this movement, where the two hands become widely divergent in working up to a climax, Corder writes over the left hand 'pleasanter an octave higher'! The resultant 'pleasantness' merely reduces an otherwise powerful climax – the apex of the movement – to an undistinguished tinkle. Finally, in a note on the scherzo the editor writes 'since the first portion has its repeat written out, it is clear that to keep the movement in proportion one should, after the Trio, go back not to the beginning, but to the seventeenth bar.' He forgets, however, that the 'repeat written out' differs appreciably from the first statement and is the third step in a crescendo of intensification, so that to omit the first two steps is to remove the foundation of the intended climax. Presumably Beethoven realised more clearly than Mr. Corder what he was doing when he wrote out this repeat in full.

However inevitable an occasional divergent reading or direction might seem in the case of the earlier masters, one would imagine that such would no longer arise as we advance into the nineteenth century. Yet the editions of Chopin's works are more abounding in contradictory details than any of Bach's. In Chopin's case not only did some early misprints escape detection and become generally accepted, but numerous later corrections and improvements were either attributed to Chopin with varying degrees of authenticity, or were boldly undertaken by the editors themselves. Of the early Chopin editors Charles Klindworth is among the most reliable and informative, and had the added advantage of having studied with the greatest contemporary exponent of Chopin – Franz Liszt. Klindworth, however, is not infallible, and as his edition has since been ousted by innumerable others, many of them less trustworthy, it was a matter for rejoicing when in 1932 Édouard Ganche and the Oxford University Press brought out a new edition which purported to be based on an exhaustive study of the original MSS. It has since transpired, however, that a large collection of autographs was not available for inspection, and that the edition is by no means as authoritative as has been claimed.[43] In 1937 the Chopin Institute in Warsaw commenced work on the publication of a new edition of Chopin's complete works, most of the autographs in question having been acquired by the then Polish government. This edition is now in the process of being completed, but in the meantime it may not be out of place to discuss some of the discrepancies or misreadings which are so widespread among editions of Chopin's works, and have proved to be a source of so much controversy.

First, some miscellaneous examples. In Klindworth's, Debussy's and most other editions the opening of the *Waltz* in G flat reads as follows:

---

[43] See *The Musical Times*, June 1939, p. 457, and September 1939 p. 677.

Ex. 136: Chopin *Waltz No. 11* in G flat, Op. 70, bars 1-2

In Ganche's edition we find:

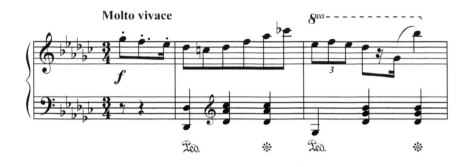

Ex. 137: Chopin *Waltz No. 11* in G flat, Op. 70, No. 1, bars 1–2, Ganche edition

Whatever the merits or demerits of the latter, it seems clear that Ganche's versions of bars 23–24 and 31–32

Ex. 138a: Chopin *Waltz No. 11* in G flat, Op. 70, No. 1, bars 23–24, Ganche edition

and

Ex. 138b: Chopin *Waltz No. 11* in G flat, Op. 70, No. 1, bars 31–32, Ganche edition

sound immature and certainly less characteristic compared to Klindworth's versions, namely:

Ex. 139a: Chopin *Waltz No. 11* in G flat, Op. 70, No. 1, bars 23–24, Klindworth edition

and

Ex. 139b: Chopin *Waltz No. 11* in G flat, Op. 70, No. 1, bars 31–32, Klindworth edition

In the Chopin Institute's edition (a) corresponds to the Klindworth edition, (b) to the Ganche edition. As regards (b) if one compares the second bar with bar 56 of the *Waltz*, in which all editions agree on A natural in the treble at the end of the bar, the A flat of the Ganche and Chopin Institute's editions sounds so inadmissible that Klindworth's version seems justified, even if ultimate authority for it were lacking.

The opening of the *Prelude* in A flat offers a similar instance for discussion. In the Chopin Institute's edition, as well as in that of Ganche, the melody begins as follows in the third and again in the thirty-fifth bar:

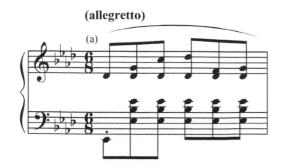

Ex. 140: Chopin *24 Préludes*, No. 17 in A flat, Op. 28, bars 3 and 35, Chopin Institute and Ganche editions

Yet the second announcing phrase of the melody and the first phrase on its last appearance in the sixty-fifth bar begin as follows:

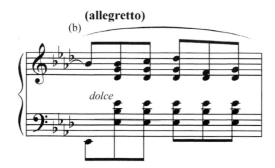

Ex. 141: Chopin *24 Préludes*, No. 17 in A flat, Op. 28, bar 65, Chopin Institute and Ganche editions

The usual reading seems preferable in which all occurrences of the phrase agree with version (b) above. In his *Studies in Musical Interpretation* Cortot supports this reading.[44]

In the following passage from the same prelude Ganche prints F natural in the first bar of the example, as against the usual F sharp, thus securing uniformity for the repetitions of the sequence:

Ex. 142: Chopin *24 Préludes*, No. 17 in A flat, Op. 28, bars 19–22, Ganche edition

---

[44] *Alfred Cortot's Studies in Musical Interpretation*, Set down by Jeanne Thieffry, Translated by Robert Jaques (London 1937), p. 50.

But in the usual reading (which is also that of the Chopin Institute's edition) the whole-tone G sharp–F sharp in bar 1 is contrasted with the augmented second B sharp–A natural in bar 3, on the logical basis that F sharp in bar 1 leads to a major key, whereas A natural in bar 3 leads to a minor key. This certainly gives a richer result.

A similar but much more obvious misreading occurs in Ganche's edition of the *Study* in E major, where the sequential repetition of bars 30–31:

Ex. 143: Chopin *Études*, No. 3 in E, Op. 10, bars 30–31, Ganche edition

is reproduced at bars 34–35 as follows:

Ex. 144: Chopin *Études*, No. 3 in E, Op. 10, bars 34–35, Ganche edition

The opening chord of bar 34 should be B major with G sharp in the alto part, to agree with the original pattern, and the repetition of the chord of B minor in both bars is without significance. The insertion of the natural sign before the D's and G in the first bar, however, may conceivably be a printer's error.

A particularly lamentable misprint prevailed in all the earlier editions of Chopin's well-known C minor *Prelude*, in the third bar of which the last melody note remains uncontradicted as E natural:

Ex. 145: Chopin *24 Préludes,* No. 20 in C minor, Op. 28, bars 3–4

Forty years ago Stavenhagen drew his students' attention to this error. It should be obvious that when the rich chord of the dominant seventh (of F minor) has already been played on the second beat of the bar, the repetition of the mere dominant chord itself on the fourth beat comes as an anticlimax, and sounds relatively commonplace. Yet E natural is usually played (witness Cortot on HMV DB 2018 and Moisiewitsch on HMV C7773). Ganche's edition is the first in which this error stands corrected, and he quotes as proof A flat pencilled before the E by Chopin himself in a copy of the original edition annotated by the composer. In his *Studies in Musical Interpretation* Cortot admits the validity of the correction.[45]

To come to a point of dynamics, most editors, including Klindworth, print a *crescendo* in the fifth-last bar of the 'Revolutionary' *Study* leading to *fortissimo* on the C major chord:

Ex. 146: Chopin *Études*, No. 12 in C minor, Op. 10, bars 80–81, Klindworth edition

I have always thought this procedure quite un-Chopin-like, though almost invariably adopted by the foremost pianists and in recordings of the *Study*. The uninterrupted semiquaver movement which persists to the end of this phrase does not lead convincingly into a violent *fortissimo* chord, but needs to be softly rounded off, so that the outburst starts with the swirling semiquavers in the treble:

[45] *Alfred Cortot's Studies in Musical Interpretation*, Set down by Jeanne Thieffry, Translated by Robert Jaques (London 1937), p. 51

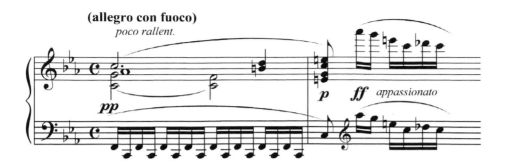

Ex. 147: Chopin *Études*, No. 12 in C minor, Op. 10, bars 80–81, Chopin Institute edition

This is the version now adopted in the Chopin Institute's edition, and it transpires that it has autograph authority.

In numerous instances variants are due to later emendations which may or may not have been endorsed by Chopin himself. Ganche, in the preface to his edition, states that in preparing his MSS for publication Chopin permitted the intervention of two or three 'ill-advised counsellors', and sometimes accepted the suggestions of these 'incompetent censors'. Anyone conversant with the biographical accounts of Chopin's character will find it hard to believe that he would easily have been persuaded to alter even the minutest detail in a composition unless he were convinced that the alteration did in fact constitute an improvement. Accordingly to dismiss all subsequent changes from the original MSS or the first French edition in the intemperate and abusive terms to which Ganche gives vent is both uncritical and unconvincing. There are few masters, if any, who would claim that the first edition of a work was incapable of improvement in any detail whatsoever.

The difficulty, however, is to decide whether Chopin did actually authorise a particular emendation and the evidence for and against may be hard of access. To take a few cases in point, the Klindworth and Debussy editions, among others, give the second and fourth bars of the *Waltz* in A flat as:

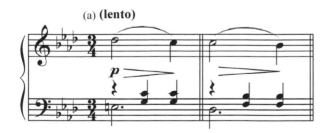

Ex. 148: Chopin *Waltz No. 9* in A flat, Op. 69, No. 1, bars 2 and 4, Klindworth edition

and the tenth and twelfth bars as:

Ex. 149: Chopin *Waltz No. 9* in A flat, Op. 69, No. 1, bars 10 and 12, Klindworth edition

the latter bars being an intensification of the former and recurring alternately with them in all repetitions of the main waltz theme save the last. Ganche, however, and the Chopin Institute print version (b) throughout, as constituting the composer's original intention. Leaving the question of authenticity aside, the alternation of versions (a) and (b) in the course of the waltz affords a welcome variety in the face of so many repetitions (the bars quoted occur no less than eight times in all) and even if it could be proved that the uniform version is authentic, and the alternating version not attributable to or authorised by the composer himself, it must be admitted that the latter is a very desirable emendation.

Again, in the last bar of the following passage Ganche prints C natural in the top part, as against C flat of the Klindworth and most other editions, which latter note imparts a far greater intensity to the repetition of the phrase:

Ex. 150: Chopin *Polonaise No. 1* in C sharp minor, Op. 26, No. 1, bars 74–77, Ganche edition

The degree of difference in effect which may be involved between the original and a later emended version of a passage can be seen from one further example. In the seventh *Prelude*, Ganche prints bars 11–14 as follows, and this approximates to the version adopted in the Chopin Institute's edition and in most other editions:

Ex. 151: Chopin *24 Préludes,* No. 7 in A, Op. 28, bars 11–14, Ganche edition

Stavenhagen, however, used to relate that Liszt had Chopin's authority for the following version in which the richer dominant seventh on F sharp is played *arpeggiata,* and G sharp in the treble of the second last bar adds poignancy by gently lifting the melody from the monotone repetitions of the other bars. Klindworth reproduces this version, except for the device of playing the top C sharp of the *arpeggiata* chord with the left hand:

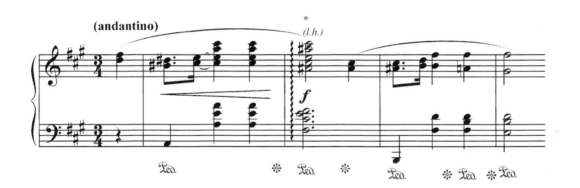

Ex. 152: Chopin, *24 Préludes,* No. 7 in A, Op. 28, bars 11–14, Klindworth edition

Sometimes, however, a variant comes into circulation as a result of squeamishness on the part of some feeble-minded editor. For instance the last bar of the introductory *Lento* of the G minor *Ballade* is printed in some editions as follows:

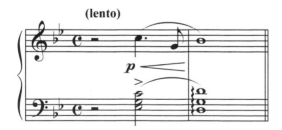

Ex. 153: Chopin *Ballade No. 1* in G minor, Op. 23, bars 6–7

Klindworth, Ganche and the Chopin Institute print the final chord as follows:

Ex. 154: Chopin *Ballade No. 1* in G minor, Op. 23, bar 7, Klindworth, Ganche, Chopin Institute editions

Taking the case on its own merits, a comparison with the harmony underlying the twenty-eighth bar of the *Moderato* and again the twenty-ninth bar of the *Meno mosso* will show that E flat is undoubtedly the note which Chopin intended. The resultant discord awakens an atmosphere of the keenest suspense, and in itself epitomises the mood of the whole *Ballade*. By comparison, the attempted emendation seems flat and colourless.

As a further instance of editorial squeamishness one might take the case of the concluding chord of the *Nocturne* in B major, Op. 32. Klindworth prints the chord as B minor, and this is the reading in the original manuscript.[46] But since the *Nocturne* is in the key of B major the majority of editors, appalled at the breach of good manners in closing a major composition with a minor chord, have corrected the offending D natural into D sharp thus introducing a note of reconciliation which is quite foreign to the gloomy *dénouement* which Chopin had conceived.

If the points already dealt with concern details only, the following case will show how editorial intervention may at times have far-reaching consequences. It has always been a tradition that Chopin's *Polonaise* in C sharp minor, Op. 26, alone among its fellows is in binary form, ending with the trio. In Ganche's edition, however, amongst others, a *da capo* repeat of the first part of the *Polonaise* is prescribed after the trio. Now it seems unlikely that a whole series of editors from Klindworth on and generations of Chopin players should have regarded the *Polonaise* as being in binary form, and lacking the usual restatement of the first part of the *Polonaise*, as a result of a mere omission of the terms *D.C.* and *Fine* in an autograph or early edition of the *Polonaise*. Such an oversight would be too obvious to remain uncorrected, unless there were some solid authority behind the omission. It seems a more reasonable inference that the *D.C.* and *Fine* marks resulted from the intervention of some such 'ill-advised counsellor' as Ganche condemns, with the purpose of rounding off the *Polonaise* as a whole in deference to formal convention, for the repeat defeats the very purpose which it should serve, the end of the first part of the *Polonaise* being in itself vague and indefinite, and leading to anything but a satisfactory conclusion. Actually it is the omission of this repeat which gives the *Polonaise* its peculiar distinctiveness, as if the gaiety of the dance were dispelled by the tender, subdued passion of the trio, to return no more. Unless definite proof should be available that Chopin himself intended or authorised the *da capo* repeat – and this is by no means the case – it seems better to defer to a tradition which has the authority of a generation of the foremost Chopin exponents behind it, and has every justification in the nature of the music itself.

---

[46] Frederick Chopin, *Nocturne* in B major, Op. 32, see footnote Imperial Edition ed. Louis Arensky (Melbourne 1924).

The above are but a few among the innumerable instances of editorial diversity to be found in Chopin's works. No other nineteenth composer has suffered from such discrepancies to the same extent. As we approach the contemporary period variant readings, for obvious reasons, become correspondingly rare.

Chapter Fourteen
General Editing:
Background Information

Apart from dealing with the text of the music itself, it is the editor's function to supply some general information with regard to the work which he is editing, especially such information as may have a bearing on its interpretation. On the whole one may complain that editors show a singular lack of appreciation of this aspect of their work. Sometimes – and this is true particularly of English editors – they go so far as to suppress information available in earlier editions.

Let us first take the case of *Erinnerung*, No. 28 of Schumann's *Album for the Young*. In the early editions underneath the title is printed the inscription '4 November, 1847. Felix Mendelssohn's Todestag' [day of Mendelssohn's death], for when the news of the premature death of his friend reached Schumann he was deeply moved, and gave expression to his sorrow by writing this little elegy in the style of the *Songs without Words*. In the last line there is a poignant progression marked with two *fermati* in which the whole pathos of his grief seems to be concentrated, and at the close there is an *Amen* cadence as though in answer to a *Requiescat in pace* for Schumann. Now that this inscription is usually omitted in present-day editions it would be safe to say that nine out of every ten pianists who play *Erinnerung* have no idea as to who is 'remembered' or why. Yet it must be obvious that to know the piece to be an elegy has some bearing on its interpretation.

Such suppression has occurred in the case of many other piano works by Schumann. In the *Davidsbündlertänze* the following old German saying is inscribed under the title in the early editions:

In all und jeder Zeit

Verknüpft sich Lust und Leid

Bleibt fromm in Lust und Leid

Beim Leid mit Muth bereit.[47]

The initials *C.W.* above the first two bars indicate that the theme is borrowed from Clara Wieck, Schumann's beloved; the different dances are signed F, E, or F and E (Florestan and Eusebius, leaders of the 'Davidsbündler'); above No. 9 is printed 'Hereupon Florestan remained silent, but his lips quivered painfully'; and above No. 18, to show that it was but an afterthought is printed 'Quite superfluously Eusebius remarked as follows, while his eyes shone with happiness.' However romantic these latter effusions – sufficiently so, perhaps, to justify their omission from the later editions – they reveal something of Schumann, an emotional hypersensitiveness which is indeed seldom reflected nowadays in the performance of his music, and any thorough editor should at least incorporate these inscriptions, together with the omitted proverb and other explanatory details, in a preface or footnote. It is surely essential for the pianist to know that the 'Davidsbündler' were members of an imaginary artistic league founded by Schumann to wage

---

[47] In every age and land / Joy and pain go hand in hand. / Keep joy from folly clear / Through pain with courage steer.

war on the Philistines; that Florestan and Eusebius were meant to represent two aspects of Schumann's own nature, Florestan being his robust self, the champion of the new tendency in music to rid itself, even with violence, of all pedantry and imitation, Eusebius on the other hand being his gentler self and a modest yet warmhearted admirer of the old masters; that the dances, which Schumann described as full of 'wedding thoughts', are meant to celebrate the festive union of his twofold nature; and finally that the connection with the proverb which Schumann chose as his text seems to be that as joy and pain are wedded together, so only the original creative spirit who has striven painfully under the curb of discipline can attain to the freedom of true joyous creation.

To take a further case, if a composition has arisen from the impact of a particular poem and the composer chooses to reproduce the poem, it shows a curious perversity on the part of a later editor to suppress it. Schumann's 'Verrufene Stelle' [Haunted Spot] from his *Waldszenen* [Forest Scenes] Op. 82, originally bore the following verses from the second of Hebbel's *Waldbilder* [Forest Images]:

> Die Blumen, so hoch sie wachsen,
> Sind blass hier, wie der Tod,
> Nur eine in der Mitte
> Steht da im dunklen Rot.
>
> Die hat es nicht von der Sonne,
> Nie traf sie deren Glut,
> Sie hat es von der Erde,
> Und die trank Menschenblut![48]

So too the following verse by Sternau, chosen by Brahms for the *Andante* of his *Sonata* in F minor, Op. 5, has been omitted from latter-day editions of the *Sonata*:

> Der Abend dämmert, das Mondlicht scheint,
> Da sind zwei Herzen in Liebe vereint
> Und halten sich selig umfangen.[49]

Without the footnote containing the gospel text in Liszt's *Les jeux d'eau*, the clue by which the spiritual background of the work is established will in all probability escape the player, yet this footnote is nowadays rarely printed. (See p. 236 below). Even titles are eliminated with the same zest, and the Liszt study originally named *La Leggerezza* [Lightness] is nowadays headed *Study* in F minor though the original title suggested the manner in which the study should be played – a necessary direction if one considers the metallic and graceless performances it usually receives. Liszt's two concert studies, *Waldesrauschen* and *Gnomenreigen* are also printed in some recent editions without their original titles.

---

[48] Literal translation: However high the flowers grow /They are here pale as death, /Only one in their midst /Stands there a sinister red. /No hue borrowed from the sun, /Whose rays it never caught, /Its hue is from the earth /That has drunk of human blood.

[49] Literal translation: Evening falls, the moon's rays gleam, /Here are two hearts united in love /And joined in a blessed embrace.

In all the above cases the omitted matter has some bearing on the actual interpretation of the work in question. Sometimes, however, explanatory or other details are omitted which, even if they do not actually affect the interpretation, are still of obvious interest. For instance three of the pieces in Schumann's *Album for the Young* lack a title but are marked with an asterisk (Nos. 21, 26, 30) and in the absence of any editorial comment pianists are not always aware that these were written for Clara Wieck, and are accordingly in the nature of love-letters addressed to her. In *Nordisches Lied* [Nordic Song], No. 41 of the same *Album*, the first four notes of the melody constitute a musical pun on the name of Schumann's friend, the Danish composer Gade, to whom he dedicates the piece with the inscription 'Gruss an G'. Without the explanatory note of the older editions the significance of 'G' and the whole point of the recurrent motif are lost to the majority of pianists. It seems almost equally pointless in the case of No. 4 of this *Album* to omit the title of the chorale *Freue Dich, O meine Seele* [Rejoice O my soul].

Again, the same composer's *Carnaval* is based on the letter-notes A-S-C-H which form the name of a small town in Bohemia where lived a lady-love of Schumann's, Ernestine von Fricken. Of the twenty-one numbers of this work, all with the exception of 'Preamble', 'Chopin', 'Paganini' and 'Pause' begin with a motif derived from these letter-notes, Nos. 2–7 and 9 being based on the four-note motif A–E flat–C–B (= Asch, since in German E flat corresponds to S and B flat to H) and the remainder, except Nos. 12, 17 and 20, on the three-note motif A flat C–B (also equivalent to ASCH, since A flat in German corresponds to As.) In Nos. 2 and 8 the motifs are transposed. As Schumann himself pointed out, the letters in question are the only musical letters in his name, and in his whimsical way he inserted three 'Sphinxes' or riddles after No. 8, the first consisting of the notes E flat–C–B–A (S-C-H-A, i.e. following the order in which they appear in his name), the second consisting of the three-note motif A flat–C–B (As-C-H) and the third of the four-note motif A–E flat–C–B (A-S-C-H). Nowadays the 'Sphinxes' are still reproduced, having by some strange chance escaped the usual process of elimination, but the riddle of 'Asch' is left unsolved, so that to the student, and indeed to the average teacher, the 'Sphinxes' present as insoluble a riddle as that with which the Sphinx originally terrified the Thebans. In fact occasions have been known when the three motifs, quite meaningless in themselves, were solemnly played as an interlude between Nos. 8 and 9. Other details needing explanation are (1) that Estrella stands for Ernestine and Chiarina for Clara Wieck; (2) as in the case of the *Davidsbündler*, that Florestan and Eusebius each stand for Schumann's 'epipsychidion'; (3) that the march theme of the finale represents the *Davidsbündler* – Schumann and his colleagues marching against the Philistines, i.e. the narrow-minded critics and conservatives opposed to Schumann's *Neue Bahnen* [New Directions].[50]

Two further instances must suffice to illustrate the needless suppression of original inscriptions, or again the frequent lack of editorial explanation. Grieg added a note to 'The Watchman's Song', *Lyrische Stücke*, Book I, Op. 12, to the effect that the piece was inspired by a performance of *Macbeth*, thus explaining the origin of the title (and possibly of the threefold repetitions of a bass-note 'Knock, knock, knock' – which occur in the middle section), but this explanatory note is no longer printed. Again, in editions of Liszt's *Funérailles*, 'October 1849' is bracketed below the title, which might at first suggest the date of the completion of the work, or,

---

[50] 'Neue Bahnen': an article on Brahms by Schumann in his journal *Neue Zeitschrift für Musik*, Vol. 39, No. 18 (Leipzig 28 Oct 1853).

if one remembered that Chopin died in this very month, that the work was a lament for Chopin's death. Actually it was written in memory of three Hungarian patriots, friends of Liszt, who were involved in the revolutionary outbreak of 1848 and executed on October 6th of that year, so that the tolling of bells, the thunder of artillery and the clarion calls which are heard in *Funérailles,* however universal the images which they awaken, have their origin in this particular tragic event.

It is, however, heartening to note that in some of the most recent editions of the works referred to above the suppressed inscriptions and explanatory details have again been restored.

DYNAMICS AND PHRASING

One of the editor's chief tasks in dealing with early piano music is the insertion or revision of dynamics and phrasing marks. Bach's use of phrasing was limited to a very occasional slur over note groups of short value, while he introduced dynamics for purposes of special contrast only. The markings in any edition of his piano music are accordingly the result of a purely individual interpretation, and the pianist who has been bred in a particular tradition, or who has definite ideas of his own, can accept or reject the editor's recommendations without undue scruple.

In the Bach-Handel period the various sections of a composition were 'terraced' in regard to their dynamics, i.e. phrases or even whole periods were customarily played at the one level, and any dynamic change made occurred at the start of a phrase or section, not in the course of it. In this regard the method of performance followed that on the harpsichord and organ, on which instruments a *crescendo* in our sense of the word was not feasible. As in the case of pedalling (see pp. 82–84) the question then arises as to whether, in playing music of this period, the pianist should imitate the dynamics of the harpsichord or whether he should avail of the full dynamic flexibility of the modern instrument. As before, it seems more reasonable to take the latter view. There seems little point in requiring one instrument to adopt the limitations of another and the texture of early eighteenth century music sounds far more live and vital on the modern piano when given a reasonable amount of dynamic shading.

Dynamics then play an important part in the editing of Bach. To take a few examples, at the end of the first prelude of the *48* many editors indicate either *forte* or *crescendo* for the concluding bars (e.g. Reinecke, Morgan, Schmid-Lindner) and again a *crescendo* at the end of the first fugue. The dynamic climax of the prelude, however, seems to occur at the seventh last bar, and it is at least equally justifiable to allow for a gradual *diminuendo* from this bar to the close. At the end of the fugue the parts taper upwards with a texture which seems somewhat too thin to bear a continuous *crescendo*. In both the above cases one might well adopt the *diminuendo* marking of the Czerny edition, which, as far as the prelude is concerned, is also upheld by Tovey.[51]

The second prelude affords an opportunity for dynamic contrasts in successive bars, such as were obtainable on the harpsichord by the use of steps or the Venetian swell. Thus the first and third bars can be played *mezzo-forte*, with the second and fourth reduced to a softer quality by means of the *una corda* pedal. A stronger contrast might then be effected for bars 5–6 (and also bars 7–8) as follows:

[51] Chopin, *Prelude No. 1*, see note to Associated Board Edition, Ed. Donald F. Tovey (London 1924)

118

Una corda

Ex. 155: Bach *Das Wohltemperierte Klavier*, Book I, *Prelude No. 2* in C minor, BWV 847, bars 5–6

From the ninth bar this alternate shading is no longer advisable if monotony is to be avoided, and in any event, it is well to change the pattern so as to prepare for the gradual *crescendo* which begins at bar 16 and mounts to a climax at bar 27 (*Presto*). In the succeeding fugue a similar series of *forte-piano* contrasts are effective in bars 9–11 (and also bars 22–23):

Ex. 156: Bach *Das Wohltemperierte Klavier*, Book I, *Fugue No. 2* in C minor, BWV 847, bars 9–10

It is a Liszt tradition to avail of such contrasts where the context allows (cf. the Czerny edition), but this practice is no longer followed by modern editors.

As an example of divergent phrasing one might take the varied specifications for the subject of the following fugue:

Ex. 157: Bach *Das Wohltemperierte Klavier*, Book I, *Fugue No. 21* in B flat, BWV 866, bars 1–5, right hand, given as presented in four different editions

None of the four editors quoted agree in the phrasing of the first two bars, and the degree of difference in the first bar, ranging from all-*staccato* to all-*legato*, is worth noting. The Schmid-Lindner version is probably the most circumspect, though he neglects to pair the quavers D and C between bars one and two, which is among the commendable features of Czerny's phrasing. Hughes agrees with Lott in the regrettable detail of detaching C, the first note of the second bar, with the effect of over-weighting the rhythm. Czerny's *staccato* opening may nowadays be regarded as affected, but it is at least vivid and imparts a lightness and lucidity when followed throughout the fugue (the third and fourth bars should, however, be joined by the one slur).

As against such varied and contradictory editorial detail Tovey has produced a text of the *48* free of all phrasing marks and dynamics. While this allows the mature and intelligent player admirable latitude and calls for a certain creative effort on his part, in the case of the majority of pianists, as well as of teachers, the lack of any guidance other than an occasional hint in the prefatory notes must prove a source of embarrassment, and must lead to more dubious results than any for which the least reliable of editors could be held accountable.

Just because Bach's music is sometimes assailed as 'sewing-machine music' (to mention one eminent composer's verdict[52]) it is all the more essential to use finely-balanced dynamics, *staccato, portamento,* or any of the means which give variety and distinction to its performance. The influence of the old belief that in playing Bach *legato* should be exclusively used still lingers, so that it is often necessary to alter and edit an editor's phrasing by introducing *staccato* or breaking up unduly long and heavy *legato* markings. For instance if the following graceful subject be played with an even *legato* throughout, as it is sometimes phrased by editors, the entire fugue is robbed of that magical lightness and transparency of texture because of which it has been aptly nicknamed the 'Butterfly' *Fugue*. The subject might well be phrased as follows, to ensure a neat and delicate execution:

---

[52] Tilly Fleischmann quotes Arnold Bax as saying this in her memoire *Some Reminiscences of Arnold Bax*, p. 21, http://www.musicweb-international.com/bax/Tilly.htm; http://www.corkcitylibraries.ie/music/aloysfleischmann/aloysfleischmann-thelife/familyandfriends/arnoldbax/

Ex. 158: Bach *Das Wohltemperierte Klavier*, Book I, *Fugue No. 3* in C sharp, BWV 848, bars 1–3, right hand

In the preceding prelude Stavenhagen used to play the quavers in the left hand *staccato* from bars 63–97 to enhance the lightness of effect. Similarly the quavers of the following theme are best taken *staccato*:

Ex. 159: Bach *Das Wohltemperierte Klavier*, Book I, *Prelude No. 17* in A flat, BWV 862, bars 1–2, right hand

As further instances of an appropriate use of *staccato* one might take the following subjects, in the first of which the isolated *staccato* note gives character and variety to the outline, and in the second of which *portamento* or *mezzo-staccato* seems called for:

Ex. 160a: Bach *Das Wohltemperierte Klavier*, Book I, *Fugue No. 1* in C, BWV 848, bars 1–2, right hand

Ex. 160b: Bach *Das Wohltemperierte Klavier*, Book I, *Fugue No. 2* in C minor, BWV 849, bars 1–3, right hand

Bach's music, then, affords wide scope for individual judgement as far as phrasing and dynamics are concerned. In the Haydn–Beethoven period, composers' markings are more frequent, but the dynamics are still limited in variety, while the phrasing is often slipshod, necessitating revision. In consequence discrepancies will still be found in different editions, and it is for the pianist to make his choice. For example, in one edition the following subject is phrased:

Ex. 161: Mozart *Piano Sonata No. 16* in C, K.545, 1ˢᵗ movement, bars 14–15, Lovelock edition

Other editions break up the phrase more neatly into its component parts – a reading which seems nearer to the true Mozart style:

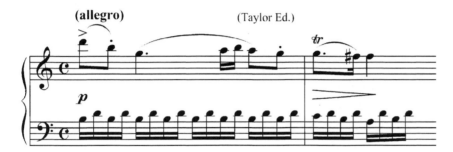

Ex. 162: Mozart *Piano Sonata No. 16* in C, K.545, 1ˢᵗ movement, bars 14–15, Taylor edition

The care which Beethoven took in his use of expression marks makes extensive editorial revision unnecessary. But occasionally some minor adjustments must be made. For instance in the score of his C minor *Piano Concerto* there is an inconsistency in the treatment of the last note of the following quotation from the first subject of the first movement – in some places it is marked *staccato*, in others not:

Ex. 163: Beethoven, *Piano Concerto No. 3* in C minor, Op. 37, 1ˢᵗ movement, bars 116–117

D'Albert, in his edition of the *Concerto*, lets this inconsistency stand, though a careful comparison of all the passages concerned (note in particular the recapitulation) will show that a *staccato* note is obviously intended. I have heard a performance in which, after the orchestra had played this note with a crisp *staccato*, the solo pianist on his entry not only played it *tenuto* but kept the pedal sustained. The effect was slovenly in the extreme.

Whereas Bach left such niceties to the performer, from Schumann's time onwards composers commence to take such pains with the smallest detail of expression as to make editorial interference a presumption. One instance, however, must be mentioned, in connection with which even the most scrupulous editor might be pardoned for taking a liberty, namely at the end of Chopin's *Study* in E minor:

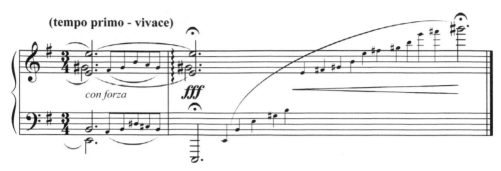

Ex. 164: Chopin *12 Études,* No. 5 in E minor, Op. 25, bars 137–138

To start *fff* and to attempt to produce a continuous *crescendo* on the single notes of the rising arpeggio is to do violence to the very nature of the progression involved and of the instrument itself. All editors agree in reproducing the *crescendo*, but even at the risk of contravening the autograph it should be necessary here for an editor to point out the impracticability of the marking as given, and to suggest a *diminuendo*. But such cases are exceedingly rare and in the romantic and modern period the editor's main contribution to the text, if any, is in the domain of pedalling and fingering.

PEDALLING

The mode of pedalling is usually left by the composer to the discretion of the performer or editor. Since the use of the sustaining pedal was not known in the Bach period modern editors either leave the text unmarked or prescribe a limited amount of pedalling according to their particular leanings towards this controversial subject. (See pp. 82–89) During the Haydn–Mozart period the piano gradually ousted the harpsichord, but special marks to indicate the pedalling were not yet devised. In inserting pedalling marks modern editors tend on the whole to allow for too much fusion, rather than too little. In the following extract from Haydn's third sonata the prescribed pedalling takes from the harmonic clarity by fusing *appoggiaturas* with their notes of resolution. With such pedalling there can be little delicacy of nuance, such as is essential for the slight and transparent texture of the music of this period:

123

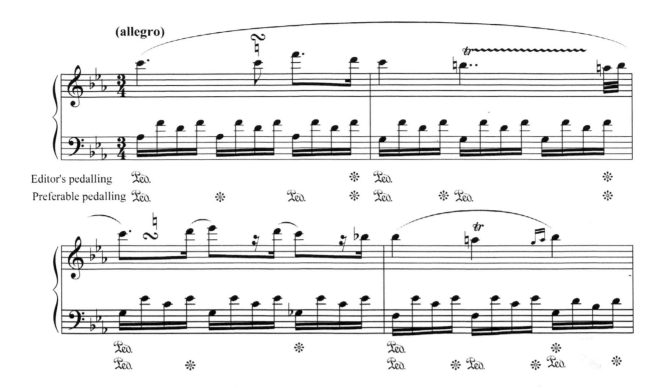

Ex. 165: Haydn *Piano Sonata No. 59* in E flat, Hob.XVI:49, 1st movement, bars 33–36, Taylor
edition

In some editions of the Beethoven piano sonatas, and notably in the very thorough edition of
the Florentine pianist Buonamici, the pedalling is also too lavish. In addition to the extracts given
in Chapter Twelve one might add the following, in which Buonamici indicates that the pedal is to
be sustained to the end of each bar, thus negativing the purpose of the phrase-marks, and of the
quaver rest in the first example:

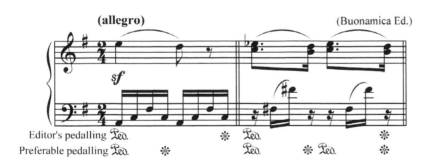

Ex. 166: Beethoven *Piano Sonata No. 10* in G, Op. 14, No. 2, 1st movement, bars 134 and 79,
Buonamici edition

Again in the following instance Buonamici indicates pedalling for no apparent reason in the
middle of a fast-moving scalic passage. Apart from any other consideration clarity of texture is
here essential to enhance the contrast with the rich *sostenuto* chords of the passage which follows,
so that the pedalling marked is quite inadvisable:

124

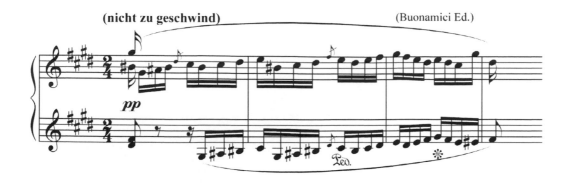

Ex. 167: Beethoven *Piano Sonata No. 27* in E minor, Op. 90, 2nd movement, bars 56–59, Buonamici edition

As further instances of muddy pedalling, one might quote from the same movement:

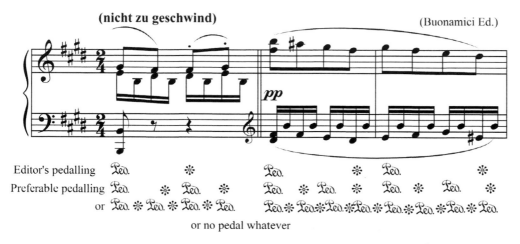

Ex. 168: Beethoven *Piano Sonata No. 27* in E minor, Op. 90, 2nd movement, bars 2 and 45–6, Buonamici edition

These examples are typical of the pedalling prescribed throughout, and not only Buonamici but many other editors tend to err in this direction. As a final example witness the following extracts from Beethoven's third *Piano Concerto*:

Ex. 169a: Beethoven *Piano Concerto No. 3* in C minor, Op. 37, 1st movement, bars 148–149, d'Albert edition

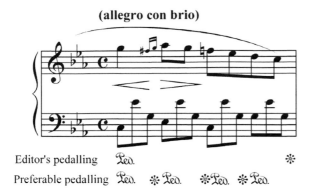

(allegro con brio)

Editor's pedalling

Preferable pedalling

Ex. 169b: Beethoven *Piano Concerto No. 3* in C minor, Op. 37, 1st movement, bar 327, d'Albert edition

It may indeed be objected that Beethoven himself, among those rare instances in which he inserted pedalling-marks into his sonatas, has used similar or even still more muddy effects, as for instance in the first movement of the 'Appassionata' *Sonata*, where he retains the minor ninth, D flat, against the root of the chord, apparently so as to give but slow release to the tension stored up by the tumultuous broken-chord passages of the preceding section:

(allegro assai)

Ex. 170: Beethoven *Piano Sonata No. 23* in F minor, Op. 57, 1st movement, bars 235–237

Another curious instance is to be found in the *Sonata* Op. 101, where he fuses a series of ascending triads so that they lead through a confused haze of sound into the clarity of a consonant chord in *pianissimo*:

(vivace alla marcia)

Ex. 171: Beethoven *Piano Sonata No. 28* in A, Op. 101, 2nd movement, bars 30–33

A further device which he occasionally specifies is the fusion of the dominant and tonic chords by sustaining the pedal for both. But it must be remembered that such instances are exceedingly rare, and, as already mentioned, that the piano of Beethoven's time, with its thin strings and small leather-covered hammers, did not allow a tithe of the resonance which our modern grand produces, so that the discordance would then have been considerably less in effect than it is now. Otherwise it would not have been possible for him in the D minor *Sonata* to mark the retention of the pedal for four bars of the recitative. To-day the pianist might preferably pedal each successive note, if the melody is to sing out with maximum clarity, and at the same time hold the chord in the left hand for three bars, so as to preserve the composer's intention:

Ex. 172: Beethoven *Piano Sonata No. 17* in D minor, Op. 31, No. 2, 1st movement, bars 143–147

It is true that pedalling is to a large extent a matter of individual taste, and can often be equally well effected in different ways. In the examples cited above, however, the limits of discretion seem to have been exceeded. The cultured pianist will pedal instinctively and will often disregard the editor's markings, however interested in these he may be. But every teacher knows the enormous difficulty which the average student experiences in learning to pedal properly. It is for such that the editor should prepare his edition, and at least indicate suitable pedalling for all those passages which present difficulty, or admit of varied treatment. Yet one finds that in the majority of editions only the most obvious pedalling is marked, and the real problems are left unsolved, while one's expectation of finding personal revelations in pedalling is often doomed to disappointment. Every great artist plays and pedals a particular master in an entirely personal way, developing a style which becomes so much a part of himself that he could not alter it even if he tried. It is this personal interpretation which one might expect to find in an edition prepared by a noted exponent. For instance it would be of interest to see how Lamond, one of the finest of Beethoven players, pedals the sonatas, yet in his edition[53] scarcely a single passage is marked which would call for any special or ingenious treatment. And if this be so in the case of outstanding executants one cannot wonder if the results are unsatisfactory in the case of editors who are not even pianists. Despite the numerous editions of the Beethoven sonatas which have appeared, that prepared by Lebert over fifty years ago in collaboration with Liszt, Hans von Bülow and others is still among the most useful and illuminating.[54] Lebert adopted the happy expedient of giving Beethoven's markings, wherever they occur, in large print, and his own

---

[53] Frederic Lamond, *Sämtliche Klaviersonaten von Ludwig van Beethoven*, Breitkopf & Härtel (Leipzig 1918).

[54] Sigmund Lebert, *Klaviersonaten von Ludwig van Beethoven*, Cotta (Stuttgart n. d.).

voluminous additions in small print – a plan having the most obvious advantages if it were but generally followed.

In the absence of some system such as that adopted by Lebert it is equally difficult in the music of the romantic period to discover what additions the editor has made to the original. Schumann, Chopin and Brahms usually inserted pedalling marks only where they desired a special effect, and editions of their works are either relatively bare of pedalling marks (particularly those of Schumann and Brahms) or worked out in detail according to the ideas and industry of the particular editor. With Chopin especially there are few editors whose directions one would follow implicitly. Chopin's own markings cannot always be adopted on the modern piano. What has already been said about the lack of sustaining power in the piano of Beethoven's period still holds good to a large extent for the Chopin period, so that Chopin's markings are liable to produce a thicker effect than that originally intended. For instance in the following passage by sustaining the pedal for the first two beats of each successive bar Chopin causes the phrasing to be altered for note-groups of the same pattern, and pedals through the rests on the second quaver of bars 2–4. Undoubtedly this gives a richer result, but the slurs and *staccato* marks are thereby ignored and the clarity of the rhythm impaired. It would be preferable to pedal each slurred group separately:

Ex. 173: Chopin *Ballade No. 3* in A flat, Op. 47, bars 54–58, Chopin Institute edition

Again, in the next passage the sustaining of the pedal for the whole of each bar blurs the melodic outline, in addition to obliterating the light, *staccato* phrase-ending towards the end of the second bar and preventing a clear start for the next phrase. By pedalling twice per bar the melody will sing more clearly, while the *legato* left hand will of itself effect continuity:

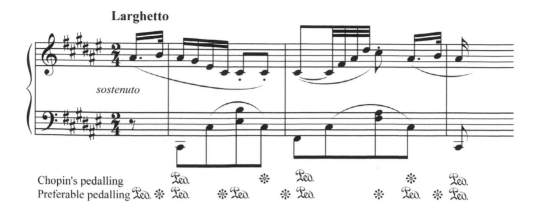

Ex. 174: Chopin *Nocturne No. 5* in F sharp, Op. 15, No. 2, bars 1–3

As noted above (see pp. 89-91) impressionists such as Debussy and Ravel seldom indicate the pedalling, which is all the stranger since pedalling plays such an integral part in their work. The same applies also to contemporary composers such as Rachmaninoff, Bartok and Bax. A few such as John Ireland and Moeran are meticulous in their markings, but they are altogether in the minority, with the result that in modern music, with its complex harmony, the student receives far less guidance than in the carefully edited classics, in which problems of tone fusion are in every way considerably less. One often finds passages in which notes are tied throughout a welter of chordal changes, and it is hard to know whether the composer intends (a) the use of the Steinway or *sostenuto* third pedal, or (b) pedal changes which make the tied note fictitious, or (c) retention of the pedal, with a possibly chaotic effect. Publishers might well insist on the composer introducing directions for doubtful passages of this kind, otherwise they must be left to the caprice of the performer, or worse still to the caprice of an editor at some future date when the music of our time will be as remote as the clavecin music of de Chambonnières is to the editor of to-day.

FINGERING

Such clumsy fingering is sometimes prescribed in editions that one doubts whether the editors, however eminent they may be as musicologists, are really pianists themselves. In quick passage work the fingering often has the appearance of having been calculated in relation to a slow tempo only and is awkward when taken up to time, while practical devices such as would occur to any experienced player are often overlooked. The reader is referred to Chapter IV, where fingering has already been dealt with under Technique and Practice (see pp. 30 seq.) and in a number of cases preferential fingering has been suggested to that taken from standard editions.

Continental fingering is now generally adopted, i.e. the thumb and four fingers are marked 1–5 respectively. The so-called English system, by which the thumb is marked with a cross and the fingers marked 1–4, is merely a source of confusion to beginners since in any event the bulk of the music they will use will contain continental fingering. In present-day editions English fingering occasionally reappears – a regrettable anachronism.

METRONOME MARKS

On one occasion Stavenhagen reproved a student for playing the Andante of Beethoven's *Sonata* in E flat, Op. 27, No.1 too quickly, and she in somewhat pained surprise pointed to the metronome marking ♩ = 84. I well remember his smile and her dismay when he told us that not only was this marking too fast (it should be nearer to ♩ = 72) but the majority of metronome marks for the works of Beethoven, Schumann and Chopin were unreliable, even when they were prescribed by the composer himself.

Such doubt about the validity of metronome marks can be justified by a variety of causes. First of all one cannot be sure whether the marking recorded on the editor's or composer's metronome holds good for one's own, unless both should happen to have been accurate. On examining three instruments, one dating from 1910, the second from 1918 and the third from 1939, I found that to achieve the same speed on all three, when the first was set at 120, it was necessary to adjust the second to 126, and the third to 128, in other words that the oldest instrument of the three moved appreciably faster than the others. Accordingly it is a wise plan to check the accuracy of one's metronome by setting it at 60, and counting the number of beats per minute by one's watch. It the beats number more or less than 60, the metronome is either faster or slower by the number of beats in question, and a corresponding allowance must be made in setting the metronome to a particular marking.

Where a discrepancy arises between one metronome and another, however, it is usually slight. A more fundamental discrepancy as regards metronome marks may be due to the change which can occur in the conception of tempo from one period to another. Thus in Beethoven's time *Adagios* were played faster and *Allegros* slower than we are accustomed to play them now. Or again in individual cases an injudicious marking may be prescribed by the composer himself. Schindler records that when Beethoven metronomed the same work twice over he marked the tempos differently each time. Again Brahms once remarked that every composer who has given metronome marks has sooner or later withdrawn them. If the composer is uncertain as to the most appropriate tempo one cannot hope for uniformity when generations have gone by, and the tradition which may have been established by some of the best exponents of the composer's own time has lapsed.

Schumann is one of the worst offenders in this respect. For instance in his *Papillons*, Op. 2, some of the markings are too slow, including the main theme, which is given as ♩ = 120, at which tempo, or at anything less than ♩ = 184, his *Butterflies* would be dull and heavy-winged indeed. Again in his *Kinderszenen*, Op. 15, the first piece *Aus Fremden Ländern* is marked ♩ = 108, a commonplace jig-like tempo which must be reduced to ♩ = 80 if the obvious intentions of the composer are to be realised.

Many of Chopin's studies are marked at too high a speed. In his book on Chopin[55] Huneker refers to Kullak's warning that Chopin should not be played according to his own metronome marks, and gives some interesting comparisons which show the degree of divergence between various editors' markings, and in some cases between the editors' and Chopin's own. For instance the F major *Study*, Op. 10, No. 8 is marked by Chopin ♩ = 96, but von Bülow prescribed ♩ = 89, and Klindworth and Kullak ♩ = 80. Huneker does not advert to quite a number of other cases in which the customary marking is still too high. For instance for the *Study* in E major, Op. 10, No. 3, marked *Lento ma non troppo*, Chopin himself, followed by all the editors, prescribes ♪ = 100. This tempo suggests a mood of jollity rather than the nostalgic melancholy with which the *Study*

---

[55] James Huneker, *Chopin the Man and his Music* (London 1921), p. 156.

is permeated and is certainly not borne out by the anecdote connected with this *Study* (see below p. 183). ♪ = 66 would be nearer to the appropriate tempo. Three further studies, very frequently played, suffer similarly from excessively high metronome marks. The 'Winter Wind' *Study*, Op. 25, No. 11, is marked ♩ = 69 in all editions, and though it is possible to play the *Study* at this tempo, above ♩ = 58 it tends to become a scramble and loses both its vitality and meaning. The *Study in the Black Keys*, Op. 10, No. 5, should not be played faster than ♩ = 112 despite the original ♩ = 116, which editors universally follow. Again the 'Revolutionary' *Study* in C minor, Op. 10, No. 12, is marked at ♩ = 160, at which tempo it is next to impossible to give adequate voice to the passionate outburst of grief and despair contained in this great *Study*. Furthermore the accentuation essential for the descending semiquaver passage at the opening and its recurrences (this characteristic and vital accent on the first note of each group is ignored by most pianists to-day) cannot be properly achieved at so high a marking. Pianists who are unwilling to sacrifice music to showmanship will not play this *Study* faster than ♩ = 152. As a general rule, when fast works are played at a slightly slower tempo than the maximum tempo possible they sound clearer and more meaningful – and ultimately just as fast. It is lamentable that so many of Chopin's studies should be played merely as a *tour de force*, with an utter disregard for their poetic qualities.

The markings for the *Nocturnes* and slower pieces are on the whole more trustworthy, but characteristically enough the tendency with pianists is to reduce them still further so that dragging results. Thus the *Nocturne* in C sharp minor, Op. 21, No. 1, is usually played far too slowly, the original marking, ♩ = 42, giving just the necessary impetus to the undulating, restlessly moving accompaniment in the left hand while the melody in the right assumes a shapely *rubato*. Still, even among the slow works instances are numerous in which the metronome marking is too high, as in the case of the *Nocturne* in E flat, Op. 9, No. 2 (♪ = 132) when the basic tempo should scarcely exceed ♪ = 116.

Even though metronome marks should always be interpreted as an indication rather than a direction, it will be seen from some of the above instances that they can lead to an entire misconception of the work to be played, particularly since markings which are quite unjustifiable still continue to appear in even the newest editions. Contemporary composers, however, are rarely inaccurate in their markings, and can be followed without the misgivings one must so often have in the case of the classical and romantic masters.

CHAPTER FIFTEEN
ORNAMENTS

The interpretation of ornaments is one of the minor problems which the pianist has to face. Here the textbook rules do not always constitute the ultimate authority, in as much as they reflect the practice of a dominant school or of a particular period, and tend to ignore the practice of other schools or the change in practice from period to period. Again, many of the rules admit of so many exceptions, even within the practice of the one school or period, that in some cases the exceptions outnumber the cases in which the rules hold good. The judgement and good taste of the executant are sometimes a surer guidance than a rule which merely codifies procedures regardless of context. In the following pages some of the points will be discussed in regard to which many pianists have come to disregard the conventional rules.

ACCIACCATURA

According to the textbook rule the *acciaccatura* or short *appoggiatura* (a grace note with a stroke through its stem) comes on the beat, thus taking time from the principal note. This practice has venerable authority behind it, and C.P.E. Bach called any other procedure '*dilettantisch*'. Speaking of this rule in the first chapter on grace notes in his *Essay on the true way of playing the Klavier,* Bach refers to the fact that people so frequently fail to observe the rule, and in the second chapter he says that the blunder of playing the *Vorschlag* or short *appoggiatura* too soon, as part of the preceding note, has given rise to 'those ugly *Nachschläge* which are now so much in fashion'.[56] From this one may gather that the rule was by no means universally upheld, and its non-observance would have been encouraged by the existence of the ornament to which Bach refers, and which, like the *durchgehender Vorschlag,* was synonymous with the *acciaccatura* played before the beat, and was written in identical fashion.[57] Admittedly the playing of the *acciaccatura* on the beat does represent majority practice in the eighteenth century and should be adopted on the whole for early keyboard music. But in the course of the nineteenth century an increasing number of executants came to adopt the practice of playing the *acciaccatura* before the beat, holding that this gives a clearer and neater result:

Ex. 175: *Acciaccatura*

---

[56] See Edward Dannreuther, *Musical Ornamentation* (London 1923), Vol. II, pp. 16 and 17
[57] Op. cit., Vol. I p. 182; Vol. II pp. 64, 80, 97.

Most pianists of the Liszt school, including Stavenhagen and Kellermann, used to play the *acciaccatura* so, under certain conditions even in Mozart's keyboard music. For instance the mode of execution prescribed for the following example according to the textbook rule:

Ex. 176: Mozart *Piano Sonata No. 11* in A, K.331, 3rd movement, bar 101

involves the difficulty of playing the *acciaccatura* in the right hand and the *acciaccatura*-group in the left hand with the chord, but unaccented, a difficulty which does not arise when these grace-notes precede the beat. Especially for rhythmic repetition of this kind, the latter mode is surer and more incisive in effect:

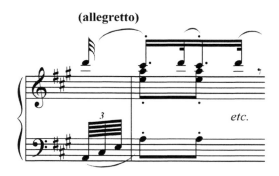

Ex. 177: Mozart *Piano Sonata No. 11* in A, K.331, 3rd movement, bar 101

As we advance into the nineteenth century the convention of playing the *acciaccatura* on the beat begins to lose its validity, though only towards the end of the century was any other procedure given theoretical recognition.[58] Schumann was sometimes careful to show by the spacing of his *acciaccaturas* whether they should precede the beat or coincide with it:

---

[58] See Louis Köhler, *Theorie der musikalischen Verzierungen* (Leipzig 1887), pp. 2–3, and Dannreuther, Vol. II, p. 129.

(leicht und mit humor)
ritard.

Ex. 178: Schumann *8 Noveletten*, Op. 21, No. 3, bars 89–90

Chopin's method of ornamentation was based on that of C.P.E. Bach, and it is assumed that he would have intended his *acciaccaturas* to be played on the beat. Yet unless the *acciaccaturas* were intended to be played before the beat it is hard to see the purpose of the difference in notation between the opening bars of the *Study* in E minor and the repetition at bar 29 ff:

Ex. 179a: Chopin *Études,* No. 17 in E minor, Op. 25, No. 5, bars 1–2

Ex. 179b: Chopin *Études*, No. 17 in E minor, Op. 25, No. 5, bars 29-30

The second mode of notation is not a short-hand way of expressing the first, since in the final statement Chopin reverts again to the first mode of notation. Both J.P. Dunn[59] and the editors of the Chopin Institute's edition suggest that the only difference between the two notations is that in the first the upper voice is *tenuto*, whereas in the second it is *staccato*, but to make this distinction it was only necessary to write the top part differently in each case. Chopin was too meticulous a craftsman to adopt a different form of notation without any particular purpose. Dannreuther seems nearer the mark in suggesting that the difference is one of nuance,[60] and a nuance in this case

---

[59] J. P. Dunn, *Ornamentation in Chopin's Music* (London 1921), p. 43.

[60] Edward Dannreuther, *Musical Ornamentation* (London 1923), Vol. II, p. 163.

could only be determined by the position of the semiquavers or *acciaccaturas* in relation to the beat.

A similar case of differentiation occurs in the following example where there would be no point in using the *acciaccatura* at all if it were played on the beat:

Ex. 180: Liszt 2 *Konzert-Etüden*, Nr. 2 'Gnomenreigen', bar 13

Where the *acciaccatura* occurs in conjunction with two or more notes of a chord it may be taken prior to the beat, though there are cases in which it must be played simultaneously with the notes of the chord, e.g.:

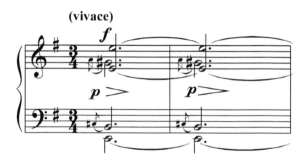

Ex. 181: Chopin *Études*, No. 17 in E minor, Op. 25, No. 5, bars 130–131

Here executants who are accustomed to take the *acciaccatura* before the beat will play as follows:

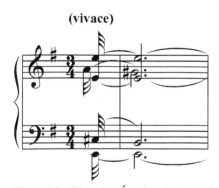

Ex. 182: Chopin *Études*, No. 17 in E minor, Op. 25, No. 5, bar 130

In the next example it is a tradition to combine the *acciaccatura* with an *arpeggiata* effect as follows:

Ex. 183: Chopin *Ballade No. 3* in A flat, Op. 47, bars 138–139

In later nineteenth century as in contemporary music the *acciaccatura* can more validly be taken prior to the beat than on the beat, though many pianists still apply to modern music what is more properly a convention of the eighteenth century.

INVERTED TURN AND SLIDE

In the case of the *acciaccatura* the difference in effect between playing the grace-note prior to or on the beat is relatively slight. But in the case of grace-note groups the difference can be considerable and aesthetic reasons can at times clearly outweigh the claims of convention. In the following example if the inverted turn be started on the beat so that the D sharp in the right hand will enter with the bass note A, even when the greatest care is taken to play the turn lightly and to accent only the principal note E, the mere fact that four notes in the right hand are played against the bass note A, means that this note will tend to be slightly prolonged, and the resultant effect is one of over-accentuation which is liable to grow more irritating with each recurrence of the figure. This context seems to justify the playing of the turn prior to the downbeat:

Ex. 184: Mozart *Rondo* in A minor, K.511, bar 1

In the next example if the first note of the turn, F sharp, be played with the chord it is given such significance even when unaccented as to anticipate the subsequent fall of the melody to F sharp, and consequently has a disturbing effect. The turn is again best taken prior to the beat:

(largo appassionato)

Ex. 185: Beethoven *Piano Sonata No. 2* in A, Op. 2, No. 2, 2nd movement, bar 29

According to C.P.E. Bach the slide is begun on the beat. Yet the ornament known as *Nachschläge* (after-beats) which is identical with the slide except that it is played prior to the beat, is recognised by Leopold Mozart and by Türk, and is admitted by Dannreuther[61] as a valid interpretation of the slides in Schubert's *Deutsche Tänze.*[62] In dealing with Chopin's ornamentation Dunn reiterates Bach's rule, but admits a number of cases in which slides should be played prior to the beat,[63] e.g.:

(allegro, ma non troppo)

Ex. 186: Chopin *Polonaise No. 9* in B flat, Op. 71, No. 2, bar 9

The above context is in no way different from dozens of others in Chopin's music, and the custom of playing the slide prior to the beat is artistically preferable except in such cases as the following, where a note of short value preceding the slide would make the ornament sound too rushed if taken prior to the beat:

(allegro, ma non troppo)

Ex. 187: Chopin *Polonaise No. 9* in B flat, Op. 71, No. 2, bar 12

---

[61] See Dannreuther, *Musical Ornamentation*, Vol. II, pp. 65 and 80.

[62] Op. cit., p. 130.

[63] Dunn, *Ornamentation in Chopin's Music*, p. 39

Nowadays the composer who wishes the slide to come on the beat will sometimes indicate this specifically as in the following example where an *arpeggiata* effect and slide are combined in the right hand:

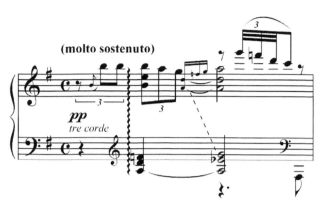

Ex. 188: Moeran *Toccata*, bar 88

UPPER MORDENT OR *PRALLTRILLER*

The upper mordent or *Pralltriller*, denoted by the sign ❧, consists of a three-note group, namely, the principal note, an upper accessory note and the principal note repeated. Its accentuation is often a source of difficulty and ambiguity. According to eighteenth-century practice the first note of the upper mordent occurs on the beat and either this note or the third note of the group may be accented, the usual distinction being that in quick tempos the accent is on the first, in slow tempos on the third note of the group:

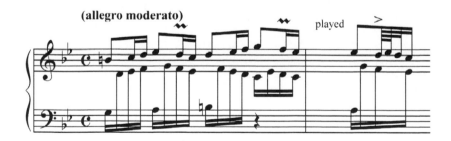

Ex. 189a: Bach *6 Partitas*, No. 1 in B flat, BWV 825, 2nd movement, bar 30

Ex. 189b: Bach *6 Französische Suiten*, No. 2 in C minor, BWV 813, 4th movement, bar 16

If the principal note of the upper mordent is preceded by the same note, the accessory note begins the group as an additional *acciaccatura*, e.g.:

Ex. 190: Bach *6 Partitas*, No. 3 in A minor, BWV 827, 5th movement, Burlesca, bar 1

The three notes of the upper mordent can combine to form virtually a triplet in fast-moving passages, as frequently in Beethoven, e.g.:

Ex. 191a: Beethoven *Piano Concerto No. 3* in C minor, Op. 37, 1st movement bars 184–186

Ex. 191b: Beethoven *Piano Sonata No. 8* in C minor, Op. 13, 1st movement, bars 80–83

In both the above examples the first note of the upper mordent should be accented, not the third, as some pianists attempt with a halting and laboured effect.

Even in slow tempo the upper mordent should be played as a triplet when a note of short-time value is involved:

Ex. 192: Chopin *Nocturne No. 19* in E minor, Op. 72, bars 35–36

When the melody-note over which the upper mordent sign occurs is part of a chord, it is customary to play the first note of the upper mordent with the other note or notes of the chord, and to accent either the first or third note of the group according to whether the tempo be quick or slow, or again whether the particular note-value be short or long:

Ex. 193a: Chopin *Mazurka No. 42* in G, Op. 67, No. 1, bars 1–2

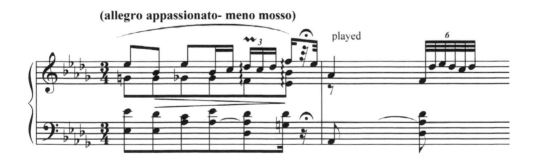

Ex. 193b: Chopin *Polonaise No. 1* in C sharp minor, Op. 26, No. 1, bars 63–64

(allegro appassionato - meno mosso)

Ex. 193c: Chopin Polonaise No. 1 in C sharp minor, Op. 26, No. 1, bars 79–80

Despite the rule that the upper mordent should be begun on the beat, it is frequently played as an anticipated ornament in Chopin (i.e. its first two notes are taken from the time-value of the preceding note). Dunn gives a list of many such cases,[64] suggesting that the ornament may be anticipated when it occurs over the first note of a phrase, or after a pause. But some of the instances he quotes do not conform to these conditions, and pianists frequently play the upper mordent prior to the beat for the sake of clarity and crispness.

At the beginning of the *Waltz* in D flat there are two occurrences of the upper mordent:

Molto vivace

Ex. 194: Chopin *Waltz No. 11* in G flat, Op. 70, bar 1

One might be inclined to assume that the difference in notation implied a difference in method of performance, and that when the ornament is fully written out it is intended to be played <u>prior</u> to the beat, but on the beat when the symbol is used. An analysis of all the other instances, however, in which Chopin uses both modes of notation in the one composition will show that no such inference can be drawn, and that he used either form indiscriminately. As a general rule one might say that if the tempo be fast, or again if the note preceding the principal note of the upper mordent be of short value, the ornament will be taken on the beat. The first note will then be accented, especially when the tempo is fast enough to cause the upper mordent to sound virtually as a triplet, as in the example just quoted. Or the third note can be accented as in the following example:

[64] Dunn, *Ornamentation in Chopin's Music*, see chapter on Transient Shake, pp. 26–29. Cf. Dannreuther, *Musical Ornamentation*, Vol. II, p. 129.

Ex. 195: Chopin *Mazurka No. 5* in B flat, Op. 7, No. 1, bars 45–46

But if the upper mordent occurs at the start of a phrase, if the tempo be slow or *moderato*, or even in fast tempos if the note prior to the principal note be a sustained one, the ornament is best anticipated, with the accent on the third note:

Ex. 196a: Chopin *Mazurka No. 42* in G, Op. 67, No. 1, bars 29–31

Ex. 196b: Chopin *Nocturne No. 3* in B, Op. 9, No. 3, bars 4–5

The sign *tr* is frequently found with Chopin in lieu of the ordinary symbol for the upper mordent, though synonymous with the latter.[65] The upper mordent is historically speaking a curtailed trill, and in the following example it is a tradition not to play merely an upper mordent, but a trill without a *Nachschlag* or turn in the manner of the old French *tremblemens*, since the upper mordent seems too slight in this context for the duration of the crotchet:

---

[65] See Chopin Institute edition, Vol. 9, footnote to *Waltz* Op. 70, No. 1.

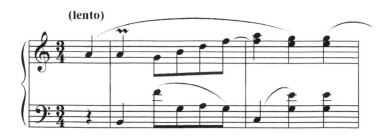

Ex. 197: Chopin *Waltz No. 3* in A minor, Op. 34, No. 2, bars 37–38

Unlike Chopin, Schumann usually writes his ornaments so as to indicate clearly how they should be played, and seldom uses abbreviations. The mordent symbol, however, is to be found in the first and last movements of the *Piano Concerto* in A minor, in the *Concert Allegro*, Op. 134, and in a few other works such as the *Abegg Variations*, mostly in fast tempos and indicating the triplet type of mordent with the accent on the first note.

Though the popularity of the mordent has declined, its symbol is still to be found in the piano music of composers such as Scriabin and Albeniz, and occurs occasionally even today (cf. Moeran's *Bank Holiday* and Bax's *Hardanger, Lullaby* and *Hill Tune*). It may be of interest to note that in traditional Irish and Scottish dance music the mordent, usually expressed by the term *tr.*, is taken on the beat, with the accent on the first note:

Ex. 198: Mordent in traditional Irish dance music

ARPEGGIO

According to the textbook rule when a chord is played *arpeggiata* the lowest note of the chord is taken on the beat. That Chopin, for instance, intended this to be so seems evident from markings in his own hand in the copies of his pupil Madame Dubois,[66] e.g.:

Ex. 199: Chopin *Nocturne No. 11* in G minor, Op. 37, No. 1, bar 5

[66] See the Chopin Institute's edition, first page of remarks appended at the end of each volume.

This would seem to settle the matter once and for all as far as Chopin is concerned, yet the number of exceptions under similar circumstances is almost sufficient to invalidate the rule. For example in the following passage, both Klindworth and Dannreuther agree that Chopin intended the notes of the arpeggiata to anticipate the beat[67]:

Ex. 200: Chopin *Variations on 'Là ci darem la mano'*, Op. 2, bars 25–26

In the next example the folly must be manifest of attempting to conceive the first arpeggio as commencing on the half-beat:

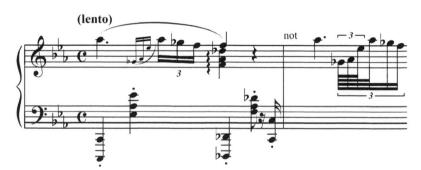

Ex. 201: Chopin *Nocturne No. 13* in C minor, Op. 48, No. 1, bar 10

Here the grace-notes have to be anticipatory and, to be consistent, so too must the arpeggioing of the D flat major chord.

In attempting to reconcile anticipatory arpeggios with those commencing on the beat in the following example from the same *Nocturne*:

[67] See Dannreuther, *Musical Ornamentation*, Vol. II, p. 166. But cf. Dunn, *Ornamentation in Chopin's Music*, p. 52.

144

Ex. 202: Chopin *Nocturne No. 13* in C minor, Op. 48, No. 1, bars 29–31

Dunn falls into the strange mistake of changing the rhythm and virtually eliminating the melody note on the first beat of each successive bar:[68]

Ex.203: Chopin *Nocturne No. 13* in C minor, Op. 48, No. 1, bars 29–31, arpeggiation, Dunn edition

Nowadays pianists normally play the top note of an *arpeggiata* chord on the beat. Where two chords are played *arpeggiata* simultaneously, as in the above example, the two upper notes coincide on the beat:

Ex. 204: Chopin *Nocturne No. 13* in C minor, Op. 48, No. 1, bar 29, arpeggiata chord playing

When the chord consists of a continuous *arpeggiata*, between two hands, it is played as follows:

[68] Dunn, *Ornamentation in Chopin's Music*, p. 48

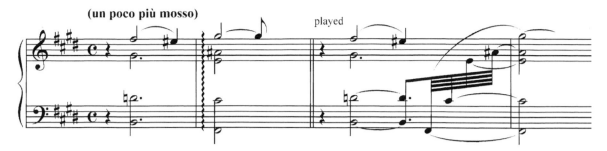

Ex. 205: Liszt *Consolations No. 2*, bars 34–35

Though the procedures dealt with above may not have been practised by the majority of pianists in the nineteenth century, they were certainly practised by a sizeable minority, and by composer-pianists of the calibre of Schumann[69] and Brahms, as may be seen from the following examples:

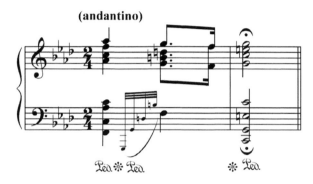

Ex. 206a: Schumann *Grosse Piano Sonata No. 3* in F minor, Op. 14, 3rd movement, bars 43–44

Ex. 206b: Schumann *Davidsbündlertänze,* Op. 6, No. 7, bars 9–10

---

[69] See Dannreuther, *Musical Ornamentation*, Vol. II, p. 157.

146

Ex. 206c: Brahms *Piano Sonata No. 3* in F minor, Op. 5, 3rd movement, bar 1 and bars 8–9

Ex. 206d: Brahms *Vier Klavierstücke,* No. 4, *Rhapsody in E flat*, Op. 119, bars 95–96

It would, however, be as unwarranted to stipulate the anticipatory arpeggio in all cases as it is to stipulate that the arpeggio always commence on the beat. In the following example the *appoggiatura* demands that the arpeggio be begun on the beat:

Ex. 207: Chopin *24 Préludes*, Op. 28, No. 8, bars 33–34

Again there are cases in which the same procedure is made necessary by the exigencies of the rhythm, e.g.:

Ex. 208: Liszt *Grandes études de Paganini,* No. 6 in A minor, bars 1–2

Frequently the best results are obtained by a combination of both methods. For instance the above example in performance probably works out best as follows:

Ex. 209: Liszt *Grandes études de Paganini,* No. 6 in A minor, bars 1–2, realisation

The lower mordent differs merely from the upper mordent in that the second note is a tone or semitone lower than the first, the distinction being indicated by a vertical line drawn through the mordent symbol. Popular in the eighteenth century, the lower mordent became virtually obsolete in the nineteenth, though it was revived by Reger and occurs frequently in his piano music.

TRILL

The majority of editors of piano music of the classical period adhere strictly to the rule that trills normally begin with the upper accessory note. Undoubtedly this was the case in the French classical school up to the end of the eighteenth century, and the rule is affirmed by C.P.E. Bach who modelled himself closely on the French masters in the matter of ornaments. But this rule, rigidly applied, must often damage the melodic or harmonic sense, for if the trill is begun with the upper note, this tends to stand out with an undue prominence. Consequently even in the performance of eighteenth century music the rule has been considerably modified. If the note on which the trill is made is the first note of a phrase, if it comes after a rest, if it be approached by leap, or from a note one degree above, or one degree below, if this note be vital to the harmonic or melodic outline – in all these cases it is the established practice that the trill commences with the principal note itself. It is only necessary to commence with the upper accessory if the preceding note is the same as, or tied to, the principal note (but again not if this note is marked *staccato*) or if the preceding note is an *appoggiatura*. Obviously the latter cases are relatively rare, so that it would be far less misleading to say that in J.S. Bach's music, and from his time on, the trill begins on the principal note, with the exceptions mentioned above.

Any attempt to adopt a rigid rule will lead to a network of inconsistencies. For instance in his article on the trill in Grove's *Dictionary of Music and Musicians* Franklin Taylor asserts that the trill commences with the upper note, though he grants most of the exceptions mentioned above. One is then not surprised to find in his edition of the Mozart sonatas diverse treatment of trills which occur under the same or similar conditions. The following examples are typical of the confusion which exists throughout.[70]

Trill approached by leap from above:

Ex. 210a: Mozart *Piano Sonata No. 8* in A minor, K.310, 1st movement, right hand part, bars 70–71

Ex. 210b: Mozart *Piano Sonata No. 8* in A minor, K.310, 2nd movement, right hand part, bars 28–29

Trill approached by step from below:

Ex. 211a: Mozart *Piano Sonata No. 10* in C, K.330, 1st movement, right hand part, bar 26

Ex. 211b: Mozart *Piano Sonata No. 1* in C, K.279, 1st movement, right hand part, bars 25–26

---

[70] Compare also Franklin Taylor's treatment of trills preceded by a rest (e.g. *Sonata* in A minor, K.310, *Andante*, figure O; and *Sonata* in F, K.332, first movement, figure H), and of trills preceded by the same note *staccato* (e.g. *Sonata* in C, K.330, *Andante*, figure D; and *Sonata* in F, K.280, *Presto*, figure C, etc.)

Such inconsistencies merely bewilder the player, and in each of the above cases it is more satisfactory to commence the trill with the principal note.

It must be remembered that, historically speaking, the trill may be derived in either of two ways – as a pulsation of any given note, and therefore starting with this note, or as a pulsation following upon an *appoggiatura*, and therefore starting with the upper note. Of these two types the first is as old or perhaps older than the second, and cannot be dismissed as a crude nineteenth-century innovation. Furthermore, with the passing of the *appoggiatura* as an ornament the *appoggiatura*-trill, commencing with the upper note, also becomes obsolete. Hummel was the first to formulate the practice of starting the trill with the principal note as a general principle, in his book on piano-playing of 1828,[71] and the date is significant since round about this time the *appoggiatura* begins to fall into disuse. As far as the trill is concerned, however, Hummel's and Czerny's precepts instead of being 'crude', as Dannreuther terms them,[72] are merely re-affirmations of a practice which had always existed, but for some two centuries had been less favoured than the *appoggiatura*-trill. In the nineteenth century the non-*appoggiatura*-trill, beginning with the principal note, emerges as the normal type, and is generally adopted for nineteenth-century piano music.

The execution of the trill in Chopin's music, however, is sometimes problematic. Chopin, as has been stated, followed C.P.E. Bach in the matter of ornaments, and his pupil Mikuli states that he generally began trills with the auxiliary note.[73] This seems corroborated by the following passage where he writes out a sustained trill in full:

Ex. 212: Chopin *Polonaise-fantaisie*, Op. 61, bars 199–201

[71] Johann Nepomuk Hummel, *Ausführliche theoretisch-practische Anweisung zum Piano-forte-Spiel* (Vienna 1828); *A Complete Theoretical and Practical Course of Instruction on the Art of Playing the Pianoforte* (London 1828), p. 65.

[72] See Dannreuther, *Musical Ornamentation*, Vol. II, p. 162.

[73] See Niecks, *Chopin*, Vol. 2, p.185

But this is an isolated case, and Dunn states that where no direction to the contrary is given, the trill in Chopin's works should invariably begin with the principal note.[74] Chopin frequently, however, indicates his intention as to whether the trill is to begin on the principal or on the accessory note by writing in one or the other as a preliminary *acciaccatura* (as at the end of the above example). An *acciaccatura* is not of course intended, the small note merely standing for the note on which the trill is to begin:

Ex. 213: Chopin *Polonaise No. 6* in A flat, Op. 53, bar 29

In the following instance Dannreuther's interpretation of the first trill is manifestly wrong:[75]

Ex. 214: Chopin *Nocturne No. 17* in B, Op. 62, No. 1, right hand part, bars 69–70

since there is no justification for starting the first trill with the upper note and the succeeding trills with the principal note, when the first trill is preceded like the others by the principal note as *acciaccatura*. The distinction may be too slight to be perceived in performance, but the notation should preferably be:

Ex. 215: Chopin *Nocturne No. 17* in B, Op. 62, No. 1, right hand part, preferable notation of the trill

Even where the upper note occurs as a preliminary *acciaccatura*, thus indicating that the trill is to commence with this note, on no account must it receive any accent, since in contexts such as the

---

[74] Dunn, *Ornamentation in Chopin's Music*, Preface, and p. 1

[75] Dannreuther, *Musical Ornamentation*, Vol. II, p.162

following prominence of the upper note would adversely affect the melodic outline. The principal note must here receive the accent, and accordingly most executants, regardless of theoretical considerations, will play the first note of the trill prior to the beat:

Ex. 216: Chopin *Waltz No. 4* in F, Op. 34, No. 3, bars 94–96

A double *acciaccatura* preceding a trill is an ornament much favoured by Chopin. Dannreuther[76] and most other theorists prescribe the following method of execution:

Ex. 217: Chopin *24 Préludes,* No. 23 in F, Op. 28, left hand part, bar 2

but executants prefer to play a preliminary triplet prior to the beat, starting the trill with the principal note:[77]

Ex. 218: Chopin *24 Préludes,* No. 23 in F, Op. 28, left hand part, bar 2, Klindworth edition

The procedure, however, of indicating the start of the trill by means of an *acciaccatura* is regrettably ambiguous, since the player cannot always be sure whether a true *acciaccatura* is not intended, as it obviously must in the following instance:

---

[76] Dannreuther, *Musical Ornamentation*, Vol. II, p. 162
[77] Cf. Harriet Cohen, *Music's Handmaid*, p. 117

Ex. 219: Chopin *Études*, No. 17 in E minor, Op. 25, No. 5, bars 131–135, Klindworth edition

and again in the following:

Ex. 220: Chopin *Waltz No 4* in F, Op. 34, No. 3, bars 123–126

Where the trill sign is not accompanied by a conventional *acciaccatura* to indicate on which note to begin, one will normally choose the principal note, as has already been stated, for even where the *appoggiatura*-trill is presupposed, the rule of commencing with the upper note is 'more honoured in the breach than in the observance'. One would necessarily start with the principal note in cases such as the following:

Ex. 221: Chopin *Polonaise No. 3* in A, Op. 40, No. 1, bar 48

The number of notes to be played in a trill will depend on the tempo. In an *Adagio* it is possible to fit into a beat from six to eight alternations (i.e. twelve to sixteen notes, excluding the turn at the end), in an *Andante* from four to six alternations, while in an *Allegro molto* or *Presto* the trill is usually played as a turn (i.e. five notes in all) or even as a triplet. In editions of Haydn and Mozart one often finds a tendency on the part of the editor to prescribe too many notes for the trill in fast movements, with the result that the trill becomes blurred, or else a slight *ritenuto* must be made in order to fit the notes in clearly. To take one example, for the following trill Franklin Taylor prescribes three alternations in addition to the final turn:

Ex. 222a: Mozart *Piano Sonata No. 10* in C, K.330, 1st movement, bars 1–2, Augener edition

to be played:

Ex. 222b: Mozart *Piano Sonata No. 10* in C, K.330, 1st movement, bars 1–2, realisation of trill, Augener edition

Apart from the inexpediency of using triplets, two alternations, i.e. nine notes in all, should here be quite sufficient, and would secure a far clearer and surer result:

Ex. 223: Mozart *Piano Sonata No. 10* in C, K.330, 1st movement, bars 1–2, alternative realisation of trill

When an accompanying figure in the left hand moves at a fast tempo, it is usually better to synchronise the trill with the accompaniment, rather than to attempt to get in too many notes, with a blurred result, as in the following example:

Ex. 224a: Mozart *Piano Sonata No. 3* in B flat, K.281, 1ˢᵗ movement, bar 58

Preferably:

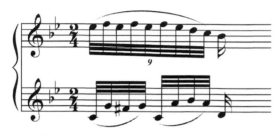

Ex. 224b: Mozart *Piano Sonata No. 3* in B flat, K.281, 1ˢᵗ movement, bar 58, realisation of trill

It is important to remember that with Chopin trills do not end with a turn unless the turn is actually written out. Furthermore, Stavenhagen used to say that when a sustained trill is used as a lead-in to the entry of a theme, a slight *ritardando* should be made as the trill draws to a close:

Ex. 225: Chopin *Grande Valse* in A flat, Op. 42, bars 1–10

BERNHARD STAVENHAGEN (1862-1914)
ROYAL ACADEMY OF MUSIC, MUNICH

Photograph: Friedrich Müller, Munich

[*Inscription*:]

Fräulein Tilly Swertz zur Erinnerung an Bernhard Stavenhagen.
[For Miss Tilly Swertz in memory of Bernhard Stavenhagen]

THE LADIESOF THE STAVENHAGEN PIANO MASTER CLASS
ROYAL ACADEMY OF MUSIC, MUNICH, 1903

The author is in the middle row, second from the right. Standing behind her is Grace O'Brien.[78]

---

[78] Though women were admitted to the Academy from 1890, they were taught separately until 1918.

INTERPRETATION AND TRADITION

Chapter Sixteen
Challenge to Tradition

Toscanini has challenged the validity of tradition, asking what tradition is, how its truth is to be ascertained, and how maintained by successive generations of interpreters.[79] According to Toscanini, tradition is to be found in only one place – in the music. This viewpoint must indeed be comforting to a pianist who has never studied with a master, who has not profited from performances by the greatest exponents of the art, who has never tried to steep himself not alone in a particular work but in the mind of its composer by studying his other works, and by studying his period and becoming acquainted with the ideals and influences which permeated his thought as a whole. For it is from such sources that a knowledge of tradition is derived. If Toscanini be right, aspiring pianists might spare themselves a considerable amount of trouble.

It is, however, manifestly false to suppose that from the mere notation of a work alone one can derive a full realisation of all that it is intended to express. If this were so a self-taught pianist in the Caucasus who has acquired a high degree of technical skill should be able to give as satisfying a performance of a Chopin *Ballade* as a cultured pianist trained in Warsaw or in Paris. One might presuppose, however, that apart from mere technical competence, which can be acquired under almost any circumstances, an alien mentality could not probe into and reproduce the real essence of Chopin's music without some guidance, either directly from an artist who possesses the necessary insight, or indirectly by a process of reconstruction out of the background and environment from which Chopin's music has sprung. To realise the effect of the lack of tradition in somewhat exaggerated circumstances, one need only recall certain performances of Wagner's operas in Paris, in which the Teutonic conception of the heroic became a ludicrous parody, or again of certain German performances of Debussy's orchestral music in which the subtle translucent texture was reduced to a muddy haze.

Toscanini's view can merely be admitted in so far as tradition is not a matter of tempo or of this detail or that, though matters of tempo or of detail may indeed be involved and may be important factors in the general result. But tradition is something more; it stands for a sum total of various qualities which are ultimately indefinable. Just as a people living in a certain region assume certain characteristics, certain inflexions of speech which mark them off from any other people, but are not easily defined, so too a particular composer's music and its true interpretation will gradually acquire a certain distinctiveness of utterance which may, for want of a better term,

---

[79] See article in *The New York Times*, 23 March 1947.

be called the 'tradition'. For the acquiring of this tradition one may point to certain conditions or requisites, none of which may be essential taken singly, but all or most of which should help towards an authentic reproduction of a particular composer's music. These conditions might be summarised as follows:

a) <u>Affinity of temperament between the performer and the composer – as revealed in his music</u>

Such affinity may be conditioned by the factor of race. Thus it will usually be more difficult for a Frenchman than it will for a German to interpret the music of a German composer, though any generalisation of this kind will of course admit of innumerable exceptions. Again, regardless of considerations of race, a performer who is temperamentally cold and reserved cannot as a rule do justice to music of the romantic period. Many of the best players of to-day, who are at one with the realism, the directness and technical exuberance of contemporary music, play the music of the romantic period in the same cold, clear-cut, matter-of-fact style in which they play Bartok or Hindemith. Romantic emotionalism is repugnant to them, with the result that they are apt to play the music of Schumann, Chopin and Liszt as they would Czerny exercises, brilliantly and efficiently it is true, but without that inner understanding of the poetic quality of the music which gives it its true significance. Pianists who by virtue of their temperament have no innate sympathy with romanticism should avoid romantic music altogether, and limit their repertoires to contemporary works or the classics. Similarly, pianists who are essentially romantic by nature and find their chief inspiration in the music of Schumann and Chopin are often incapable of appreciating early eighteenth-century music, or again are antagonistic to the idiom and methods of modern composers, and consequently lack both the disposition and the understanding with which to approach their work.

In all such cases where the vital factor of temperament is a stumbling block no amount of technique or acquaintance with tradition will enable the pianist to give a really adequate performance.

b) <u>Knowledge and guidance derived from a teacher, through whom is transmitted the accumulated interpretative detail gained from the best exponents of the past</u>

One would imagine that the tradition of how to play a particular composer's music should necessarily derive from the composer himself. But this is not always the case, for composers are notoriously poor interpreters of their own works. The ideal fountain-head of a tradition is that in which the composer himself shares in determining how his music shall be played, and at the same time some of the chief exponents of his day, and their disciples, gradually form a style of performance which both in its broad characteristics and in specific details may be enriched by later performers, who are steeped in the earlier tradition and add to it their own contribution. In this sense a tradition is always in the making. It may abate and decline according as players of the best calibre lose touch with the earlier tradition, or again become revitalised according as some new personality finds the old threads and re-weaves them into the traditional fabric.

The essential thing is continuity. The secrets of a craft are handed down from father to son; a succession of *seanchaithe* or peasant story-tellers will perpetuate a mass of lore gathered through the generations; and so too the artist-teacher will transmit his experience and that of his predecessors to his pupils, who will in turn transmit them further. Certain interpretative details will be lost, others may be lost and then rediscovered, new devices, new modes of giving point and significance to the interpretation of a passage will be invented, and accepted if they conform to the general traditional pattern. Consequently there is no 'modern' way of playing Mozart, or Beethoven or Chopin. If the performance of an earlier composer's work is to be authoritative it needs to be the outcome of a mould that has been fashioned bit by bit out of the experience of generations of the best minds which have lent themselves to its interpretation.

c) Knowledge of the *Zeitgeist* or spirit of the period in which the composer of a particular work lived, of his environment, of the literary and other influences by which he was affected and of his output as a whole

The pursuit of such a broad field of study may well seem futile to the average plodding pianist. The true artist will nearly always penetrate to the core of the music itself, but even in his case the realisation of the proper background against which the music has to be viewed and felt will be valuable in kindling and at the same time directing his imaginative insight. How much more will such knowledge help those who lack the ultimate artistic vision, but who may be able to acquire a certain measure of vision synthetically, through a study of these sources!

In playing Mozart it cannot but be a help to visualise the life of his period, both in its outward trappings of powdered wig and buckled shoe, of polished manners and high living, and in its inner characteristics mirrored in the elegance, incisive wit and irony of some of the literature of the period (Voltaire and Rousseau in France, Goldsmith and Johnson in England, Wieland in Germany). Admittedly the relationship between music and literature in the latter half of the eighteenth century is slight as compared with the relationship of these two arts in the romantic period which followed. When we come to Chopin, it is almost essential to know something of the world in which this composer lived and moved. With Chopin the personal background to his music – his friendship with George Sand, the inspiration of the poetry of Mickiewicz, national poet of Poland and fellow-exile of Chopin's – is perhaps more significant from the interpreter's viewpoint than the background of any other composer, but whether he be Bach, Beethoven or Debussy, an insight into the mind of the man himself and of his times can but stimulate and enrich the pianist's imagination and illuminate his playing.

d) Knowledge of the origin of a particular work – of any literary, biographical or other details which may throw light on it, or help towards its true interpretation

Here we come counter to the tendency in modern editions of romantic works to suppress literary or explanatory matter printed in earlier editions, a tendency already dealt with in some detail in Chapter 14. The reason for the lack of information concerning the genesis of compositions, or the actual suppression of such information, seems to lie in the present-day dread of suggesting, no matter how remotely, a 'programme' basis for music. This tendency, itself a reaction against the excessive image-hunting of the past generation, has now become so extreme as to cause the suppression of even the legitimate lore associated with many works, lest it interfere with their appreciation as abstract music. And so the majority of present-day pianists know next to nothing about the works they play. Any schoolboy studying English literature will be informed about the sources from which the plots of *Hamlet* or *The Merchant of Venice* are derived, nor will any educationalist think it strange that he should be encouraged to know more about the drama than the text itself. Yet pianists will play Liszt's *St Francis Preaching to the Birds* or *St Francis Walking over the Waves* without any inkling as to the source or nature of these legends and with no opportunity given them of gaining such information. It may be reprehensible to read into a work programme details which the composer never intended, and to insist on their validity, but it is surely equally reprehensible not to know the most elementary facts concerning the work's genesis, or as in the case of the Liszt *Legends* not to know the story which the music is intended to portray. Even if the composer chooses not to disclose the source of his inspiration, or in writing programme music not to publish the full background, afraid lest the public should pay more attention to fitting in the programme details than to absorbing the music itself, this does not say that we must refrain from learning all we can about the work's sources, since what we learn will illuminate for us the mind of the composer, and help us to come closer to the orbit of his vision. If it should be discovered that a work arose out of a concrete experience or was based on a particular programme which the composer had in mind, it does not necessarily follow that we must interpret the work in terms of that particular experience or programme. Chopin at first intended to inscribe the words 'After Hamlet' under the title of his *Nocturne* in G minor, Op. 15, No. 3, but subsequently changed his mind, deciding 'Let them guess for themselves'. The interpretation of the *Nocturne* is a matter for the individual player or listener, and Chopin himself wished this to be so, but who can deny that it is of interest and possibly of importance to know the orientation of Chopin's own mind when engaged in its creation.

Research of this kind can have a wider scope. Every commentator on Chopin mentions the influence of Mickiewicz on his work, yet not one in a hundred pianists will have read a line of the Polish poet's verse. One may indeed play Chopin admirably without the help of Mickiewicz. But in acquainting oneself with the background of passionately patriotic poetry, with the messianic spirit of Mickiewicz and his fellow exiles, one deepens one's sensitivity to the inner core of Chopin's music, reaching perhaps for the first time to an awareness of that vision, of an oppressed people's unconquerable spirit, from which the composer drew his chief inspiration.

So far we have been referring to biographical or descriptive matter which may to a greater or lesser extent affect the interpretation of a work. A further source of guidance may be derived from a stray remark of a composer's which has been recorded, a passage in one of his letters, or a hint passed on to one of his pupils or friends, which will give the clue to the best solution of a problem of interpretation which might otherwise be solved in several different ways. For instance in the article quoted at the outset of this chapter Toscanini admits that on hearing Weingartner take the second 'banner' or 'fanfare' theme of the *Meistersinger* overture in a light, lively and *staccato* manner, he almost jumped from his seat. Presumably Toscanini did not know, as Weingartner must have known, that in his treatise on conducting Wagner expressly states that this part of the overture should be taken at a really lively pace ('*wirklich lebhaftes Allegro*') and that only on its reappearance at the end should the 'fanfare' theme be taken *pesante* ('*die in wuchtigen Vierteln auszuführende Fanfare*').[80]

To give some comparable instances from piano literature, pianists are apt to rattle off the opening figure of Chopin's *Scherzo* in B flat minor, Op. 31, as if it were a scherzo of the

---

[80] Richard Wagner, 'Über das Dirigieren', *Gesammelte Schriften und Dichtungen*, Vol. 7 (Leipzig 1898), pp. 327, 329.

boisterous, rollicking type. Even if they were unable to divine the mood of the *Scherzo* instinctively, a knowledge of tradition would have taught them Chopin's real intentions here. For him the opening was never played *piano* enough, it was never 'vaulted' enough, never important enough. 'It must be a charnel-house', he said on one occasion.[81] And so the opening notes should be played in a hushed, sinister *pianissimo*, like a frightened question, to be answered by the succeeding *fortissimo* as by a thunder-clap.

Again, in the following passage the bracketed sub-phrase is usually played trippingly, pertly, if anything quicker than in strict time:

Ex. 226: Chopin *Nocturne No. 14* in F sharp minor, Op. 48, No. 2, bars 57–58

But Chopin once told his pupil Gutmann that this section of the *Nocturne* should be played 'like a recitative'. 'A tyrant commands' (the first two chords) he said, 'and the other asks for mercy'.[82] Accordingly the bracketed sub-phrase should be played lingeringly, appealingly, with the utmost expression, to secure the necessary contrast to the loud imperious chords which precede it.

Such allusions, either quoted in biographical studies or handed down by word of mouth, are of the utmost importance to the pianist who has a sense of reverence for the works he is studying and a genuine desire to give them authentic utterance. They disprove Toscanini's statement that tradition is to be found in the music alone, and the dull, insipid or robot-like performances one may hear by pianists who profess to be literal and objective provide sufficient proof that the printed notes are merely the bare bones of a work, and that its living soul must be created by the artist's imagination. Between the playing of two sensitive pianists, each of whom genuinely believes that he is merely reproducing what the composer has written, there can be a world of difference. Only the possession of rare artistry, coupled with the guidance of tradition, will enable a pianist to give the ideal performance.

In the chapters which follow, an attempt will be made to deal with a certain number of well-known works in terms of the tradition which has become associated with them, under one or more of the headings suggested above.

---

[81] Wilhelm von Lenz, *Berliner Musik-Zeitung Echo*, Vol. XXVI, 1876.
[82] James Huneker, *Chopin: The Man and His Music* (London 1903), p. 264

BEETHOVEN PLAYING FOR A BLIND GIRL ('MOONLIGHT' SONATA)

PAINTING BY WENZEL ULRIK TORNØE (1844-1907)

BORNHOLMS KUNSTMUSEUM, GUDHJEM, DENMARK

CHAPTER SEVENTEEN
BEETHOVEN

SONATA IN C SHARP MINOR, OP. 27, NO. 2 (THE 'MOONLIGHT')

Biographers and critics are accustomed to dismiss with scorn the various versions of the legend concerning the origin of the 'Moonlight' *Sonata*. Though some of these are sentimental in the extreme and all are unauthenticated, it is a mistaken viewpoint to dismiss any legendary matter which has grown around a work of art, simply because it is not verifiable, or indeed even if it can be refuted. From such legends one can gain an estimate of the popular reaction to the work, and this too is of importance. The most acceptable version of the legend relates how Beethoven, while staying at Heiligenstadt, heard one evening a fragment of his F major *Sonata* badly played as he passed an open window. As he listened he overheard the player saying she would give anything to hear the *Sonata* properly played. Entering the house and following the sound of the poor, worn-out instrument, he discovered to his surprise that the pianist was a blind girl who had been playing his sonata by ear. Moonlight filled the room, showing her dreamy, absorbed expression. Moved by the sight, Beethoven sat down and improvised the strains which were later to become incorporated in the *Sonata* Op. 27, No. 2.[83] Actually, however, the title 'Moonlight' *Sonata* seems to be derived from a remark of the contemporary critic Rellstab, who wrote that the opening movement reminded him of moonlight on the Vierwaldstätter See [Lake Lucerne].

However hackneyed the simile and however much this title has been derided, it is certainly apt for the exquisite first movement, calm and resigned, with its poignant melody singing out above the *pianissimo* triplets. In the majority of editions common time is given as the time signature instead of *alla breve*. As a result the first movement is usually played too slowly. Earlier editors such as Reinecke and Lebert and a few present-day editors such as Lamond prescribe *alla breve*, and this is undoubtedly correct.

The real art in this movement lies in playing the triplets with perfect *legato* and as softly as possible, while the melody above should be taken somewhat *rubato*, but never sentimentally. The semiquaver G sharp in bars 5 and 6 should be slightly lengthened so as to allow maximum intensity. At the same time the octaves in the left hand should be played *legato* and *sostenuto*, and careful pedalling should be used so as to acquire a rich, sonorous but subdued bass. It could be amusing, if it were not so pitiful, to hear the movement mutilated by pianists of European reputation, who strive to make even this idyllic music a vehicle for showmanship. The sonata has been filmed with a ponderous pianist hammering out the triplets and lifting his left arm high into the air before attacking each successive octave.

In the twelfth bar either B or C may appear as the second note of the second triplet:

---

[83] See August Göllerich, *Beethoven* (Berlin 1903), p. 12

(adagio sostenuto)

Ex. 227: Beethoven *Piano Sonata No. 14* in C sharp minor, Op. 27, No. 2, 1st movement, bar 12

Reinecke gives C, Lebert and Tovey B, while Lamond also gives B, but in a footnote says 'the editor plays C' without stating his reason. This irritating divergency might be cleared up by a simple statement, namely that the autograph gives B, but C seems more logical and consistent and is customarily adopted, since the outline of the figure then corresponds to that of the first three bars on which it is obviously based, in diminution.

It is also customary, though seldom indicated by any editor, to arpeggio the ninths quickly and almost imperceptibly in bars 16 and 18 and on their recurrence in bars 52 and 54, in order to bring out these melody-notes more clearly and with more poignant effect:

(adagio sostenuto)

Ex. 228: Beethoven *Piano Sonata No. 14* in C sharp minor, Op. 27, No. 2, 1st movement, bars 15–16

Another traditional device is to accentuate the F sharp in bar 35, and to hold the sustaining pedal until the third beat of bar 37:

(adagio sostenuto)

Ex. 229: Beethoven *Piano Sonata No. 14* in C sharp minor, Op. 27, No. 2, 1st movement, bars 35–38

If we choose to retain the imagery suggested by the popular title of the sonata, this gives the effect of the moon gradually flooding the whole landscape with light, and then darkening again for the four sombre bars which follow. In these the inner melody should be brought out so as to suggest a mood of utter forlornness, with a subtle diminution of tone and *ritardando* as the melody changes to D natural, so as to effect a still darker hue. Pianists sometimes use the soft pedal throughout the whole of the movement, but this makes for a certain monotony of colour, and lessens the contrast between the numerous *crescendos*, and in particular the effect of the gradual fading away in bars 19–23.

The second movement is generally played too quickly, due to the metronome marking ♩.= 76, which is given in most editions. The tempo should not exceed ♩. = 66, since this is no gay scherzo, but merely a lilting *allegretto*, mainly wistful in mood, which serves as a link between the two major movements of the sonata. Carl Reinecke mentions in one of his letters that after sixty years he still remembered Liszt's playing of this sonata and the way in which he used the scherzo as a bridge between the first and last movements, playing it slowly and almost like a conversation between two people. The first two four-bar phrases are each divided into a *legato* section and a *staccato* section, the one separated by a crotchet rest from the other. The phrasing is accordingly automatic, but one can underline it by a subtle use of dynamics, making a slight *crescendo* each time at the end of the *legato* section, and playing the answering *staccato* section *pianissimo*. In the next two phrases the same sub-divisions are retained in the left hand, but the melody in the right hand moves continuously above the intervening rests. It would, however, be inartistic to play this melody *legato* throughout. The top E flat in bar 10, the A flat in bar 12 and the A flat in bar 14 should be played *staccato*, so as to allow a clear if quite minute break between the two sections of each phrase, with each two-bar section answering the other, as in the first two phrases of the sentence, according to the plan *mf, p, f, dim*. After the double-bar the rests between the sub-phrases no longer occur, but it is all the more important to delineate the latter by pointing and by dynamic contrast. It is not sufficient to observe the slur in bar 2 after the double bar; the second sub-phrase, beginning with the A flat minor chord of bar 2, must be clearly detached from the first and also from the ensuing phrase by breaks between the second and third beats of bars 2 and 4. This sub-phrase (bars 3–4) should also be played more softly, and even with a suggestion of *rubato*, if the sudden change of colour which it introduces is to be given its proper value. As a rule pianists play straight through here without making any demarcation or differentiation between the sub-phrases, and the result is to divest the passage of its meaning and make it commonplace. In the next four-bar phrase the sustained chord in the left hand with held pedal bridges the slight break caused by the phrasing in the right hand. Clear breaks must again be allowed between the second and third beats of bar 8 and of bar 12 after the double bar. Towards the end of bar 17 and in bar 18 there should be an appreciable *ritenuto* to secure a climax which will crown the whole period, after which the cadence should be played in strict time. In the fourth last bar of the trio the D flat in the left hand is usually tied, as in the Reinecke and Buonamici editions, but this is ineffective in view of the *crescendo* marked and it is preferable to omit the tie, as in the Lebert edition, so as to allow the accent which seems necessary here.

The last movement, *Presto agitato*, is usually not played quickly enough, again because of the metronome marking ♩ = 84. As has already been suggested, conceptions of speed vary from one generation to another, and a speed which might have completely satisfied the musician of Beethoven's period might not be acceptable to us now. Stavenhagen used to demand a tempo of 88–92 at the least. The two-bar ascending passage with which the movement begins should be played *pianissimo* on its first two occurrences, with soft pedal and without the sustaining pedal, so as to achieve a sinister 'forked lightning' approach to the two 'thunderclaps' by which it is surmounted, and these should be played *forte* with the sustaining pedal. On its third occurrence in the fifth and sixth bars the figure should be played *piano*, while in the seventh and eighth bars a *crescendo* should be made and the pedal used to build up a climax of tone. In bar 17 after the double bar F sharp is given in the Lamond edition instead of G natural in the right hand, as first note of the last beat – obviously a misprint, yet of the type which can easily become perpetuated. But the most debatable point is the trill above the octave which occurs in the course of the second subject:

Ex. 230: Beethoven *Piano Sonata No. 14* in C sharp minor, Op. 27, No. 2, 3ʳᵈ movement, bar 30 as given in six different editions

Lebert allots eight notes to the trill beginning with the upper auxiliary note, Buonamici seven notes, beginning with the principal note. In each case if all these notes are to be clearly filled-in, either the movement must be taken at a slower tempo than it should properly be played, or the semiquaver group in the left hand must be unduly slowed up. Of other editors, Corder invents a novel and thoroughly unorthodox procedure by beginning on the lower note and then jumping the octave, and a similar procedure is recommended by Tovey for a small hand. An anonymous editor prescribes four notes beginning with the auxiliary note, while Klindworth, Reinecke, Köhler and Lamond each prescribe five notes, beginning with the principal note. The latter, according to Stavenhagen, was Liszt's method, and it seems by far the most satisfactory. Lamond, however, commences the trill on A sharp six bars later with the auxiliary note, a procedure which is inconsistent with the preceding instance, and even with the text-book rules, since the note concerned is approached and quitted by step from underneath.

An interesting point as regards accentuation occurs in the passage commencing at bar 43. Many pianists accent the first chord of each bar in this passage, despite the fact that it is as a rule inartistic to hammer out the last note of a phrase or a sub-phrase:

Ex. 231: Beethoven *Piano Sonata No. 14* in C sharp minor, Op. 27, No. 2, 3rd movement, bars 43–45

Rhythmically it would be more legitimate to accent the first chord of the second group of four chords in each bar – if any marked accent is to be employed at all – but it is perhaps preferable tomake a slight *crescendo* towards the middle of each bar, with a *diminuendo* again towards the end, whereby the problem of accentuation will be naturally solved.

The tumultuous arpeggio passages before the *Adagio* are traditionally accented as follows:

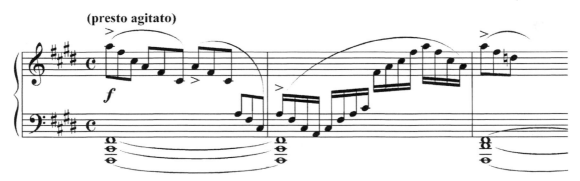

Ex. 232: Beethoven *Piano Sonata No. 14* in C sharp minor, Op. 27, No. 2, 3rd movement, bars 177–179

In the bar before the chromatic run the left hand can be used to bring out the first note of each group:

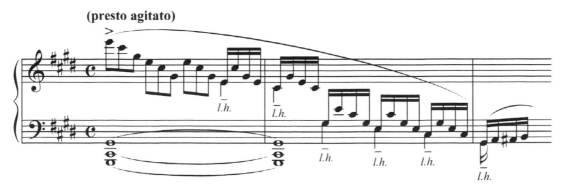

Ex. 233: Beethoven *Piano Sonata No. 14* in C sharp minor, Op. 27, No. 2, 3rd movement, bars 183–185

As regards the cadenza, pianists often play this in one downward rush, stopping abruptly when they come to the crotchets. Though this passage is always printed as a series of twenty-seven quavers followed by three crotchets, the following Stavenhagen version will be of interest, since it shows clearly the best mode of *ritardando* to follow:

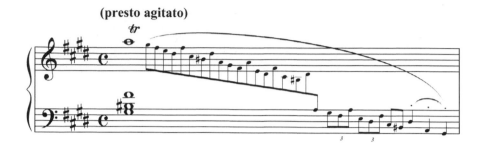

Ex. 234: Beethoven *Piano Sonata No. 14* in C sharp minor, Op. 27, No. 2, 3rd movement, bar 187

The relationship of the ensuing *Adagio* to the cadenza has already been discussed (see p. 77).

Finally, in the third and fourth last bars the first notes of each group should be accentuated, with the pedal sustained for the whole of the two bars. The last two chords may be played without pedal, so that by means of hard percussive tone the relentless *dénouement* may be more effectively realised:

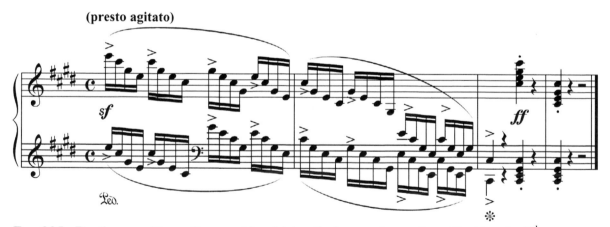

Ex. 235: Beethoven *Piano Sonata No. 14* in C sharp minor, Op. 27, No. 2, 3rd movement, bars 197–200

SONATA IN F MINOR, OP. 56 (THE 'APPASSIONATA')

The 'Moonlight' *Sonata* has been dealt with in some detail to indicate the wealth of minute points which the pianist must consider – and the points referred to constitute, of course, only a small portion of those which he will be called upon to solve. For the 'Appassionata' *Sonata* a broader basis will be adopted leaving aside technical detail and considering questions of tempo and of the interpretation as a whole.

When Schindler, Beethoven's friend, asked the composer what he had in mind when he wrote this and the D minor *Sonata*, he brusquely said: 'Read Shakespeare's *Tempest*!' On another occasion he said to some friends: 'If they knew what I am thinking about when I write, they would be terror-stricken'.[84] To play a work then such as the 'Appassionata' *Sonata* efficiently and neatly, without turbulence or passion, gainsays its very nature. Again, if we are to credit Beethoven with any acumen in commenting on the sources of his own creation, or on a literary analogy which occurred to him, it is worth while pursuing his reference to *The Tempest* to discover whether any specific points of contact may be found.

For the first movement one might consider Miranda's words (Act I, scene II):

> O I have suffered
> With those that I saw suffer! A brave vessel
> Who had no doubt some noble creature in her,
> Dash'd all to pieces. O the cry did knock
> Against my very heart. Poor souls they perish'd.
> Had I been any god of power, I would
> Have sunk the sea within the earth.

Some players alter the tempo drastically for the second subject (bar 36) of this movement – Bülow, for instance, in his edition prescribes ♩ = 112, as against a main tempo of ♩ = 126, resumed again at bar 51 for the third subject. This, however, is not to be recommended, as it impairs the unity of the movement, and for the second subject no more is necessary than a change of tone to *dolce tranquillo*. Stavenhagen used to grow indignant at the least suggestion of a *ritardando* in the final bars, on the grounds that Beethoven himself had here created the effect of a *ritardando* by proceeding from crotchets to minims in the bass, and that superimposing any further *ritardando* merely weakened the stern, relentless ending.

The *Andante con moto* should be played with the utmost restraint, and the tempo held at a solemn march-like pace, without *ritardando* at the cadences. Some pianists are inclined to overdo the *con moto*. Compare Ferdinand (Act I, scene II):

> Sitting on a bank
> Weeping again the king my father's wrack,
> This music crept by me upon the waters;
> Allaying both their fury, and my passion
> With its sweet air. ...

The first of the two *arpeggiata* chords before the finale should be played as distantly, as dreamily as possible. Then suddenly, as with a rude awakening, the second chord should be attacked, taking the top D flat with the left hand in order to secure maximum force, before plunging into the passionate and feverish finale. This movement should be rather too quick than too slow – it must suggest nature herself in her most violent mood. According to Ries, the movement was actually inspired by a storm which Beethoven experienced while on an outing near Döbling. Journeying home while the storm raged, on his arrival Beethoven dashed to the piano and for a whole hour, forgetful of Ries' presence, thundered out the themes which were subsequently incorporated into the finale of the sonata.[85] As for *The Tempest*, witness Prospero (Act V, scene I):

---

[84] Anton Schindler, *Biographie von Ludwig van Beethoven* (Münster 1840), p. 199
[85] Franz Gerhard Wegeler and Ferdinand Ries, *Notizen über Ludwig van Beethoven* (Koblenz 1838), p. 99.

> I have bedimn'd
> The noontide sun, call'd forth the mutinous winds,
> And 'twixt the green sea and the azur'd vault
> Set roaring war: to the dread rattling thunder
> Have I given fire, and rifted Jove's stout oak
> With his own bolt: the strong bas'd promontory
> Have I made shake and by the spurs pluck'd up
> The pine and cedar; graves, at my command,
> Have wak'd their sleepers, op'd, and let them forth
> By my so potent art.

A generation ago no woman could play this sonata without being exposed to adverse criticism, for it was the attitude of the critics that only a man can play Beethoven, and in particular the 'Appassionata'. The answer, of course, is that if a woman cannot play Beethoven, no man should attempt Chopin. But every great interpreter must have a dual nature, something of the male and something of the female; he must, to borrow a phrase from Schumann, combine the qualities of a Florestan and Eusebius. A man cannot interpret Chopin if he is coldly intellectual, and lacks a high degree of poetic warmth. A woman cannot interpret Beethoven unless she has exceptional physical as well as intellectual strength. Hans von Bülow used to say that no one under the age of forty should play Beethoven, and it is true that for Beethoven above all a full and varied experience of life is necessary, if justice should be done to his all-embracing style.

CHAPTER EIGHTEEN
SCHUMANN

PAPILLONS, OP. 2

To illustrate the wealth of tradition associated with Schumann's music we shall take one of his most frequently-played works, the *Papillons*, dedicated to his three sisters-in-law Therese, Rosalie and Emilie, and inspired by the second-last chapter of Jean Paul's *Flegeljahre*. As he himself says, this is an attempt to turn a masked ball into music. The title seems to be a fanciful reference to the dances themselves, which are as light and aerial as butterflies.

One rarely hears a performance of this work which shows that the pianist has an intimate knowledge of the traditional interpretation. To begin with, the work should not take longer than fifteen minutes at most to play, but one hears performances lasting twenty and even twenty-five minutes, presumably due to the observance of Schumann's own metronome markings, which are in a few cases too high, but in the majority of cases too low. Apart from the question of the main tempos, within each dance there are numerous minor variations to be made. In the notes which follow, approximate metronome markings are given to indicate the most important of these variations, but only as a rough guide, since the whole work must be played with the utmost freedom and elasticity.

Then again, the *Papillons* are seldom played with sufficient sensitiveness or imagination, such as would reveal a spontaneous personal reaction to the poetic basis of the work – for programme music of a kind it assuredly is. As a possible help in this direction a purely individual interpretation of each number will be given, not for the purpose of dogmatising as to its content (every artist will have his own picture of this, be it abstract or concrete) but to stimulate such players as seem immune, by temperament or experience, to the romantic spirit of Schumann and his circle.

<u>Introduction and No. 1</u> After a brief introduction the *Papillons* theme is stated – a captivating waltz theme which heralds the opening of the ball, and to which the dancers gaily circle. The metronome marking here should be ♩ = 184, rather than ♩ = 120 as given. In order to play the octaves lightly and accurately at this speed it is best to use the first and fifth fingers in bars 1, 5 and 7, though in all editions the fingering 4, 5, 3 is indicated. According to Stavenhagen, Liszt used to play the octaves so, and after the double bar he would hold the G sharp in the left hand in the third bar as a dotted minim, emphasising both it and the G natural in the fourth bar and holding the pedal from the latter to the seventh bar, to secure rich colour:

ROBERT SCHUMANN (1810-1856)

LITHOGRAPHY BY JOSEF KRIEHUBER (1800-1876), VIENNA 1839

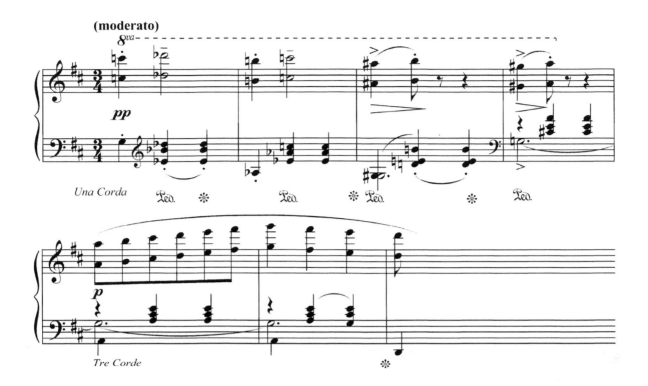

Ex. 236: Schumann *Papillons*, Op. 2, No. 1, bars 9–15

<u>No. II</u> Pierrots come whirling in. After the double bar one of them stands out alone and performs a provocative step. The metronome marking should be ♩ = 132 rather than ♩ = 116.

As given in modern editions the second half of the section after the double bar is merely a repetition of the first half. But in earlier editions an alternative version appears for the melody of the second half, which is far preferable, namely:

Ex. 237: Schumann *Papillons*, Op. 2, No. 2, bars 9–11, right hand part, alternative version

<u>No. III</u> Enter the figure of a knight in armour. This dance should not be taken too ponderously, and the tempo should be ♩. = 72 (rather than ♩ = 120).

<u>No. IV</u> A coquette trips past, with figures in pursuit darting in and out of the throng (middle section). The initial tempo is best as given at ♩. = 108. Liszt used to play the octaves in the second and tenth bars *staccato* and without pedal, thus giving the theme a delightful piquancy:

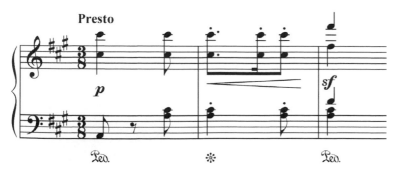

Ex. 238: Schumann *Papillons*, Op. 2, No. 4, bars 1–3

He took the middle section *pianissimo* at ♩. = 168, far faster than the opening section, using the *una corda* but without sustaining pedal. In this way the fugitive effect is intensified. Incidentally in bar 14 after the double bar the lower note in the left hand should read E sharp, not E natural.

No. V Romance – with a rude interruption (middle section) disturbing the lovers' tryst. The initial tempo should be ♩ = 66 (rather than ♩ = 80). The interruption, consisting of the four bars after the double bar, should be played loudly and at a much faster tempo, namely at ♩ = 104. From the fifth bar after the double bar, beginning *pianissimo* and, as it were, tentatively, one should lead up in a gradual *crescendo* to the opening theme, playing it now with greater animation and passion than before, but dying away again in the last four bars.

No. VI Once more the tumult of the dance, riotous fun alternating with the gently swaying rhythms of the statelier steps. The initial tempo should be ♩. = 72 (rather than ♩ = 152). The second section is taken at a slow, quiet pace (♩ = 126), with the sustaining pedal held for the first two bars, and the *una corda* pedal held throughout. In the fourth section (at ♩. = 72) no sustaining pedal should be used in the first, third, fifth and seventh bars; the right hand part should be played pertly, the *sfzorzando* suggesting the effect of an impudent swish of skirts.

No. VII A tender vision of youthful ardour and innocence – perhaps the 'angelic love' of Wina in *Die Flegeljahre* to which Schumann alludes in a letter in which he describes the *Papillons*.[86] The tempo should be ♩. = 42 (rather than ♩. = 58). According to Stavenhagen, Liszt used to repeat the A flat major section, playing it the second time *pianissimo*, with *una corda* pedal, at a somewhat slower tempo and with more *rubato*, accentuating and prolonging very slightly the second semiquaver of the middle part in each bar. This fascinating effect, he used to say, had Schumann's own approval:

---

[86] See Frederick Niecks, *Robert Schumann* (London 1925), p. 137

Ex. 239: Schumann *Papillons*, Op. 2, No. 7, bars 9–12

In bar 10 after the double bar Stavenhagen used to play B natural in the middle part, not B flat as printed:

Ex. 240: Schumann *Papillons*, Op. 2, No. 7, bar 18

<u>No. VIII</u> Boldly each cavalier steps forward, but soon he is merged in the dissolving rhythms of the waltz. Tempo ♩. = 76 (rather than ♩ = 132).

The D flat section should be light and delicate, the chords played *staccato*, with pedal used only on the first crotchet. The first chord of the last bar in this section, as in the foregoing bar, should be played *arpeggiata*. In the following section there should be a gradual broadening as the *forte* chords are approached, and the *sforzando* chord should be played *arpeggiata* and prolonged, after which the waltz theme should be played not *piano* as printed, but with full sonority and vigour, as if it were taken up by the whole orchestra.

<u>No. IX</u> Fleeting glimpses of fair forms and mischievous eyes that lurk beneath the masks. Tempo ♩. = 116.

The second section, with *una corda* and without sustaining pedal, should sound like a *pizzicato* passage played by strings. A slight hesitation before the final chord will give a roguish effect, and avoid an unduly abrupt ending.

<u>No. X</u> After an introductory measure a summons to the waltz is solemnly given out and the waltz itself follows, tenderly expressive and flowing.

The metronome markings are as follows: *Vivo* ♩. 100; *Più lento* ♩ = 120; waltz section proper ♩. = 60 (faster than the *Più lento* section). For the repeat of the first section of the waltz Stavenhagen used to obtain a charming rhythmical effect by very slightly accenting the third beat of each bar in the left hand:

Ex. 241: Schumann *Papillons*, Op. 2, No. 10, bars 25–26

Bars 25–29, marked *pianissimo*, should lead with a finely graded *ritardando* into the repeat of the waltz theme. In the concluding bar Stavenhagen used to repeat the dotted minim C in the right hand very softly, despite the fact that it is tied, finding this necessary for the completion of the melodic line.

No. XI Height of the carnival – the merry-makers frolic with abandon. Tempo ♩ = 120. The chords with *acciaccaturas* in the right hand which occur two bars before the *Più lento* section in G major should be played very lightly with no sustaining pedal and with a slight *accelerando*, perhaps so as to suggest the effect of laughter, while in the bar preceding the *Più lento* section the initial pause may be momentarily prolonged and the semiquaver B played *staccato* so as to accentuate the piquant finish. In the first four bars of the *Più lento* section itself (♪ = 120) the upper as well as the lower notes in the right hand should be equally accentuated. Then for the next four bars the accentuation should be transferred to the topmost note of the left hand. The four bars before *Tempo vivo*, with *acciaccaturas* in the right hand, should be played just twice as fast (♩ = 120) as the *Più lento*. Stavenhagen used to repeat these four bars, the second time *pianissimo* with *una corda* and without sustaining pedal.

No. XII Finale. The philistines, old and peevish members of the party, who are represented by the opening part of the 'Grossvater Tanz' [grandfather dance] (a seventeenth-century German dance which usually terminated the evening), think it high time for the ball to end, but the young bloods merely tease them, and dance some impudent steps (second and livelier section than the 'Grossvater Tanz' in 2/4 time). The dance goes on, with the philistines demurring (combination of philistine and Papillons themes), but the philistines have their way. The notes of the Papillons theme disappear one by one, while the philistine theme is doggedly retained. The town clock strikes six and all together fade into the distance. The last dancer leaves the ball-room, a rustle of silk, a retreating footstep and the carnival is over.

The main tempo of the finale should be somewhat on the heavy side (♩. = c. 76). The 2/4 section is then played quicker in a teasing, provocative fashion (♩ = c. 144). To obtain this effect

Stavenhagen used to play all the quavers in the right hand of this section *staccato*. At the *poco rit.* in bar 19 of the *Più lento* the Papillons theme is taken daintily again, but from bar 23 to 25 there is a *crescendo* and *accelerando* to *forte* and full tempo at bar 25 as if the philistines, whose theme now recurs with full vigour, had rushed in, insisting that the dance must stop.

As already mentioned in the chapter on pedalling, a problem is here presented by the tying of the low D in the left hand for 26 bars, with the pedal sustained throughout. Stavenhagen used to break the tie at the ninth D and strike the note *fortissimo*, omitting the initial upper chord of the left hand part. Just before the pause bar he silently depressed the low D and then pedalled again, allowing the note to sound alone for the larger portion of the *fermata*. This gives a curious effect and evokes a more intense sense of the lull after the confused medley of sounds has died away, leaving only this faint shimmer of tone which then merges into complete silence. On a Steinway grand the held D's could of course be retained by the *sostenuto* pedal, thus allowing pedal changes in the upper part, but the result would be much less colourful.

With regard to the performance as a whole, Schumann himself marks *fermatas* at the end of Nos. 2, 3, 6 and 7, but in view of the fact that No. 5 is relatively slow-moving and intense it would be well to precede this number also with an adequate pause. Nos. 8, 9 and 10 are grouped together almost without a break, but at the end of No. 10 a *fermata* is again prescribed owing to the dying away of the waltz theme. No. 11 is the climax of the work, with No. 12 as its aftermath. The real art lies in stringing all the pieces together, so that they will sound as one whole – a difficult task in view of the slightness of the connection between them and the short duration of each.

Stavenhagen's *Meisterklasse* always looked forward to someone playing the *Papillons*, there was so much to be said about the interpretation, so much to be read into each episode of this romantic work. The closest attention was paid to every detail. For instance Stavenhagen was very particular about the chimes of the town-clock. They had to be played in absolutely strict time, with the same metallic tone for each stroke, for the *diminuendo* refers only to the Papillons and philistine themes, which die away to a whisper while the clock chimes on with automatic clang. One pianist had conceived the *diminuendo* as applying to all the parts and had worked hard to secure the smoothest possible gradation of tone from *forte* to *pianissimo*. 'Did you ever hear a clock do that?' asked Stavenhagen sarcastically. And complete humiliation awaited the pianist whose clock only struck five![87]

[87] 'That must be a Cork clock,' was Stavenhagen's remark on the writer's first attempt to strike six. If anyone brought him a poor edition of some work or other, he would say maliciously, 'That must be a Cork edition'. His notions about Cork were formed while on a European tour shortly after Liszt's death in 1886. He played in London and Dublin. (Edward Martyn thought him the finest pianist he had ever heard, having superb technique, intense vision, in fact all the essential qualities of a great artist.) Afterwards Stavenhagen proceeded to Cork to give a recital there. To his amazement there was no grand piano to be had in the city, and he returned to London without performing. He never forgot this experience, and would still ask fifteen years later how it was possible that a city with eighty thousand inhabitants did not possess one decent instrument.

FRYDERYK CHOPIN (1810-1849)

PAINTING BY EUGENE DELACROIX (1798-1863)
MUSEE DU LOUVRE, PARIS

CHAPTER NINETEEN
CHOPIN

It is always necessary for the pianist to be in sympathy with the mood and style of the composer whose work he undertakes to interpret, but with no composer does lack of sympathy on the interpreter's part show up so clearly as in the case of Chopin. On the other hand one hears performances by players who have little inner refinement or sensitiveness, little poetic vision, and who are temperamentally alien to the romantic mode of thought, so that the impression left on the mind of the hearer is one of mere mechanical efficiency. On the other hand one may hear performances which through lack of artistic restraint reduce Chopin's music to a caricature. Quavers may then be prolonged into crotchets or capriciously shortened into semiquavers, straight-forward melodies broken up into wayward snippets, simple rhythms distorted, chords played *arpeggiata*, or again the treble limp behind the bass or vice versa – all in the name of expressive playing, but with merely maudlin results.

Of these two extremes the latter is probably the more regrettable, for Chopin's music is essentially aristocratic, and however overcome with emotion the true aristocrat may be, he still preserves that sense of restraint which precludes sentimentality. Lack of balance in the treatment of the emotional qualities of Chopin's music was largely responsible for the criticism of effeminacy which used to be levelled against it. But in a properly balanced performance the virility of the G minor *Ballade* or the F minor *Fantasia* alone should have been sufficient answer to Berlioz' sneer 'Il se mourait toute sa vie' [he spent a life-time expiring].

Nowadays, it is true, the sentimental manner of playing Chopin has largely gone out of fashion, and survives for the most part only in a kind of eccentric *rubato*, such as has already been discussed (see p. 63). The main defect in Chopin-playing today arises from a cold, dry approach to music which is warmly romantic. Pianists whose playing of this master suffers from anaemia, or who are allergic to romanticism, can only be advised to delve into the environment amidst which Chopin's music was produced – Paris of the eighteen-thirties and forties with its brilliant galaxy of musicians, poets and painters – to read Balzac, Victor Hugo, Lamartine, George Sand, to study the work of the painters Delacroix and Ingres, and above all to gain some knowledge of the poetry of Mickiewicz and the other Polish *émigré* poets such as Slowacki and Krasinski. It is unquestionable that one of the main driving-forces behind Chopin's inspiration was a passionate love of his native country and its people, and through the poetry of his fellow-exiles one may sense in a more concrete way the images and ideals which haunted Chopin's memory and are expressed so consummately in his music.

TWENTY-FOUR PRELUDES, OP. 28

In his book on Chopin, Liszt summarises his impression of the *Preludes* as follows: 'No work of the master affords better insight into the astonishing richness of his thought than the *Preludes*. Tender and often quite miniature in form, they are so intense in mood that it is scarcely possible, when hearing them, not to be aroused by the poetic ideas which begin to throng the mind. Though intended to suggest musical material rather than to develop it, they conjure up lively images, or if you will, spontaneous poems, which seek to give equivalent expression to the feelings and emotions which have been awakened.'[88] Every player or listener, if he is so disposed, will create his own poem to satisfy his particular conception of each prelude, yet a few details have been handed down relating to the interpretation of some of the preludes which may be of interest to the executant.

Prelude No. 1

It has always been a Liszt tradition to repeat the first prelude, which is otherwise so short and fleeting that it is over before the mood has had time to establish itself. Less *ritardando* and *diminuendo* should then be taken at the close for the first playing than for the repeat.

Prelude No. 3

In contrast to the gloom and morbidity of the second prelude, the third is all airiness and grace. Just one detail calls for comment – bars 9 and 10 might be taken as a *pianissimo* echo of bars 7 and 8, with *una corda* pedal and slight *ritardando*.

Prelude No. 4

The melody in the fourth prelude should be played *rubato*, so that a slight prolongation occurs on the last crotchet of each bar. Again, a *crescendo* towards the beginning of each new bar should be succeeded by a *diminuendo*, for by this rise and fall in tone the sense of weariness and sorrow which pervades the whole piece will be brought out to the full. Of the three last chords, the first two should be played *arpeggiata*, the third and last non-*arpeggiata*, *ppp* and without the sustaining pedal. This final chord should be so played as to suggest a sense of numbness, of void, as if the chasm had suddenly opened to which the prelude seems to lead. After a few seconds, however, the sustaining pedal might be depressed, so as to give the chord a slight after-glow.

Prelude No. 6

The fourth and sixth preludes were played at the funeral service for Chopin at the Madeleine Church in Paris on October 30th, 1849. Of all the preludes they are the most uniformly tragic and forlorn.

The origin of the sixth prelude has been the centre of some discussion, and even if this has little bearing on its interpretation it is well for the pianist to know the story involved. In her *Histoire de ma vie* George Sand relates how during the sojourn of Chopin, her children and herself at the deserted Carthusian Monastery of Valdemosa on the island of Majorca, from November 1838 to February 1839, she and her son journeyed one evening to Palma, but were detained by a storm, and their lives placed in considerable danger. They returned at last to Valdemosa to find the invalid Chopin in a state of 'tranquil despair' into which he had fallen after he had spent hours of anguish fearing for their safety. While in this state he had been playing his 'admirable Prelude'. At first when they appeared he would not believe they were of this world, but presently he recovered himself and confessed that in a vision he had imagined himself drowned in a lake, with ice-cold waters beating regularly on his breast. George Sand drew his

---

[88] Franz Liszt, *Friederich Chopin* (Leipzig 1896), p. 165

attention to the rain-drops which were falling monotonously on the roof, but he denied having heard them, and was vexed by her use of the term 'imitative harmony' in regard to his prelude, in fact he protested with all his might against this suggestion of a puerile imitation of external sounds. George Sand adds that his composition of that evening was full of the sound of rain-drops, but transfigured by his imagination.[89]

Now there is a controversy as to which 'admirable Prelude' is here in question. Most writers hold it be to No. 6, others again No. 15. Liszt, however, connects the incident with No. 8, in F sharp minor. He makes no reference to the suggestion of rain-drops, but tells how Chopin in his anxiety for George Sand worked himself into a terrible state of agitation. Before her return, and once the thunder-storm had passed, he recovered and seating himself at the piano improvised the F sharp minor prelude. Liszt goes on to relate how Chopin played this prelude for George Sand next day and on several occasions afterwards, but she was merely irritated by it and showed no comprehension of the anguish of mind which it revealed, fearing that Chopin's devotion and solicitude would act as a check on her adventurous excursions and on the freedom which was so essential to her nature.[90]

Though George Sand is not always a trusty narrator (the *Histoire de ma vie* was written fifteen years after the events described) her testimony in regard to the rain-drops must be given priority. Only two preludes can be associated with this idea, namely Nos. 6 and 15. Apart from the tradition that No. 15 is connected with a vision of a ghostly *cortège* of monks passing through the cloisters, No. 6 more fitly suggests that state of 'désespérance tranquille' in which George Sand found Chopin on her return from Palma, and its gloomy foreboding is more in accordance with the details she gives of Chopin's trance.

At the same time the turbulent eighth prelude could well be associated with Liszt's description of the event, which was written in 1850, a few years before George Sand's. To complicate matters still further, it is certain that the majority of the preludes had been completed or were at least substantially complete before Chopin came to Majorca, and that his work on them there was chiefly one of revision. George Sand states that the most beautiful of the preludes were composed in Majorca, but however that may be, most biographers agree that at least a few (including Nos. 2 and 4) were composed on the island. In view of the evidence quoted above, it seems possible that either No. 6 or No. 8, or even both, may have been the outcome of the storm scene so graphically described by George Sand.

Prelude No. 7

See Ex. 151 and analysis p. 111.

Prelude No. 9

It is of this prelude that Liszt must have been thinking when he said, in reference to the preludes as a whole, that at times the tones of the organ seem to roll through the spaces of some vast cathedral.[91]

[89] George Sand, *Histoire de ma vie*, Vol. IV (Paris 1855), p. 438.
[90] Franz Liszt, *Friedrich Chopin*, p. 189.
[91] Liszt, *Friedrich Chopin*, p. 166

Prelude No. 15

In the passage from her *Histoire de ma vie* already referred to, George Sand relates that at Valdemosa Chopin was unable to overcome his restless imagination. The cloisters were for him full of terrors and phantoms. Returning from her nocturnal explorations among the ruins one evening she found him at his piano, pale, his eyes wild, his hair almost standing on end – for some moments he failed to recognise her. It was inevitable that the gloomy atmosphere of the deserted monastery should have played on his mind, for his health was already in decline and his condition only aggravated by the winter on Majorca. In many of the preludes one may picture the effect of these sinister visitations at Valdemosa, but in none is the impression so clear as in the middle section of this prelude. It seems to suggest a ghostly procession of monks moving through the cloisters chanting a solemn dirge – which the delicate and graceful opening and close serve only to throw into still darker relief.

Prelude No. 17

George Sand remarks of some of the preludes that they occurred to Chopin 'in the hours of sunshine and health, amidst the noise of children's laughter under the window, the distant sound of guitars, the singing of birds amidst the moist foliage and the sight of pale little roses full-blown on the snow.' Of all the preludes, No. 17 seems to tally best with this description, though it does not follow that the prelude was one of those actually composed in Majorca.

The last appearance of the main theme is accompanied by a deep bell-like effect – eleven repetitions of low A flat in the left hand. Each A flat should be played with equally rich and sonorous tone while the other parts sound *sotto voce* and *pianissimo* above. Paderewski relates that Madame Dubois (*née* O'Meara of Limerick), Chopin's last pupil, told him that Chopin used to play these bass notes with great strength, and always with the same strength, since they represented the sound of an old clock in the castle striking the eleventh hour – and a clock knows no *diminuendo*.[92] An analogy immediately suggests itself with the six strokes of the town-clock at the end of Schumann's *Papillons*, with the difference, however, that in the *Papillons* the clock-chimes are an explicit and dramatic detail of the programme underlying the music, and have little meaning unless heard as such, whereas in the Chopin prelude the repeated A flats do not necessarily convey any meaning outside the music, and, if never associated with clock or bell effect fit unobtrusively into the design as a rich tonic pedal. Hence it seems necessary to allow for a *diminuendo* in the case of the last two A flats. With the upper parts dying away to *ppp* it is inartistic to keep the A flat reiterations booming at a tone-level at which they make no sense unless the programme detail is understood or explained. Actually the effect more aptly suggests the pealing of a bell than the chiming of a clock, and the final peals might then with still greater justification fade into the distance. In any event Chopin, unlike Schumann, was entirely averse to the imitation of external sounds in his music, and Madame Dubois' story, which one would be disposed to accept, is curiously at variance with his known attitude in such matters.

This divergence can serve to illustrate the point that guidance derived even from a reliable source should not be followed if it seems to contravene artistic principles. In other words tradition is not a code of procedures handed down impersonally, and blindly adopted but, as was pointed

---

[92] Ignace Jan Paderewski, Mary Lawton, Eds., *The Paderewski Memoirs* (London 1938), p. 154

out before, it is a living code which continues to be modified and improved upon from one generation to another.

Prelude No. 19

In his book on Chopin, Liszt mentions, whether as a surmise or as a fact, that the E flat prelude was written in Majorca on a stormy day. He compares the even flowing movement to the ceaseless patter of rain-drops from the eaves, which continues in stormy weather, even amidst the sunny intervals.[93]

Prelude No. 20

See pp. 107-8.

The twenty-four preludes are often played as one work. Though it seems hazardous for concert purposes to group together so great a number of short and unrelated pieces, most of them apparently drawn by Chopin from old notes and sketches made at various times, the effect as a whole can be surprisingly successful, and each individual prelude seems to gain by being associated with its fellows. But it is essential to time the transition from one prelude to another so that the continuity of effect is not broken. In accordance with the general principle already stated, a longer pause should be made after the slower preludes than after those that are either quick-moving or gay.

STUDY IN E MAJOR, OP. 10, NO. 3

The *Study* in E major contains one of the loveliest melodies Chopin ever wrote. He himself thought it finer than any other, and his pupil Gutmann relates that when he (Gutmann) played it once at a lesson, Chopin lifted up his arms with hands clasped, and exclaimed: 'Oh, my fatherland!' The deep expressiveness and nostalgia of the first section gradually seems to give way to foreboding and fear, after which the middle section with its fierce sequences of diminished sevenths gives the sense of conflict and turmoil unresolved, to be followed by the first section again, now seeming to suggest a mood of sorrow and resignation. If ever Chopin epitomised in music an exile's dream of his native country it is here. The study will repay a detailed discussion, because of the many fine points of interpretation for which it calls, especially with regard to *rubato*-playing.

The apparently straightforward character of the opening is full of pitfalls for the insensitive pianist, and needs the most careful planning. First of all the tempo is far slower than the original metronome mark would suggest (see pp. 129-130). Secondly the melody must sing with vibrant intensity throughout the first section, each note being given a carefully-graded value – for instance the F sharp in the first bar should get slightly more weight than the other notes. Thirdly the phrasing must be clear-cut and pliant. As has already been remarked (see pp. 66-7 above) a rather pronounced *ritardando* should be made on the first four semiquavers of the second bar, after which the semiquaver accompaniment must be resumed immediately in strict time and the following two bars played in free *cantabile* style, basically, however, in strict time also, until the *ritardando* is made even more markedly than before in the first half of the fifth bar. From the

[93] Franz Liszt, *Friedrich Chopin*, p. 166.

beginning of the sixth bar there is a *stretto*, i.e. the first two semiquavers are played in the basic time, but immediately the tempo begins to increase. It seems regrettable that Chopin should have inserted the *stretto* marking above the second half of the seventh bar, where actually the flow of the *stretto* should begin to abate, to prepare for the pronounced *ritardando* at the end of the eighth bar. In making this cadence one should emphasise slightly the descending line B–A sharp–A natural–G sharp. The opening phrases, now repeated, must be played even more expressively and softer than the first time. At bar 15 a further *stretto* begins, which resolves at bar 16 into a *ritenuto* whereby the movement broadens as the chords grow louder, until after the first chord of bar 17 the semiquaver figure is resumed in strict time. From bars 17–21 there is a gradual *ritardando*, so that the groups of four semiquavers in the second half of the bar are played on each appearance more softly and lingeringly. Of the two grace notes at the beginning of bar 21 the G sharp (notwithstanding the omission of the tie in the Ganche and Chopin Institute's edition) should be tied to the preceding minim, if an effect of utter bathos is not to result, while the F sharp has practically the value of a semiquaver, though a very slow one, owing to the *ritardando*, coming, out of time as it were, after the last semiquaver of the preceding bar and before the sounding of the E major chord.

For the middle section, from the second half of bar 21, one should begin *pp*, with an appreciably quicker tempo (the indication *poco più animato* as found in the Klindworth and Ganche editions is usually lacking in present-day editions). At the first half of bar 23 the player should hold back somewhat and make a slight break before the beginning of the next phrase. This procedure is repeated at bars 25 and 27, but not in bar 29, because of the necessity for unimpeded forward movement at this point. Bars 31 and 35, being repetitions in the minor of the bars preceding them, should be placed with *una corda* pedal and with a slight *ritenuto* which is then compensated for by the sweep of the succeeding passage in each case. In the *fp* of bars 32 and 36 if the octave in the left hand be brought to the fore, while the *una corda* pedal is still retained, a curiously ominous effect can be produced, which helps to prepare the way for the strife and tumult which is shortly to come. Throughout the passage-work which follows here Chopin phrases against the metrical stress, and unless certain of the phrases are clearly demarcated by making slight breaks between them, the pattern will remain unclear. Thus, breaks equivalent to the insertion of a semiquaver rest should occur after the first semiquaver of bar 32, after the fifth semiquaver of bar 33, and the corresponding places in bars 36 and 37, and again after the first semiquavers of bars 42 and 44, with slightly lesser breaks after those of bars 43 and 45. The tempo will have increased somewhat from bar 38 on, but at bar 45 it is essential to make a *ritenuto*, despite the *con fuoco* marked here, in order to give proper weight to this full and trenchant cadence. It seems clear that *con fuoco* should only apply from the following bar (bar 46), lasting until bar 53, where a very slight *ritardando* and *diminuendo* may be made. The stretch from this bar until the repeat of the first section should resemble a falling curve as regards speed and dynamics. It is fatal, however, to over-emphasise the cadence at bars 53 and 54, or at the latter bar to change to a sudden *piano* as indicated, and to a slower tempo, for the whole effect of the middle section depends on achieving a great climax, with a very gradual release extending from bars 53 to 61 in one unbroken line.

From bar 62 on the playing will be identical with that of bars 9–20, except that in the few bars which Chopin adds to make a close the first A (in the middle part of each of bars 73 and 74) and the first G sharp (bars 74 and 75) might be slightly emphasised so as to give a darker colour.

The above may be taken as a general plan for the *rubato*-playing in this study, but it must be carried out with subtlety, so that the variations in speed will appear natural and inevitable, not forced or arbitrary.

———————

Descriptive titles for some of Chopin's studies and also of his polonaises have been handed down by successive generations of players, as distinct from sentimental absurdities such as 'Souvenir de la Pologne' or 'Murmurs de la Seine' which Chopin's English publisher, to the composer's great annoyance, affixed to some of his works for the purpose of helping their sales. The traditional titles are not of intrinsic importance – Chopin himself disapproved of any descriptive matter which would lay down a definite programme for his music (see pp. 159-160 above), but all such matter is of interest to the student, and it is culpable ignorance on the pianist's part not to know the lore which may be associated with the work he is playing.

The *Study* in G flat, Op. 10, No. 5, is known as the 'Study in the black keys', since the right-hand part is exclusively pentatonic, i.e. from the notes G flat, A flat, B flat, D flat and E flat.

The *Study* in C minor, Op. 10, No. 12, perhaps the most frequently played of all the studies, is known as the 'Revolutionary' Study, since it was composed after Chopin heard of the taking of Warsaw by the Russians on September 8th 1831. Its sustained and noble vehemence suggests the *saeva indignatio* of a patriot who despairs at his country's downfall, but whose defiant spirit still remains uncrushed.

The *Study* in A flat, Op. 25, No. 1, is sometimes called 'The Shepherd Boy' because of the following programme which Chopin himself is supposed to have suggested for it: 'I imagine a little shepherd who takes refuge in a peaceful grotto from an approaching storm. In the distance rushes the wind and the rain, while the shepherd gently plays a melody on his flute.'

The *Study* in G flat, Op. 25, No. 9, has been called 'Butterfly Wings', because of its delicate, fugitive movement.

The *Study* in A minor, Op. 25, No. 11, is known as the 'Winter Wind'. Around a rigid, march-like motif, swirling figures play with the chill, devastating breath of winter, now howling, now whispering, seldom relaxing their vehemence. It is a study in *crescendo* and *diminuendo*, but is too often turned into a mechanical show piece by distinguished virtuosi, so that the wind begins to whistle with the effrontery of a steam engine. There is a limit to the speed at which the purely musical context of this study will survive.

(Reference to some of the above studies will be found on p. 108, pp. 133–4, pp. 151-3.)

The *Polonaise* in E flat minor, Op. 26, No. 2, has been called the 'Siberian' or 'Revolt' *Polonaise* because of its sinister, turbulent mood. Associating this music with its Polish background one cannot but hear the uncanny sound of muffled drums, the murmurings of revolt, the groans of prisoners, but all this amid the invincible will to liberty of an oppressed people.

The *Polonaise* in A, Op. 40, No. 1, with its martial rhythms and drum effects, is popularly know as the 'Military' *Polonaise*. Rubenstein saw in this polonaise a picture of Poland's greatness, just as he saw in the C minor *Polonaise*, Op. 40, No. 2, a picture of Poland's downfall.

The *Polonaise* in F sharp minor, Op. 44, is sometimes called the 'Dream' *Polonaise* as the result of a description of it by Liszt, who speaks of it as one of Chopin's most forceful compositions. He goes on to say that 'it excites us like the story of some broken dream ... a dream-poem in which impressions and objects follow each other with startling incoherence and with the strangest transitions.'[94] In the middle of the polonaise proper, with its booming of canon and thunder of horses' hooves, there comes as middle section a tender and graceful mazurka. Chopin himself said that this was a fantasia rather than a polonaise.

The *Polonaise* in A flat, Op. 53, has been named the 'Heroic' *Polonaise*, and is usually regarded as the finest of all Chopin's polonaises in the richness and splendour of its texture. It may here be mentioned that the *staccato* octaves of the trio of this polonaise are often begun too loudly and played too quickly. Chopin himself protested against the exploitation of the octave accompaniment, for the purpose of making a tour de force of the polonaise. Obviously one must begin with a *pianissimo* such as might suggest the sound of galloping cavalry barely discernible in the distance, using *una corda*, but at first no sustaining pedal, and then working up gradually to a great climax.

Stavenhagen once showed us an effect obtainable in this polonaise by slipping one's foot off the sustaining pedal and making it clang for the opening *sforzando* and for the release after the trill in bars 33 and 34. I cannot now remember whether the effect was intended to be taken seriously or not, but even if it should help to emphasise the military character of the polonaise – and the effect was frequently used for this purpose by some of the virtuosi of the last generation – it must be admitted that such tricks are in dubious taste. (For reference to the *Polonaise* Op. 26, No. 1, see p. 110 above.)

NOCTURNE IN B, OP. 32, NO.1

Poetry frequently inspires music, but it is rare enough to find an instance of music directly inspiring poetry. Paul Verlaine's poem 'Colloque Sentimental' was written as a literary counterpart to Chopin's B minor *Nocturne*, and though the interpretation is, of course, entirely subjective, the poem achieves a close parallel to the mood of the music. The nocturne readily suggests a dialogue, with its frequent outbursts as if one of the speakers were to become irritated and to cry out angrily, while some of the phrases seem to be related as if question were followed by answer. Just as the form of the nocturne is novel, so too is that of Verlaine's poem, in which the ghosts of two lovers discuss their past, he with fervent appeal, she unresponding and cold. Like the music, with its sinister coda, the poem ends in unrelieved gloom.

Colloque sentimental[95]
Dans le vieux parc solitaire et glacé
Deux formes ont tout à l'heure passé.

Leurs yeux sont morts et leurs lèvres sont molles,
Et l'on entend à peine leurs paroles.

---

[94] See George Charles Ashton Jonson, *A Handbook to Chopin's Works* (London 1905; 2nd revised edition 1908), p. 145

[95] *A Mirror for French Poetry 1840-1940: French poems with translations by English poets*, Selected and edited by Cecily Mackworth (London 1947)

Dans le vieux parc solitaire et glacé
Deux spectres ont évoqué le passé.

--Te souvient-il de notre extase ancienne?
--Pourquoi voulez-vous donc qu'il m'en souvienne?

--Ton coeur bat-il toujours à mon seul nom?
Toujours vois tu mon âme en rêve? --Non.

--Ah! les beaux jours de bonheur indicible
Où nous joignions nos bouches! --C'est possible.

Qu'il était bleu, le ciel, et grand l'espoir!
--L'espoir a fui, vaincu, vers le ciel noir.

Tels ils marchaient dans les avoines folles,
Et la nuit seule entendit leurs paroles.

Paul Verlaine, *Fêtes galantes* (1869)[96]

The opening of the nocturne should be played simply, with a slight *rubato* for the semiquavers of the second beat of bars 2 and 4 (see p. 67). In the sixth (*stretto*) bar there occurs the sudden impetuous question and in the seventh (*poco rit.*) bar the quiet restraining answer which are mirrored in the Verlaine poem. After the tune has been heard in the next two bars singing out softly in the right hand it is an effective contrast for its repetition in the following two bars (bars 10 and 11) to reduce the general level to *pp*, and bring out the left-hand melody with rich though subdued tone – a beautiful effect usually overlooked:

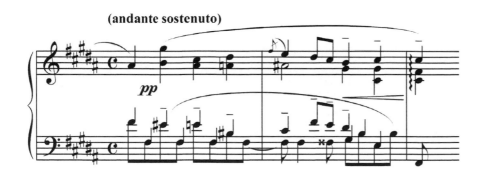

Ex. 242: Chopin *Nocturne No. 9* in B, Op. 32, No. 1, bars 10–12

Much the same procedure applies to bars 33 and 34, and again to bars 54 and 55.

[96] A translation of 'Colloque sentimental' by Arthur Symons published in *The Savoy* of 1896: 'Sentimental Conversation': In the old park, solitary and frozen, /Two figures have just passed by. /Their eyes are dead, their lips are flaccid, /And their words are hardly heard. /In the old park, solitary and frozen, /Two spectres called up the past. / – Do you remember our one-time ecstasy? /– Why do you want me to remember? / – Does your heart still beat at my mere name? /Do you still see my soul in your dreams? – No./ – Ah! the glad days of unspeakable happiness /When our lips were joined! – Perhaps./ – How blue was the sky, how high our hopes! / – Hope has fled, vanquished, towards the black sky. /Thus they walked again through the wild oats. /And only the night overheard their words.

Bars 23–26 are almost Brahms-like in their sonority, and are followed by the upsurging question of bar 27 (*mf*) and the sad, poignant answer of bar 28 (*p*, with *una corda* pedal and a slight *ritenuto*, and with the notes F sharp–E sharp–D sharp in the left hand brought slightly to the fore).

In bar 61 the first two notes prior to the trill should be played slowly, as quavers, and the trill itself should contain a *crescendo* and *diminuendo*, fading away into a triple *pianissimo* on the hushed chord which follows. This is the commencement of the coda, a tragic recitative. The repeated E sharps in the left hand should be played slowly and eerily like a death-knell, with a slight *ritardando* on the last triplet. The demisemiquavers in the next bar should be played quickly and impetuously, with the minims G and B held in each case after the chords are struck, and the pedal taken again on each note alone, so as to heighten the effect of the note and give it intensity. If we accept Verlaine's imagery, these phrases seem to express an outburst of anger on the part of the two ghostly disputants – their parting, as the chill light of dawn breaks, brings no reconciliation, but merely bitterness and reproach.

In most editions the notes of bar 63 (recitative) are reproduced as an unbroken succession of quavers, but the passage undoubtedly needs the grouping given in the Klindworth edition:

Ex. 243: Chopin *Nocturne No. 9* in B, Op. 32, No. 1, bar 63–64

The last two bars, marked *Adagio*, should be played relentlessly (as already pointed out on p. 110 above, the final chord should be minor, not major). Then, as already mentioned in the case of the minims of bar 63, the pedal might be taken on the ultimately sustained B's after the minor tonic chord has been released.

Here we have an example of Chopin's dramatic power and his ability to evoke the most sombre moods. The nocturne may well be studied by students as a preparation for greater works such as the ballades or the B flat minor *Sonata*.

NOCTURNE IN C SHARP MINOR, OP. 27, NO. 1

This nocturne is another sombre work, but broader in its outlines and more impassioned in its climaxes.

The cadence in bars 6–7 and its recurrences should be taken *ritenuto*, with the upper notes C sharp–D sharp–E as a clear melodic progression in the left hand. Bars 15–18, being closely modelled on bars 11–14, are best taken at a softer tone-level, or even as an echo of the latter. The two bars before the *Più mosso* tend to sound somewhat thin unless the pedal is retained throughout, and the upper notes D in the first bar and F sharp in the second bar should be slightly accented and held. Incidentally, the approach to the double-*forte appassionato* passage in the *Più mosso* section is made difficult by an exceedingly wide leap in the left hand, but this difficulty is obviated by taking the penultimate C sharp with the thumb of the right hand:

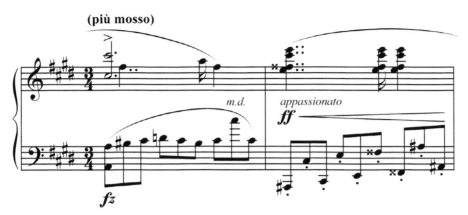

Ex. 244: Chopin *Nocturne No. 7* in C sharp minor, Op. 27, No. 1, bars 44–45

Stavenhagen used to make a point of beginning bar 67 *pianissimo*, and taking the quaver chords *leggiero* and *staccato* for the start of the *crescendo* which leads to bar 69. The *accelerando* which begins at bar 78 must at the *fortissimo* chords, three bars before the cadenza, give way to a most pronounced *allargando*, with a pause on each beat of the bar before the cadenza, the last being appreciably sustained. The octaves of the cadenza itself should not be begun at full strength, which would sound abrupt and inartistic, but at a lower tone-level with a *crescendo* to *fortissimo* between the first and fourth octave.

Stavenhagen used to tell us of a special effect which Liszt obtained towards the end of the nocturne. Bars 94–95 and 96–97 are in apposition, but to make the contrast more effective Liszt used to play the latter bars *pianissimo* and with more *rubato* than in the previous two bars, slightly accentuating the top note of the accompaniment in the left hand, and at the same time playing the chords in the right hand *arpeggiata*, upwards for the second and fourth chords, downwards for the third chord in bar 96 and the first and third chords in bar 97. The result is delicately expressive and adds a richness to the intense tranquillity which pervades the end of this nocturne.

Ex. 245a: Chopin *Nocturne No. 7* in C sharp minor, Op. 27, No. 1, bars 96–98

Liszt's version

(tempo primo - larghetto)
rall. -

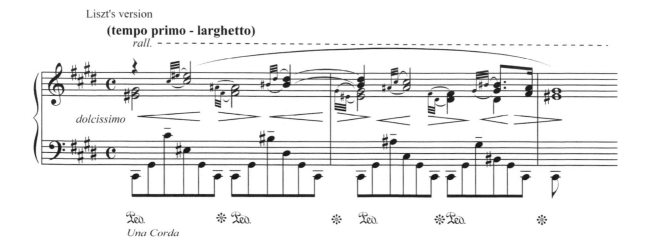

dolcissimo

Una Corda

Ex. 245b: Chopin *Nocturne No. 7* in C sharp minor, Op. 27, Liszt's version of bars 96–98

Stavenhagen used to add that Chopin himself approved of Liszt's rendering of this passage, and that though Liszt was sometimes accused of tampering with Chopin's music, it was only an occasional effect such as this which he had known him to introduce, and in each case one which greatly enhanced the context.

(For references to other nocturnes see p. 56: *Nocturne* in F sharp, Op. 15, No. 2; p. 64: *Nocturne* in G, Op. 37, No. 2; p. 65: *Nocturne* in D flat, Op. 27, No. 2.)

WALTZ IN A FLAT MAJOR, OP. 42

Chopin's waltzes should be played with simplicity and delicacy and with ample variety of tone colour. They are salon music par excellence, and the majority are French rather than Polish in their spirit.

The trill with which the A flat major waltz begins often proves a stumbling-block, for it is not so simple to interpret as it looks. The traditional way of playing the trill is to begin *pianissimo* with *una corda* pedal, to release the latter after the second bar and make a *crescendo* which reaches its climax with the chord C–A flat in bar 7, and then a *diminuendo* together with a slight *ritardando* up to the commencement of the main theme (the practice of making a slight *ritardando* towards the end of a trill was customary with Chopin). The main theme with its delightful combination of duple and triple rhythm can well be studied *legato* at first, with the top notes held. Then when played up to time it must be taken *portamento*, for since the theme is mostly played by the fifth finger, each note must be released before the next is sounded, but the *legato* practice will ensure a rich and clear singing-tone. The theme itself should be played *pianissimo* and *leggiero* with *una corda* pedal, and when it reappears an octave higher it should be played *piano* without the *una corda* pedal for the first eight bars, but reverting to *pianissimo* again with *una corda* pedal for the ensuing eight bars.

The section in D flat major from bar 89 should be slightly slower. Stavenhagen took no pedal in bars 91 and 92 of this section, thereby getting a brighter and gayer effect for the descending passage in the right hand, as it if were a brief peal of silvery laughter. In bar 104, the second of the *fortissimo* bars, and again in bar 164, he sustained the last chord momentarily before rippling into the *leggiero* section. In bar 160 the *arpeggiata* chord preceded by an *acciaccatura*, reproduced in most editions as:

Ex. 246a: Chopin *Waltz No. 5* in A flat, Op. 42, bar 160

should be played as follows:

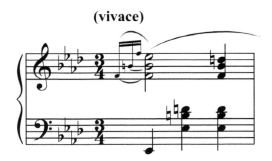

Ex. 246b: Chopin *Waltz No. 5* in A flat, Op. 42, bar 160 as it should be played

A rich effect can be obtained by playing the ascending scale passage, which commences in bar 239, *pianissimo* with *una corda* pedal and with sustaining pedal sustained throughout and released only on the top *staccato* note. The octave on the third beat of this bar (bar 244) should be prolonged very slightly before resuming the waltz movement in the next bar, for to play this bar in strict time sounds commonplace.

In the bars which follow, the octaves in the left hand forming a descending scale should be well brought out and accented, to ensure a full resonant bass for the rich superstructure. On its last appearance the *leggiero* section (from bar 261) should be played with more excitement and *élan* than on its previous appearances, and the repeated pedal note E flat should be well accentuated. For the precipitous descent towards the end the following fingering might be taken:

(vivace)

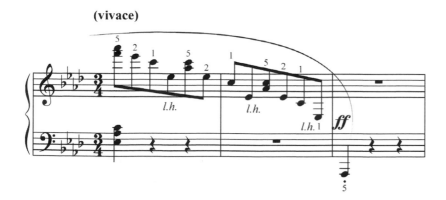

Ex. 247: Chopin *Waltz No. 5* in A flat, Op. 42, bars 283–285

No vestige of a *ritardando* should be contemplated for the final bars (despite the habits of some pianists to the contrary) and the waltz ends on a note of unrestrained gaiety and abandon.

(For further reference to the waltz see p. 69 above.)

WALTZ IN C SHARP MINOR, OP. 64, NO. 2

Of Chopin's waltzes, two, namely the *Waltz* in C sharp minor and that in A minor, Op. 34, No.2, are markedly Polish in character.

The first two bars of the *Waltz* in C sharp minor are in waltz rhythm, the third and fourth in mazurka rhythm, and the interplay between these two rhythms gives the waltz its peculiar and essentially Polish charm. Stavenhagen used to say that to bring out the contrast more clearly, and to emphasise the mazurka rhythm, Liszt used to make a slight *tenuto* on the second beat and to a lesser extent on the third beat of bars 3 and 4, and to accentuate the third beat of each bar:[97]

(tempo giusto)

Ex. 248: Chopin *Waltz No. 7* in C sharp minor, Op. 64, No. 2, bars 3–4

In the *Più mosso* section commencing at bar 33 he used to hold over the last notes of bars 33–36 and the second last notes of bars 37 and 38 into the following bars, thus securing a delightful rhythmic effect. The held notes should sing out softly as they descend, though any exaggeration should of course be guarded against:

---

[97] That Chopin himself adopted such rhythms is shown by Hallé's assertion that he proved Chopin to be playing 4/4 instead of 3/4 time in a mazurka (see James Huneker, *Chopin* (London 1903), p. 345) and by the story of the altercation with Meyerbeer on the same point (op. cit., p. 362).

Ex. 249: Chopin *Waltz No. 7* in C sharp minor, Op. 64, No. 2, bars 33-40

The suspension effect might be used again in this section from bars 41–45, but should then be discontinued. Bars 49–56 should be taken *leggiero* with *una corda* pedal and without the sustaining pedal, which for the *crescendo* in bar 57 the *una corda* pedal should be released and the sustaining pedal used from this bar to the *staccato* note at the end of this section.

In bars 82–89 (*Più lento* section), which are a modified restatement of bars 65–73, the rising chromatic progressions in the left hand should be brought out more clearly and expressively than in the first statement (see pp. 60-1 above). In fact it may be stated again as a general principle that when a passage is repeated, variety of colour may best be obtained in the repetition by slightly underlining any inner melodies which may be present, such as will enrich the texture.

In Ganches's edition and in many others the F's in bars 70–71 and 81–82 and the D flats in bars 75–76, 76–77, 91–92 and 92–93 are repeated, not tied. The repetition of these notes sounds crude, whereas when they are tied, as in the Klindworth and Debussy editions, the syncopated effect lends a subtle rhythmic distinction. The Klindworth and Debussy editions are here corroborated by the Chopin Institute's edition, which as in the case of the Debussy edition goes still further by tying the E flats of bars 66–67. In regard to this one point, however, one cannot but prefer the repeated E flats of the Klindworth edition which seem necessary to balance the repeated F's of bars 74–75.

Ganche prints an autograph version of the waltz which in bars 93–96 reads as follows:

Ex. 250: Chopin *Waltz No. 7* in C sharp minor, Op. 64, No. 2, right hand part, bars 93–97, Ganche edition

The accepted version seems far preferable (the penultimate note, G natural, is often wrongly printed as G flat):

Ex. 251: Chopin *Waltz No. 7* in C sharp minor, Op. 64, No. 2, usual rendering, right hand part, bars 93–97

(For references to other waltzes see p. 140: *Waltz* in A minor, Op. 34, No. 2; pp. 69 and 108: *Waltz* in F minor, Op. 69, No. 1; pp. 69 and 154: *Waltz* in A flat, Op. 42; p. 140: *Waltz* in G flat major, Op. 70. No. 1)

IMPROMPTU IN F SHARP, OP. 36

To interpret this impromptu adequately the pianist must work in terms of the finest gradation of tone. The opening has already been dealt with (see pp. 67-8 above). It is a Liszt tradition, in the *coloratura* passage of bar 17, to make a slight *crescendo* to the upper A sharp on the second beat and to hold this note slightly before cascading down in *pianissimo* to the low A sharp at the start of the next bar. The *una corda* pedal should be depressed throughout the bar (Liszt nearly always used the *una corda* pedal for *coloratura* passages of this kind). The same procedure applies to bar 29. From the end of bar 33 to the middle of bar 36 it is important to bring out the middle voice of the left hand, which moves mostly in thirds with the theme on top.

The martial section in D major is far more effective if begun *pianissimo*, as if from the distance, with a gradual *crescendo* to the double-*forte* of bar 51. Klindworth marks the opening of this section *mf*, Ganche inserts no marking and the Chopin Institute's edition is the first to adopt the *pp* marking, on the authority of a pencilled insertion in the copy of Madame Dubois, Chopin's pupil. In bar 46 the rising bass in the left hand should be well brought out, and towards the end of the bar there should be an almost imperceptible *ritardando*, though the semiquaver upbeat should, of course, be taken in strict time. From bar 47 on it is advisable to emphasise the octaves in the left hand on the first and third beats to secure a fully vigorous and martial effect. Students often have difficulty in dealing with the rhythm of the second half of bar 57, but, as explained on p. 15

above, the solution is to practise the right and left hand parts separately and then combine them in strict time.

The celebrated transition to the next section:

Ex. 252: Chopin *Impromptu No. 2* in F sharp, Op. 36, bars 58–61

has been variously held to be a dire miscalculation – Professor Gerard Abraham considers it to be the clumsiest transition in the whole of Chopin[98] – or a flash of genius. The latter view will seem the more justified to listeners who hear the passage properly shaped from the dynamic point of view. The first of the two bars should not be commenced *piano*, as indicated, but *mezzo-forte*, which should be the stage reached at this point in the course of the *diminuendo* from the previous double-*forte*, and the *rallentando* and *diminuendo* should then be continued and the *una corda* pedal used in the second bar, so that the subtle harmonic change will be matched by an equally subtle change of colour. If Chopin's *piano* marking is adopted, the sudden drop in the dynamic level after an unbroken stretch of *fortissimo* playing, coming together with the unexpected harmonic shift, must inevitably prove too violent for the listener. But by keeping an even grade of *diminuendo* from the previous double-*forte*, the abrupt harmonic turn is less liable to sound strained, and can be felt as a highly-charged, original continuation rather than an eccentric veering off the course. The insertion of an *a tempo* marking at the commencement of bar 59 in the Chopin Institute's edition (apparently without autograph authority, as it occurs within brackets) seems both inartistic and entirely wide of the mark.

In the F major section, where the melody is quiescent in the right hand from bars 65–66, it is necessary to bring out the left hand part by slightly underlining the note E on the third beat of bar 65 and the notes D and E on the first and third beats of bar 66. In the *coloratura* passage of bar 71 (see pp. 69-70 above) the procedure already adopted for bars 17 and 29 is no longer applicable, but the tenor progression in the left hand, E–D sharp–D natural–C, should be allowed to make itself felt.

The shading and balance necessary for the opening bars of the next section in F sharp major has already been discussed (see pp. 59–60 above). At the end of bar 74 a *diminuendo* and slight *ritardando* should be made, and from bars 76–78 a *crescendo*, with a *subito pianissimo* and slight *tenuto* on the fourth beat of bar 78. A *crescendo* from here to the fourth beat of bar 81, and a

---

[98] Gerard Abraham, *Chopin's Musical Style* (London 1939), p. 53.

diminuendo and *ritardando* at the end of this bar will give the section its proper dynamic and agogic shape.

The section which follows is marked both *forte* and *leggiero*, a contradiction in terms. In any case it is more in keeping with the context (and a tradition with Chopin players) to begin softly, using the *una corda* pedal, and to make the various *crescendo*s and *diminuendo*s from a basic level of *piano*, rather than of *forte* tone. The bass should sing out clearly underneath and the two-part chords should be kept appropriately subordinate – it is a common fault to accentuate these unduly. A proportionate balance must then be preserved between the rippling scale-passages in the right hand and the singing bass, through the varying gradations of tone. Moreover, the scale passages should not be played too quickly or *con bravura*, as they usually are played, but delicately and limpidly. In bar 90 the melody in the left hand involves a slight change from that of the corresponding bar 84, and should sing out more broadly, for it involves an intensification such as Chopin is always able to achieve with such telling effect and with a minimum of means. In bar 94 the notes A sharp–F sharp–E sharp–B–A sharp etc in the right hand should stand out (in the Klindworth edition these notes are printed as quavers, with separate down-stems). A *ritardando* should be made on the last two beats of bar 97 to round off this section, since the ensuing three bars are merely cadential extension. The concluding section (from bar 101) must then sound quieter and dreamier than on its earlier appearance, a reverie rudely cut short by the loud assertion of the tonic chord.

FANTASIE-IMPROMPTU IN C SHARP MINOR, OP. 66

This impromptu is usually played too quickly, as an exercise in velocity rather than as the poetic expression of two contrasted moods – that of an *Allegro agitato* and a broadly lyrical middle section. When played too fast, the finely-etched contours of the swirling passage-work become blurred and ineffective other than as a technical display. For the return of the opening section after the *Moderato cantabile* Chopin actually adopts the marking *Presto*, which is not possible if the maximum speed be employed at the outset.

After the introductory *sforzando* octave the accompanying figure in the left hand begins *forte*, but a *diminuendo* should be made to the beginning of bar 5. This *diminuendo*, though given by Klindworth, is not to be found in Ganche's and other editions, and is seldom observed in performance. It is so vital, however, that one would be justified in retaining it even if it is not to be found in the autograph – to thunder an arpeggio for two bars and then begin the main theme *subito piano* just sounds crude and inartistic. This main theme should actually be started *pianissimo* with *una corda* pedal and with the most delicate tone, so that when it returns in bar 9, where the *una corda* pedal should be released, the *piano* marking will then mean a slight increase in volume. As in nearly all Chopin's passage-work of this kind, dynamic shading is essential; for instance in the first two bars of the theme there should be an increase of tone for the first half of each bar, and a decrease in the second half, while one rise and fall in tone should cover the whole of the next two bars.

At bar 13 the melody should be brought out richly in the alto with the thumb of the right hand, while from bars 17 to 23 – a delightful change – the melody appears on top as the second semiquaver of each group, held and accented (Klindworth adds crotchets with up-stems), and then for two further bars (bars 23–24) changes back to the alto again. It is technically difficult to secure an even emphasis on the upper melody notes without increasing the tone elsewhere, and one must regretfully record that too many pianists are content to evade the issue and leave the melody-notes virtually unmarked. Bars 17–25 should be played with limpid tone (the first two bars with *una corda* pedal) and with slightly lingering effect, until with the return of the opening theme in bar 25 the full tempo is resumed.

The *Largo* commences *forte* and *pesante*, after which there should be a *diminuendo* and slight *rallentando* into the *Moderato cantabile*. In these two introductory bars of the *Largo* the basic speed of the accompanying figure of the *Moderato cantabile* is set up and the only justification for a change of tempo from *largo* to *moderato* would be a change of time signature from *alla breve* to common time at the commencement of the *Moderato* as in the Klindworth edition. In the Chopin Institute's edition the change is made at the commencement of the *Largo*, which seems illogical. But Ganche and most other editors insert no change of time signature whatever, with the result that pianists usually take the *Moderato cantabile* at too fast a speed, and make insufficient allowance for its broad, flowing character. Incidentally the trill or mordent in bar 43, etc., should be played as an anticipated upper mordent (see p. 140 above). The middle section of the *Fantasie-Impromptu* is perhaps rather long drawn-out, and involves too much repetition, for which reason it is all the more important that variety of colour and nuance be given to the many re-statements of the main theme. For instance in playing bar 53, which but for the turn is a repetition of bar 45, the tenor doubling of the melody in the left hand might be reinforced, commencing with the upbeat (A flat), and for further repetitions of this bar, right and left hand colour might predominate alternately, with *una corda* pedal for the left hand reinforcement, and without it for normal balance.

With regard to the final section it need only be said that the *Presto* tempo should not be overdone, and it is sufficient if this section is played with still more verve and *élan* than at the outset. In bars 118–119 there should be no *ritardando* such as some pianists are wont to make; if anything one should move with headlong and increasing pace into a *molto agitato* at bar 119.

SCHERZO IN B MINOR, OP. 20

In his scherzos Chopin retains the outlines of classical scherzo form (Op. 31 has much the same sonata-cum-scherzo form as the scherzo of Beethoven's *Ninth Symphony*), but he breathes into them such desolate despair or grim demoniacal energy as makes the title seem a paradox. Here we have the Polish 'Zal' – the gloom and bitterness, the disillusionment, the irony and reckless gaiety of a long-suffering and oppressed nation.

In the B minor scherzo the mood ranges from the opening 'shriek of despair', as Niecks calls it, and the turbulence of the scherzo proper, to the tranquil nostalgia of the trio, a nostalgia which was so completely a part of Chopin the exile, and so often seems to have sprung from recollections of his childhood and its deeply-felt associations.

The dynamics of the main theme must be carefully graded – a sudden *sforzando* in the left hand in bar 9 is followed by a *subito piano* and *crescendo* to a further *sforzando* in both hands on the first beats of bars 11 and 13. Pedalling should be confined here to a *staccato* pedal on the first quaver of bar 9, with no pedal in bars 11, 13 and 16, in order to secure a more abrupt cut-off for the violent accent in both hands at the end of each phrase. In bars 10 and 12 the pedal should be taken on the first crotchet and released on the second. In bars 14 and 15, the pedal should be taken on every alternate beat, commencing with the first. The same pedalling scheme applies to bars 17–24.

At bar 44 the tempo suddenly broadens, and the utmost expressiveness is called for. The *ritardando* of bars 56–57 might well be accompanied by a *crescendo* from *piano* to *mezzo-forte*, with a *poco sforzando* on the first chord of bar 57. A *diminuendo* and change of pedal are necessary on the third beat of this bar, and a complete break should be made before the held octave of bar 58 is sounded. The phrase commencing with this latter bar might be played *pianissimo* with *una corda* pedal the first time, and repeated *piano* without the *una corda* pedal. A *diminuendo* can be secured on the held chord of the first-time bars (bars 65–68) by the use of 'tremolo' pedalling, as described above (see p. 39 above).

On the return of the *Agitato* section one should begin *pianissimo* with *una corda* pedal for the first four bars. Starting at *piano* level in bar 77 and at *mezzo-forte* in bar 81, there is then a *crescendo* for three bars followed by a *diminuendo*, and from the beginning of the latter (bar 85) the top notes of the left hand should be emphasised. From bars 89–105 the left hand should be emphasised. From bars 89–105 the left hand melody should be brought out with rich singing tone, with a continuous *crescendo* from *piano* to double-*forte*. From bar 105 the first note of each chord in the right hand should also be emphasised. The *ritenuto* section, commencing at bar 164, might be played as before. At the end of the next *Agitato* section the extension leading over to the *Molto più lento* should be played with the most intense concentration, ever more quietly and slowly, so as to prepare the hearer for the dreamy, tender mood which is now to follow.

The *Molto più lento* is based on an old Polish Christmas carol, a lullaby for the Infant Jesus. The melody notes are best held as follows in the alto part for the first five bars and in the top part for the next three, though this entails a wide stretch for the right hand:

Ex. 253: Chopin *Scherzo No. 1* in B minor, Op. 20, bars 307–314

All eight bars might be played *pianissimo* with *una corda* pedal and with *cantabile* tone for the melody notes. At bar 9 of the *Molto più lento* section the *una corda* pedal should be released and the next section should be begun *piano*. From bars 17–23 there should be a gradual increase in tone and speed. The combination of grace notes and mordent in bar 20 is executed as follows:

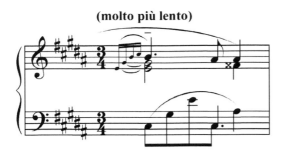

Ex. 254: Chopin *Scherzo No. 1* in B minor, Op. 20, bar 326

In the course of the repeat of this section a variant of the first statement is to be found in bars 54 and 55:

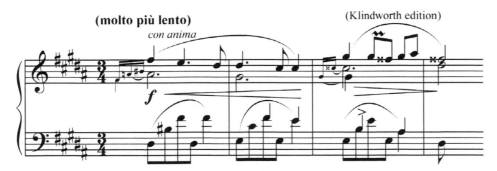

Ex. 255: Chopin *Scherzo No. 1* in B minor, Op. 20, bars 359–362

The progression F sharp–E in bar 54 greatly enhances and intensifies the expression, but it is missing in the Ganche edition and many others. It has been adopted in the Chopin Institute's edition, though without the upper stems inserted by Klindworth. On its last statement, from bar 65, the lullaby theme should be played with the utmost tenderness, *pianissimo* and with *una corda* pedal. The dream-like quiet is then shattered by the agonised cry of bar 81, and again by the deep-toned *sforzando* of bar 83, and after a further *ritardando* and *diminuendo* the *Agitato* section reappears. At each successive recurrence the theme should be played more wildly and fiercely. To secure sufficient force for the chromatic scale passage at the end of the impassioned coda, Liszt used to play interlocked octaves:

Ex. 256: Chopin *Scherzo No. 1* in B minor, Op. 20, bars 611–612

SCHERZO IN B FLAT MINOR, OP. 31

The *Scherzo* in B flat minor is the finest of the four scherzos which Chopin wrote, by reason of the depth and variety of its moods, the broad sweep of its melodies and the eloquent vehemence of its climaxes.

The sinister opening figure has already been referred to (see pp. 159-160 above). It should be played mysteriously and *pianissimo* with *una corda* pedal – not in the dry, mechanical fashion which is usual even with well-known virtuosi. Four times this furtive questioning figure is followed by an imperious answer, and on the second and fourth occasions the subsequent descent (bars 18–22 and 42–46) should be make precipitously and with a slight *accelerando* to give the effect of urgency which is needed here (see pp. 77-8 above). Reference has already been made to the danger of accenting the last note of the phrase in each of bars 54 and 56 (see p. 56 above); in bar 55 a barely perceptible broadening might be made sufficient to give a certain hesitancy to this answering phrase. The whole passage might be shaped and pedalled as follows:

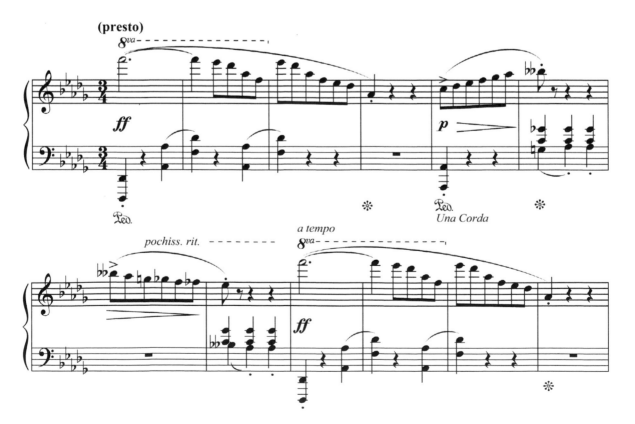

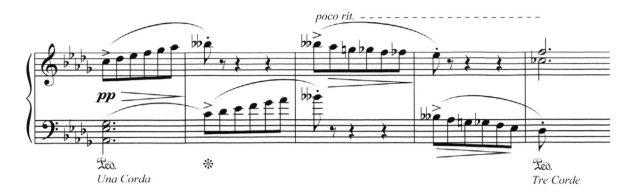

Ex. 257: Chopin *Scherzo No. 2* in B flat minor, Op. 31, bars 49–65

The mordent in bar 74 is taken prior to the beat (see p. 140 above). In bars 79–83 the initial note in each bar in the left hand (A flat–G–G flat–G flat–F) might be held to enrich the texture. A slight *rubato* towards the beginning of bar 81 and a sudden drop in the dynamic level will help to intensify the melody at this point and give it new colour. There should be a further *rubato* in bar 88 and the corresponding bar 104, while in bars 97–100 (an intensification of bars 81–84) the lower melody note might be played with more tone than the upper note of each octave in the right hand, so as to achieve a warmer colour, which can be enhanced by lingering very slightly over these bars. From bar 108 both speed and tone should increase up to the *fortissimo* of bar 117. A *cantilena* as long as this – it covers no less than 53 bars – cannot be played in an unbroken, unvarying line; it needs elasticity of treatment and intense expressiveness, though one must beware of exaggeration and above all of sentimentality. The whole section is *con anima* and the basic speed should be a lively one despite the agogic variations which it undergoes. From bar 117 strict time is, of course, vital. Bars 117–121 in *fortissimo* might be answered by bars 122–126 in *piano* with *una corda* pedal – it is monotonous in the extreme to play these eight bars with the same tone and colour. The tone might be increased at bar 126 with the slightest of *ritardandos* and a *diminuendo* for bars 128–129, and with the final octaves played *pianissimo*. The fingering of this passage has been referred to on p. 35.

The trio (*Sostenuto* section in A major) is in a quiet reflective mood, and should be played with *una corda* pedal for the first twelve bars. A *diminuendo* should be observed from bars 265–266 and 269–270 and the second chord in each case with its dissonant element is then given more intensity than the first by the expedient of reducing the tone and by allowing a very slight delay intervene before sounding it – an important interpretative effect which is seldom observed in performance. The *una corda* pedal might be taken on the last beat of bar 280 to prepare for the *coloratura* passage of bars 281–285, which should be played evanescently, with a slight *ritardando* on the last four quavers, for the petering-out of this rippling wavelet. Observe how in the repeat of the first section the note A in the left hand is tied from bar 285–286, a tiny detail which shows Chopin's sensitive craftsmanship, and serves to indicate the pains which the pianist should take in delineating the minutest points of the texture.

From bar 310 the tempo should be strict with the exception of a slight *rubato* in bars 314 and 321. This section is somewhat difficult to play because of the held dotted minims, but with practice they can be manipulated even by a small hand. It is reprehensibly careless to release the minims just to make the fingering easier. The balance of parts in this section has been dealt with above (see pp. 61-2). From bars 326–332 the tenor progression D sharp–E–F sharp–E–D sharp–E–B might be brought slightly to the fore, these eight bars being played softly and with *una corda* pedal. Again in bars 342–346, a repetition of bars 334–338, variety of colour can be obtained by bringing out the bass notes to a somewhat greater extent than on the first statement of this passage. Bars 334–349 should be played lightly and delicately and with *una corda* pedal. The fingering has been dealt with above (see p. 31). In bar 353 (as in bar 357) it is simplest to take the last three quavers in the left hand.

Later, in the *Agitato* section in G minor commencing at bar 492, a series of two-bar phrases answer each other continuously. It is inartistic to play this stretch at an even tone-level, as one often hears it played; rather should every alternate two-bar phrase be played *forte* and *mezzo-forte* so that the one phrase clearly answers the other. The two phrases commencing in bars 507–508 should then form part of a *diminuendo*, and from bar 512 a *crescendo* starts again.

As in the opening section of the scherzo (bars 53–57) a slight broadening should be allied with reduced tone in bars 520–524. In the *Sempre con fuoco* section commencing in bar 544 (reversion to B flat minor) the descending octaves in the bass should be well marked. In the final *Più mosso* section, the apex and culmination of the whole scherzo, a great climax can be built up by depressing the pedal on the low A flat of bar 744 and sustaining it as far as bar 748, while half-pedalling at bars 749, 751, 753 and 755, so that the low octave is still retained as a bass, giving a foundation to the brilliant superstructure of clashing chords until the tonic is reached in bar 756.

THE FOUR *BALLADES*

Writers who deal with the *Ballades* usually refer to an alleged connection between the *Ballades* and certain of Mickiewicz's poems, but dismiss the subject on the grounds that the connection cannot be adequately authenticated, and that in any event such programmatic explanations are irrelevant, or even misleading and harmful. These objections, however, do not seem to allay the references to Mickiewicz's poems, which continue to be named even in the latest works of reference, and to be dismissed, often – one may suspect – without having been read or the possibility of their being related to the *Ballades* examined.

Accordingly in the following pages the poems associated with the *Ballades* will be dealt with and summarised, so that instead of a vague and exasperating allusion to the mere title of a poem, the pianist will gain some idea of what the poem is about, and will have some opportunity of judging whether there could be any inherent validity in the tradition connecting the poem and the ballade concerned. This does not mean that the *Ballades* are to be interpreted as programme music in the strict sense of the word, i.e. following a poetic narrative detail by detail. If Chopin was in fact inspired by a particular poem in writing each of his *Ballades* he would merely have reproduced the general spirit of the poem in his own terms, and possibly illustrated such elements in it as moved him most, much in the same way as Liszt in his *Faust Symphony* interpreted Goethe's *Faust*, not as a play but as a psychological study of the chief characters involved. It is on such lines that the relationship between each *Ballade* and the relevant Mickiewicz poem will be discussed before details of interpretation are dealt with.

BALLADE NO. *1* IN G MINOR, OP. 23

The G minor *Ballade* is generally believed to have been inspired by the poem 'Konrad Wallenrod', written by Mickiewicz shortly before the ill-fated Polish rising of 1830, and hailed as a national epic by the Polish patriots. It is a historical poem dealing with the wars in the fourteenth century between the Teutonic Knights of the Cross and the Lithuanian pagans. The hero, Konrad Wallenrod, symbolises the love of the patriot for his fatherland, and his determination to overcome its oppressors even at the risk of his own life and honour. Konrad, the Lithuanian pagan, sets himself to avenge his devastated country by rising to power within the Order of the Knights, until as Grand Master he leads their army against his kinsmen and wilfully brings about its destruction, dying in the end as a traitor at the hands of the knights themselves. 'Play the fox as well as the lion', the poem seems to say; 'treachery is the only weapon of the slave'. Such was Mickiewicz's outcry against the three powers which had partitioned his native Poland, and 'Wallenrodism', as it was called, rapidly became the fashion among the young Polish officers in the Russian army.

Once can imagine how the poem must have stirred the Polish exiles, Chopin in particular. Most writers who deal with the G minor *Ballade* refer to 'Konrad Wallenrod', and most pianists know of the reference, yet few, as we have said, have any inkling as to the nature of the poem. This may be summarised as follows:[99]

As a child Konrad had been captured and reared as a Christian by the Teutonic Knights, but in the first raid against the Lithuanians in which he takes part he deserts to his kinsmen, and ultimately married Aldona, daughter of the Lithuanian prince Kiejstut. They are not long together when the knights again invade the country, overcoming all resistance. Konrad in his despair decides that the only hope of saving his people is to wreck the Order of the Knights from within. He leaves Lithuania, wins renown as a warrior in foreign lands, joins the order, and after some time is elected Grand Master. In the meantime Aldona, resolved to share his fate, has immured herself as a recluse in a tower near the chief city of the order, where Konrad visits her secretly, hearing her voice and speaking to her, but never seeing her. A banquet is held on the feast of the patron saint, and a Lithuanian minstrel sings the story of Walter (Konrad's native name) and of Aldona to the uncomprehending knights. But Witold, a Lithuanian noble who had been deposed and sought the protection of the order, is afflicted with remorse on hearing the minstrel's ballad. Leaving with his warriors he enters several strongholds of the knights by guile and slaughters their garrisons, before marching into Lithuania to join the forces of his fellow-countrymen. The order now decides to embark on a crusade against the treacherous pagans, and the army, led by Konrad, lays siege to Vilna. But Konrad plays into the hands of the Lithuanians, remains inactive while they cut off all supplies, is surrounded and defeated, and returns, the first to tell the tale of the disaster. He hastens to Aldona's tower to tell her that his vow has been fulfilled and Lithuania avenged, and asks her to flee with him to their native land. But she refuses, unwilling to break her vows and emerge as a wretched phantom of her former self. Meanwhile a secret conclave of judges has condemned Konrad as a traitor. An armed party surprises him in a bastion where he has shut himself up and, exultantly recounting the havoc and destruction he has wrought upon the order, Konrad dies.

---

[99] See *Gems of Polish Poetry: Selections from Mickiewicz*, translated Frank H. Fortey (Warsaw 1923).

The fact that there is a strong tradition connecting the G minor *Ballade* with Mickiewicz's poem (a tradition vouched for by Stavenhagen, independently of Huneker's testimony on the subject) does not mean that there is necessarily any close relationship between the poem and the music. Professor Gerald Abraham goes so far as to say that 'there is about as much connexion between the G minor *Ballade* and Mickiewicz's grim narrative poem with its exceedingly tough and unpleasant hero as between *Macbeth* and Chopin's *Barcarolle*.'[100] Professor Abraham can have little appreciation of the spirit of Mickiewicz's poem or of the *Ballade*, for it is easy to conceive how the one could have inspired the other. In fact, many possible points of contact can be sensed. The opening of the *Ballade* could well evoke the scene in which the Lithuanian minstrel at the banquet of the knights begins his song of Lithuania's sufferings and of Konrad's deeds, while the dissonant E flat (see p. 112 above) seems to suggest that note of apprehensiveness, of uneasy tension which underlines the poem, and emanates from Konrad's treachery. Again, the *meno mosso* theme, tender at first, rises then to such heights of passion that it seems as if the figure of Aldona in the poem had become a flaming symbol of deliverance to the rest of humanity. Here we have the Messianic note so characteristic of the poetry of Mickiewicz and of the other Polish poets of the period. Lastly one cannot but feel that the final *Presto con fuoco* portrays a terrible triumph, culminating as it does in these crashing octaves which move inexorably closer and then career downwards with headlong violence to the close. Even though Chopin did not intend his *Ballades* to be regarded as programme music in a literal sense, their title alone suggests some uncommunicated programme basis, and one can feel the G minor *Ballade* to be permeated with subjective sentiment. What more appropriate background for the player to delve into than that which may well have inspired the composer? No one would be foolhardy enough to assert dogmatically that any section of any detail of the *Ballades* refers to any particular part of the poem, but the poem can serve as an apt introduction to the *Ballade*, kindling the player's imagination with that sense of 'old, unhappy far-off things and battles long ago' which seems so inherent in the music.

For the G minor *Ballade*, perhaps more than for the other *Ballades*, the pianist must possess great imaginative power and the ability to build up the whole work dramatically in waves of increasing or lessening tension. The numerous changes of tempo must be plastically treated; thus the *a tempo* of bar 36 should be taken at an appreciably faster speed than the opening of the *Moderato* section itself, and many other adjustments of speed are necessary which are not specifically indicated. But if there is an unusual amount of freedom in this *Ballade*, it is all the more necessary to mould it in such a way that all its parts unite into a whole.

At the commencement of the *Moderato* (i.e. bar 8) some pianists linger on the initial five-note figure. This is the merest sentimentality – *rubato* must indeed be used, but only to shape the close of each two-bar phrase, so that there will be a very slight *ritardando* covering the second half of bar 9 and the first half of bar 10, and similarly covering bars 11–12, 13–14 and so on. Rigid time is then necessary again from bar 21 on, since from this point a more sustained line begins to take shape.

In bars 61–64 the notes D–G flat–D–F–G–A in the bass should be brought out melodically. The notes D flat and C flat in the right hand of bar 85 and the note B flat in the left hand of bar 86

[100] Gerald Abraham, *Chopin's Musical Style* (London 1939), p. 58.

should be held a little longer than the given crotchet value, and should form a clear progression. In bars 97–98 the *diminuendo* which it seems natural to make might be offset by slightly emphasising the left hand notes F sharp, G sharp, to secure darker colour. The mordent in bar 113 is anticipated (see p. 140), i.e. the two grace-notes precede the beat, while the mordents in bars 119 and 123 are played as triplets, the first note of the triplet being accented and coming on the beat. In bar 135 the omission of the flat before A in the left hand is a misprint which still reappears in most editions. In bar 137 a slight *ritardando* is called for and some emphasis for the notes A natural, A flat at the end of the bar.

Clear phrasing is secured in bars 159 and 160 by accenting the third note A in each bar (see p. 48 above). In bar 166 the low B flat *sforzando* is best taken by the right hand as a continuation of the preceding scale passage:

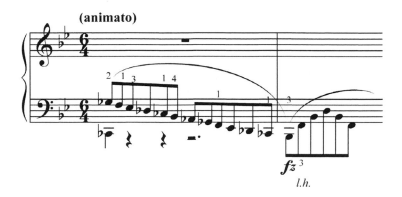

Ex. 258: Chopin *Ballade No. 1* in G minor, Op. 23, bars 165–166

In bar 179 the trill is played as a triplet, and the two upper notes of the chords after the octaves in the right hand should be repeated, not tied as in some editions.

In bars 192–193 Chopin has marked *dim. e rall.* as a lead-in to the *Meno mosso* section. Stavenhagen, however, told us that Liszt used to make a considerable *crescendo* here and to play the theme (from bar 194) *forte*, instead of *pianissimo* and *sotto voce* as marked; further that Chopin approved of the suggestion and subsequently adopted it himself. The progression D–E in bars 199–200 was suddenly taken *pianissimo* by Liszt and from then on he made a continual *crescendo* to the *Presto con fuoco*. The forcefulness and the sense of strife can be increased by accenting the off-beats (bass notes) in the left hand, as well as the chords on the weak beats in the right hand, from bar 208 on. In bars 234–235 the first and third beats receive an intense accent and so do the successive beats of bars 236–237. Such accentuation is absolutely essential for the achievement of a proper climax, but it is too often disregarded in performance.

If the rising scale passages in bars 251 and 255 are practised in groups of four they will be much more accurate and brilliant when played up to time. The soft G minor chords after each scale passage should be played slowly and ominously, and the subsequent group of six quavers played with impetuous excitement. The dissonant converging octaves need maximum force, and the descending octaves in both hands should then thunder downwards with the relentless force of an avalanche.

BALLADE NO. 2 IN F, OP. 38

In his *Music and Musicians*[101] Schumann, to whom the second *Ballade* is dedicated, says that Chopin himself acknowledged the *Ballade* to have been 'inspired by some of Mickiewicz's poems'. It has always been a tradition, however, that this *Ballade* was inspired by one poem in particular, namely, 'Switez', or 'The Legend of Lake Switez', adapted by Mickiewicz from a popular ballad. This is presumably the poem to which Huneker refers when he says that Chopin admits to have written the *Ballade* 'under the direct inspiration of Adam Mickiewicz's 'Le Lac de Willis',[102] Willis, Vili or Vila being terms for various kinds of female sprite in Slavonic mythology. The poem may be summarised as follows:[103]

Often at night out of a thick enveloping mist the lake of Switez emits the hum of a city, the tumult of warriors, the cries of women, the tolling of bells and the clash of arms. The lord to whom the lake belongs, eager to probe its mystery, assembles a fleet of barges to drag the water's depths. When the nets are drawn to the surface a woman is revealed, of luminous complexion, with lips of coral and flaxen hair. She speaks to the terrified crowd telling them that where this lake now stands there once stood a city famous for the valour of its warriors and the virtue of its women. One day its ruler, Prince Tuhan, and his knights were called away by the Lithuanian king to help him give battle against the invading army of the czar. The prince was sorely grieved to leave Switez unprotected, but his daughter – the lady of the lake herself – bade him go without fear, for in a vision she had beheld an angel bare his sword and spread his golden pinions over the town as a symbol of protection. That very night the Russians battered their way into Switez. Rather than suffer death at the hands of the invader, the defenceless inhabitants resolved to slay themselves. But the princess prayed that the Lord himself would destroy them. Suddenly the town disappeared, swallowed into the earth. In its stead a lake arose margined with water-lilies, into which the wives and daughters of Switez had been changed. As the Russians touched these lilies, thinking to adorn their helmets, they were struck down with sickness and perished. The poem ends abruptly, telling us that this tale is still preserved among the people, and that the lilies of Lake Switez are still called 'czars' – the flowers that foiled the Russians.

Here again, the music must of itself arouse the imagination. But just as there are possible links between the G minor *Ballade* and 'Konrad Wallenrod', so one may feel that the opening *Andantino* just catches the simple pastoral mood suggested by the description of the lake at the beginning of Mickiewicz's poem, while the recurrences of the turbulent *Presto* could suggest the various stages of the story's progress, culminating in the great climax of the coda, and rounded off by the absolute tranquillity of the last few bars – the lake at peace again.

BALLADE NO. 3 IN A FLAT, OP. 47

According to Kleczynski[104] the third ballade was evidently inspired by (Mickiewicz's) 'Undine', and Huneker states its derivation from the latter poem quite categorically.[105] It seems

---

[101] Robert Schumann, *Essays and Criticisms: Music and Musicians*, First series, trans. ed. annotated by Fanny Raymond Ritter (London 1876), p. 203.

[102] James Huneker, *Chopin: The Man and His Music* (London 1921), p. 281.

[103] See *Selections from Mickiewicz*, transl. F.H. Fortey (Warsaw 1923), p. 25 ff.

[104] Jan Kleczynski, *Chopin's Greater Works* (London n. d.) p. 68.

clear, however, that the virile rhythms and elated moods of the third *Ballade* could have no possible connection with the shadowy, dream-like atmosphere of 'Undine'. If the latter poem be connected with any of the *Ballades*, the connection, as we shall see, is probably with the fourth *Ballade* in F minor. Again, the legend is manifestly absurd which connects the fourth *Ballade* with a poem by Mickiewicz in lighter vein, a Lithuanian ballad named 'Trzech Budrysów' (The Three Brothers Budrys), and it seems likely that Kleczynski or some source which he was following, and other writers after him, have confused the two *Ballades*, so that the fourth *Ballade* should have been stated to have associations with 'Undine' and the third *Ballade* with 'Trzech Budrysów'. This is all the more likely since the key-signatures of the two *Ballades* are the same.

The poem 'Trzech Budrysów'[106] and the third *Ballade* undoubtedly seem to have much in common. The poem has a gaiety and humour rare with Mickiewicz, while the third *Ballade* is the only one of the four Chopin *Ballades* which is consistently light-hearted. The poem tells of how old Budrys summons his three sons and bids them ride off to battle, one to the Russian front:

<blockquote>
There are sable's black tails, there are silvery veils,
There are coins shining brightly like ice
</blockquote>

one to the Prussian front, to

<blockquote>
…trample
That dog's breed, the Knights of the Cross;
There lie amber thick-strown, vestments diamond-sown,
And brocades all a marvellous gloss
</blockquote>

the third to the Polish front, and he is to bring home a bride:

<blockquote>
For 'tis Poland the world over that's the land for a lover:
All the maids are like kittens at play;
Faces whiter than milk, lashes soft as black silk,
And their eyes – like the star-shine are they!
</blockquote>

The sons ride away, autumn and winter pass without news of them, and old Budrys thinks them dead. Then one day the first son returns, then the second, then the third, all three of them bearing beneath their mantles – not booty, but a Polish bride!

It would be easy to read into the A flat *Ballade* a programme which is close to the plot and spirit of the poem. The first theme might stand for old Budrys himself, more especially in relation to the eighth verse of the poem:

<blockquote>
Fifty years are now sped and my bride is long dead,
The bright Pole I brought home from a raid;
And yet still when I stand and gaze out toward that land,
I remember the face of that maid.
</blockquote>

The martial rhythms and trumpet calls which follow could suggest old Budrys summoning his sons to battle; the lilting second theme, almost unmistakably equestrian, could suggest the three sons starting off on their adventures; the episode (commencing bar 115) the old man's dreaming of his own Polish bride; the recapitulation, the return of the three sons with their Polish brides;

[105] James Huneker, *Chopin*, p. 283.
[106] See *Poems by Adam Mickiewicz*, ed. G.R. Noyes (New York 1944), p. 162.

and the coda (*Più mosso*) the old man's dream relived anew. However one may wish – or not wish – to interpret the details, poem and *Ballade* seem closely related.

To come now to matters of interpretation, in the second bar of the third *Ballade* a quite incongruous effect is produced by playing the last chord of the bar *arpeggiata*, as usually marked, in contrast to the enhanced effect obtained by playing the second chord *arpeggiata*:

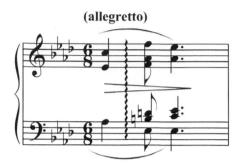

Ex. 259: Chopin *Ballade No. 3* in A flat, Op. 47, bar 2

The same progression occurs at bar 38, and again at bar 46, with a repetition *in alt* at bar 46–47. Liszt used to play the first progression of bar 46 as marked, non-*arpeggiata*, but the repetition *in alt* was played by him as a delicate echo of the preceding progression with both chords *arpeggiata*:

Ex. 260: Chopin *Ballade No. 3* in A flat, Op. 47, bars 46–47

From bar 52 the pedal might be depressed for the first note of each slurred group, and released for the second (see p. 127). After the repetition, from bars 109–112, and again from bars 150–153, Liszt used to pedal on each successive chord without releasing for the slurs, getting a rich effect by fusing the chord and its resolution, and at the same time bringing out the upper note in the left hand:

Ex. 261: Chopin *Ballade No. 3* in A flat, Op. 47, bars 109–113

In bars 130–131 a firm bass line is essential, and in bars 132–133 the top notes of the left hand should be emphasised, and the two bars played lingeringly, if the shapely melodic curve here is to be given its due value. In the original German edition, the Klindworth edition, and many recent editions, bars 136–137 read as follows:

Ex. 262: Chopin *Ballade No. 3* in A flat, Op. 47, bars 136–137

But in the autograph and the original French edition there is an extra bar, which has been adopted in the Chopin Institute's edition:

Ex. 263: Chopin *Ballade No. 3* in A flat, Op. 47, bars 136–138, Chopin Institute edition

The omission of this bar in the previously-named editions is hardly a mistake, as the editors of the Chopin Institute's edition suggest, but more probably the result in the first instance of an emendation, since repetition of this kind seems peculiarly un-Chopin-like, and has a weakening rather than a strengthening effect in view of the further repetition woven into the descending line which follows. Aesthetically (a) seems superior to (b) and here the pianist must balance the issue for himself.

At bar 156 (157) marked *mezzo voce*, it is advisable to begin *pianissimo* with *una corda* pedal, and then gradually to work up to the *fortissimo* of bar 172 (173).

BALLADE NO. 4 IN F MINOR, OP. 52

If the explanation given above be correct concerning the confusion of the third and fourth *Ballades* in regard to the Mickiewicz poems traditionally associated with them, there may be grounds for connecting the fourth *Ballade* with 'Switezianka'[107] (i.e. 'Undine', or 'The Nixie'), a companion poem to 'The Legend of Lake Switez'. The story of the poem is as follows:[108]

A young huntsman falls in love with a water nymph who appears to him at night among the groves of Lake Switez and disappears at dawn. She rejects his offer of marriage, declaring that treachery lurks in the heart of man. Presently another maiden appears out of the lake, and lures him to sport with her and exchanges caresses. Suddenly she reveals herself to be none other than the first nymph. She denounces his infidelity, a storm arises and increases in fury until an abyss opens among the waters, and both are engulfed. On a moonlight night the forms of the nymph and her lover may still be seen gliding dimly over the lake.

The haunted questioning main theme of the *Ballade*, the seductive second theme, the triplet figuration in the latter part of the *Ballade* which seems to suggest swirling water, the dramatic outburst before the coda, followed by the series of tense *pianissimo* chords, and the coda itself which sweeps with ever increasing velocity to the *dénouement*, are among the features which may have a bearing on the poem. This should serve as an excellent introduction to the *Ballade*, more particularly for such pianists as are lacking in imaginative insight, and the ability to clothe a sustained narrative with the necessary dramatic and poetic qualities.

FANTAISIE IN F MINOR, OP. 49

To Liszt has been attributed the notion that the *Fantaisie* in F minor was the outcome of a quarrel and reconciliation between Chopin and George Sand.[109] Kellermann used to deny this story with its melodramatic details as both unworthy and untrue, and to declare that if the opening of the *Fantaisie* had any extra-musical associations at all these could only be with some phantom procession, some sinister episode out of Poland's past. It is true that the *Fantaisie*, like the *Ballades*, seems to spring from some deeply felt poetic background, and even though the nature of this must be left to the imagination, the player will come nearer to the music according as his imagination is nourished by sources which also influenced the composer. If 'Read Shakespeare's *Tempest*' was Beethoven's answer to Schindler's query about the 'Appassionata' *Sonata*, then 'Read Mickiewicz's *Ancestors*' might well be the advice to any pianist who wishes to prepare

---

[107] Professor Gerald Abraham strongly suspects that 'Lac de Willis' and 'Undine' are one and the same poem' (*Chopin's Musical Style*, p. 58), not realising that 'Switezianka' is synonymous with 'Undine'. Though he is right in suggesting that 'Switez' is synonymous with 'Lac de Willis', he does not attempt to sort out the tangle, or examine the possibility of a relationship between the *Ballades* and their associated poems.

[108] See *Poems by Adam Mickiewicz*, ed. Noyes, 'The Nixie', p. 71.

[109] See Huneker, *Chopin*, pp. 384-5.

himself in a general way for the mood-cycle of the *Fantaisie*, for there is a remarkable affinity between the spirit of both works. Part III of Mickiewicz's fantastic drama *Dziady* (*Ancestors* or *The Festival of the Dead*) was published in Paris in 1832 after the final defeat of the Polish insurgents. As it happens, we know that Chopin received a copy of *Dziady* at Marseilles on March 9th, 1839,[110] on his return journey from Majorca, and the *Fantaisie* was completed at George Sand's *château* at Nohant and first published in November, 1841. The drama must have made a profound impression on Chopin. His preoccupation with Polish poetry just about this time may be gauged by the fact that he translated Mickiewicz's works for George Sand, and that both attended the Polish poet's lectures on Slavonic literature at the Collège de France in December, 1840. But even if *Dziady* had nothing whatever to do with the genesis of the *Fantaisie*, it is worth reading for the insight it gives into the ideals and aspirations of the exiled Polish romantics. As the play is hard to come by, the following synopsis may prove useful:[111]

The hero of the drama, Gustavus, is a Polish patriot interned as a political prisoner by the Russians. In Part III, Scene 2, we find him dreaming of all he has yet to suffer, imagining himself in exile amid his country's enemies with song as his only weapon, and none to understand. (How this must have awakened echoes in the mind of the exiled Chopin!) Suddenly aroused, Gustavus determines to become a new man with a changed name – Konrad, a sort of Prometheus unbound, the champion of his fellow-prisoners. And after the most harrowing stories have been told of the maltreatment of Polish compatriots Konrad interposes with a song of diabolical vengeance against his country's executioners. Then, alone in his cell, he gives vent to the famous 'Improvisation', an exalted and rhapsodic invocation of his own powers as poet and creator. Pouring scorn on all other poets he asks the Almighty for dominion over souls and he will build

Poland ... A Living Song! Create a greater glory than 'Creation' – Poland – A Song of Joy!

But God is silent, and Konrad with impious irony asserts Him to be Intellect rather than Love. Amidst the antiphonal chanting of an Evil Spirit on the poet's side, and a Good Spirit praying and pleading for him in his blasphemies against God, Konrad, prostrate with grief for Poland, cries out:

> Now is my soul incarnate with my country,
> My body is all spirit with her soul,
> For I and my dear fatherland are one: .....
> O my beloved country, tried and true!
> I gaze at thee, matchless 'mid matchless wrongs!
> Even as a son gazeth upon his father
> Broken on the wheel; ....
> And thou, O God! art wise and calm and bright,
> Thou smil'st serene with azure skies serene,
> (The azure heavens are the smile of God!)
> Thou seest – rulest – judgest everything,
> And the world says 'Thou art infallible!'

Then Konrad challenges the Almighty, threatening that he will send his

[110] Niecks, *The Life of Chopin*, Vol. II, p. 52.
[111] See Adam Mickiewicz, *Gems of Polish Poetry – Selections from Mickievicz*, translated by Frank H. Fortey (Warsaw 1923), pp. 75 seq.

> Voice through all the world,
> Strong with the righteous wrath of the oppressed,
> Reaching the generations yet unborn,
> Piercing like a tremendous trump of doom,
> And rocking all Thy palaces in Heaven,
> And everywhere proclaiming that Thou art
> Not the father of the world, but…

and the voice of the Demon interposes

> The Czar!

whereupon Konrad stops a moment, staggers and falls.

The prison chaplain, a friar, enters and prays over the prostrate form. Konrad recovers, at first still impiously demented, but finally penitent and submissive to the supernatural ways of the Almighty. And in the process of his conversion, sweet memories steal upon him: Eva, a young girl, praying for him, and Maryla sighing in vain for her lover. It is All Souls' Night, when even the dead come back, but Maryla's lover never! No longer is he Gustavus as in the days she first knew him, but Konrad, and sadly changed at that. 'Thy lover hath changed his ancestral name. The Festival of the Dead is over. Thy lover shall never come.'

Equate the imagery of this play with parts of the *Fantaisie* and one must be struck by the sinister opening (the phantoms of Part II of the play), the passionate singing theme commencing at bar 68 (Konrad's improvisation), the great outburst of bars 109–126 (Konrad's challenge to the Almighty), the *Lento sostenuto* (Konrad's conversion, his thoughts on All Souls' Night), and above all by the resignation of the *Adagio* towards the end ('The Festival of the Dead is over. Thy lover shall never come!').

The pianist who comes to interpret the *Fantaisie* after having read and assimilated the play should not go far wrong in his approach to the music, even though he discards all the details of the play and thinks now in terms of the music only. For one, he will not play the opening *Tempo di Marcia* section in that irritatingly jaunty fashion which is so usual. Even without any sense of tradition here, the context should be sufficient to warn him that this section should be played with solemnity and dignity, beginning with a mysterious *pp* and rising ultimately to a great *crescendo* at bar 19.

In bar 9 the chord on the fourth beat should be played *arpeggiata*, the D flat in the right hand coming with the A flat octave in the bass. In bar 10 the last chord should again be played *arpeggiata* and the triplet taken appreciably slower. The bass in bars 15–16 is customarily played in octaves. In bar 18 the top left-hand part should be brought out, from the A flat of the third beat to E flat in the following bar, thus obtaining a sonorous *crescendo* to the *forte* chord on E flat. It may be remarked in passing that the bass must usually make the chief contribution towards the achievement of a full, rich *crescendo*, if the result is not to be hard and dry. For lack of a rich bass and of a properly worked out colour scheme Chopin's music too often sounds anaemic.

From bar 21 the bass notes are marked *staccato*. The *staccato* here and in all such cases should not be taken literally, or else the sonority of the texture will suffer. These bass notes should be played *portamento*, i.e. practically held until the hand moves to the succeeding chord, and even when released by the fingers they should be retained by the sustaining pedal. The following dynamic scheme might be adopted in bars 21–29:

Ex. 264: Chopin *Fantaisie* in F minor, Op. 49, bars 21–29

With regard to the sudden *pianissimo* of bar 28, Kellermann once said: 'It should give the effect of light suddenly penetrating through a stained-glass window'. In bar 29 the entire chord on the second beat is played *arpeggiata*, B natural and D being taken by the thumb and second finger respectively of the right hand to ensure an even flow.

Using the *una corda* pedal from bar 37 on, Stavenhagen used to play the chords of bar 37 *mf* and the three *staccato* chords of bar 38 *pp*, without sustaining pedal, securing an effect like muffled drums. He adopted the same procedure at a lower dynamic level for bars 39–40. A rich effect is obtained by retaining the sustaining pedal for the full value of each of the minim chords of bars 41–42. At bar 43 one should begin slowly and *pp*, then quicken slightly and make a *ritardando* on the last three notes before the pause of bar 44. The next bar should be begun *piano*, with somewhat more *accelerando* and *ritardando* before the pause of bar 46. From bar 47 the pace is gradually increased to double, with a broad *ritardando* at bar 52. Throughout this section, from bars 43–49, it is essential to hold the notes written with downstems in the right hand.

In the passage marked *a tempo doppio movimento* (bar 64) the dramatic chords in the left hand should be played with great force and clarity. In bar 66 the right hand should take over the top A flat of the left hand part with a sharp accent (first, second and third fingers – see p. 35) and then continue the scale passage for the first two groups of bar 67, the last two groups being played by the left hand with mounting *crescendo*. The *agitato* section should be played imaginatively and with much passion, the melody singing out freely above the triplets in the left hand. In this section (bars 68–72) very few hands, especially women's hands, have sufficient stretch to allow the minim notes to be held in the bass. When this is so these notes should be accented and held as long as possible, and, when released, retained by the pedal, which should be held for each minim. The lovely *cantilena* which follows (bars 77–84) is one of those passages which, though marked *dolce* by Chopin himself, serves insensitive pianists with an opportunity of showing off their technique – and how brilliantly they hammer it out! The passage should be played delicately and smoothly with *una corda* pedal for the first four bars, and somewhat more tone for the repetition an octave lower. This passage is tender and lyrical in feeling, in contrast to all that has gone before and to the tortuous and violent passages which follow. The arpeggios in the left hand of bars 87–88 and 91–92 should be played *forte* and markedly, the top note always accented and *staccato* (though these chords should be practised *legato* in slow tempo), while the first note of each triplet in the right hand should be forcibly accented and the last note released *staccato*.

Bars 93–94 should be played a little slower and with dramatic emphasis, while bars 95–96 should be lighter and slightly quicker. For the tense passage commencing at bar 101 it is a Liszt tradition to make a barely perceptible *rubato*, so as to suggest a slight hesitation at the end of bars 102 and 104, while from bar 105 there is continuous onward-sweeping movement to the *ff* octaves of bar 109. The pedal as usually given should obviously be emended as follows:

Ex. 265: Chopin *Fantaisie* in F minor, Op. 49, bars 109–111

At bars 118–119 the third of the three repeated phrases should be played more slowly and heavily as if to convey a sense of exhaustion. From the next *forte* chord one should then work up gradually to a great climax, making a slight *ritardando* with the last pair of majestic chords which precede the mysterious section in E flat. The opening of this section should be played *pp*, the octaves in the bass and the middle notes *staccato*, with the melody *legato* and *marcato* in the right hand. No sustaining pedal, only *una corda* pedal, should be used for the first eight bars, and the chords should be played in strict time and in a strange, relentless way as if the forces of destiny were taking shape, secretively at first, then more openly and inexorably. Only from the ninth bar should there be a *crescendo*, and from here the sustaining pedal should be depressed on each chord.

After the tempestuous passage which follows, one should linger on the octave A flats and G's (bar 154) before resuming the main theme. This should be played with greater intensity and richer tone than before. The triplets of bars 180–182 should be played *mf*, and be answered by *pianissimo* chords and a slight *ritardando* in bars 181 and 183. At bar 187 this dialogue should become softer and dreamier. At bar 188 one should begin slowly and softly, then gradually quicken with slight *crescendo*, dying away at bar 191 and retarding again from bar 194–196.

The *Lento sostenuto* which follows is one of the most beautiful reveries which Chopin wrote. It should be played softly at first with *una corda* pedal, simply, and with great depth of feeling, as if something treasured had been irretrievably lost. The new phrase commencing at the end of bar 8 should be begun *ppp* and hesitatingly, as if one were afraid to disclose one's sorrow, but from this point onwards there should be a gradual awakening and increased intensity of expression. At bar 17 the opening theme recurs at *mf* level, but at the end of bar 18 the tone should be reduced again. I still remember how Stavenhagen brought out the progression F sharp–F double sharp–G sharp–A natural in the left hand in bar 18, and the progression D sharp–E–G sharp–F sharp in bar 20, and how he emphasised and lingered slightly on the last named G sharp, playing the whole passage with such subdued tenderness. Listening to the *Lento sostenuto* played nowadays one might sometimes think that pianists, both male and female, were made of cast-iron, so impervious do they seem to its message, as indeed to the romance and poetry of Chopin's epoch.

With the *sforzando* chord of bar 25 (Tempo I) comes a rude awakening. This chord should be played *staccato* in the right hand, and almost roughly, without pedal, and the left hand chords in the next bars should be heavily accentuated. Little remains to be said about the recapitulation, except that the descending triplets in bars 118–121 (counting from the *Lento*) should be played with fury, and the first four chords of the *Adagio* with maximum power. Stavenhagen always made a slight pause before commencing the recitative, of which he played the first phrase *pp*, the second *p* and the last *ppp*, leading up to the three crotchets which should be played like a sigh, slowly and regretfully. After a *tenuto* on the dominant seventh the triplets of the *Allegro assai* move slowly at first, gradually quickening with a surging *crescendo* to bar 128 and then dying away again. The last two chords should be played with great force and finality.

SONATA IN B FLAT MINOR, OP. 35

Of all Chopin's works this sonata has given rise to the greatest amount of controversy. When it first appeared critics saw in it Chopin's failure to cope with the framework of the sonata, and the structure of the first movement was seized upon as evidence of incompetence simply because the development and recapitulation are foreshortened – due to the extensive working-out of the first subject in the development, the recapitulation commences with the second subject. Such a procedure is frequently to be found in the works of Schubert and Schumann (it was actually the norm in pre-classical sonata form) and the structure of the first movement of the B flat minor sonata is in fact masterly.

No exception could be taken to the structure of the scherzo and the funeral march, but the real bone of contention was the strange and unexpected finale. This prejudice against the finale seems to have been extended to the other movements, so that even Schumann could write 'The idea of calling it a sonata is a caprice, if not a jest – for he had simply bound together four of his wildest children to smuggle them under this name into a place to which they could not else have penetrated.'[112] It is difficult to understand how the first three movements could have been referred to in such terms. As regards the finale, Chopin later showed in the B minor Sonata, Op. 58, what

[112] Robert Schumann, *Music and Musicians*, Second Series, p. 277.

he could write in the way of a finale if he chose, but for the B flat minor Sonata his teeming, if capricious, imagination devised a *dénouement* the relationship of which to the other movements seems to require a programmatic explanation. To Rubinstein the sonata was 'a poem of destiny', and all four movements might be interpreted in elemental terms such as the struggle with fate, the grim humour of life, death and the aftermath.

The first movement opens with a tragic motto theme, which should be played freely and with great expression, befitting the introduction to the tense drama which now begins. From bar 25 the accentuation as given is unnatural and cannot be observed. One should accent the first, not the second half of each first and third beats:

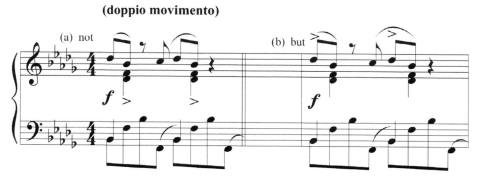

Ex. 266: Chopin *Piano Sonata No. 2* in B flat minor, Op. 35, 1st movement, bar 25

The Chopin Institute edition retains the accents as in (a), since they are clearly marked in the autograph, but refers to Brugnoli as insisting on the accentuation in (b). At bar 41 the second subject (*sostenuto*) should be played in fairly strict time, not sighed over and prolonged, as so many pianists affect. The fourth bar (bar 44) should be played without *rubato*; if a *rubato* is called for at all it might be applicable at bar 46, but only to a barely perceptible degree. At bar 76 Ganche's version is drab as compared with Klindworth's (endorsed by the Chopin Institute's edition):

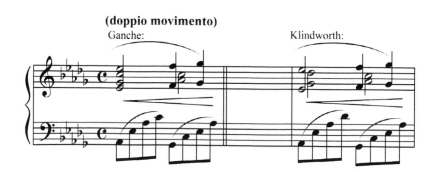

Ex. 267: Chopin *Piano Sonata No. 2* in B flat minor, Op. 35, 1st movement, bar 76 Ganche edition, bar 76 Klindworth edition

The change in rhythm at bars 81, 126, 134, 162, 210 is best thought of as being a change of time from 2/2 to 6/4, and Klindworth introduces the latter time signature at these points, reverting to 2/2 at bars 101, 130, 154, 170 and 230. Bars 109–112 and bars 117–118, allusions to the opening motto theme, might be taken slightly slower with *a tempo* in bars 112 and 119. At bar 157 the 8va marking as given by Ganche is clearly absurd. For the concluding section beginning at bar 230 it would be wiser to begin *mf*, to allow for an adequate increase of tone to the *fff* of the last three chords.

The scherzo is usually played too quickly. This movement should be demoniacal in its effect, not brilliant and boisterous. It is a mistake to play the first eight bars at a uniform level, and wiser to commence *p* with an immediate *crescendo* to *f* in the second bar; then to start the third bar *mf*, with *crescendo* to *f* in bar 4, similarly in bars 5–6, followed by continuous *crescendo* to the *ff* of bar 8. From bars 17–20 the *una corda* pedal should be used, and each octave in the left hand pedalled. The octave figure of bars 35–36 should stand out in a relentless *ff* both here and for its subsequent recurrence at bars 78–79. The chromatic first inversions which commence in bars 37, 41 and 45 are best begun *pp* with *una corda* pedal for the first bar and a half, with a mounting *crescendo* each time, as if to convey the tormented sighing and moaning of wind. The broad theme to which this leads at bar 50 should be rich and full and the first five bars should be played *espressivo* despite their weight of tone.

At the *Più lento* the tenor part in the left hand at bars 88–90 should sing out softly with slight *rubato*, and from the second beat of bar 90 to bar 92 the alto part in the right hand might be weighted above the others. A similar procedure should be adopted from bars 96–100. Pianists with small hands may find it difficult or impossible to play bar 86 as written:

Ex. 268: Chopin *Piano Sonata No. 2* in B flat minor, Op. 35, 2nd movement bar 86

and the same difficulty arises at bars 94, 102, 130. The solution is to take the lowest notes of the right hand part as inner notes of the left hand chords. At bar 112 a misprint is usually to be found – C natural, not C flat in the left hand.

The section commencing just before the double-bar should be played tenderly and dreamily, and though the left hand should be prominent, its general level should be *p* rather than *mf*. At bar 160 a pronounced *ritardando* is necessary before the re-entry of the first theme. The dramatic reappearance of the scherzo theme at Tempo I necessitates a *forte* start, unlike the procedure suggested for the opening of the scherzo.

Of the *Marche funèbre* Liszt wrote that he once heard a young Pole say 'only a Pole could have written this'.[113] One feels, Liszt continues, that it is not the death of a single warrior which is

---

[113] Franz Liszt, *Friedrich Chopin*, p. 14.

here being mourned, to be avenged by other heroes, but rather the passing of a whole generation of warriors, with none but women, children and priests to survive them.

The main theme should be played *legato*, with slightly increased weight on the second and fourth beats so as to suggest more effectively the clangorous tolling of death-bells. At bar 15 I think it more artistic to begin *mf* and thus secure a greater *crescendo*, which should swell out like a cry of despair to the first chord of bar 16. Here the left hand should take up the melodic line at *ff* level, diminishing in tone again towards the end of the bar. The same procedure should be adopted in bars 17–18. For the trill in bar 19 as many alternations as possible of the two notes should be secured so as to give the effect of a full, deep rolling of kettle drums. At bar 28 this roll diminishes to a dim muffled tone, and a *ritardando* is necessary in this bar for the approach to the last two bars. These should sound quite forlorn, and should be played *pp* and with *una corda* pedal.

The trio section, beginning at bar 31, should be played simply and plaintively and without any *rubato* in the first bar. The *una corda* pedal should be used for the first four bars, and a slight *crescendo* made for the upsurge in bars 32 and 34. A *rubato* is necessary in the second half of bar 37 in order to underline the cadence. The best dynamic scheme to adopt after the double bar (bar 39) is to begin *pp*, swell to *p* at bar 41 and to *mf* at bar 43, giving full weight to each of the melody notes in the second half of this bar, and making a poignant accent at the beginning of bars 44 and 45. At bar 46 there should be a *ritardando* leading to the return of the main theme.

Many distinguished pianists use excessive *rubato* in the trio, lingering on the important melody notes and making dotted quavers, even crotchets, out of quavers. The result is artificial in the extreme, and every vestige is forfeited of the tenderness and simplicity which are so essential here.

For a finale Chopin gives us no triumphant paean, no resounding hymn of faith and hope. As Liszt – quoted by Rubinstein and others – once said: 'after the desolation of death, only the night winds whispering over churchyard graves'. To Schumann the finale seemed 'more like a joke than a piece of music … yet we must confess that even from this joyless, unmelodious movement an original, a terrible mind breathes forth.'[114] One can understand that after the profound funeral march this amorphous patter would seem almost an impiety to the German romantic outlook, yet it would be true to the nature of Polish romanticism, its irony and self-mockery, to pass abruptly from a genuine outburst of sorrow to a sinister epigram or riddle. Chopin himself says of the finale that 'the left hand *unisono* with the right hand are gossiping after the March.'[115]

Liszt used to play the whole movement in a breathless *pianissimo*, except for one big *crescendo* and *diminuendo* from bars 13–16 inclusive (as reproduced in the Klindworth edition), and for the sudden thunder of the final tonic chord. One should use the *una corda* pedal throughout, without any sustaining pedal, and the right hand should dominate slightly over the left. Above all the player should aim at securing an uncanny, spectral effect. Then only will the finale make a telling end to the sonata as a whole.

---

[114] Robert Schumann, *Music and Musicians*, 2nd Series, p. 280.

[115] See James Huneker's introduction to the American edition of Karol Mikuli's Chopin Sonatas.

FRANZ LISZT (1811-1886)

BUST BY MAX KLINGER (1857-1920), 1904
UNIVERSITY OF MUSIC AND THEATRE 'FÉLIX MENDELSSOHN BARTHOLDY' LEIPZIG

LISZT – VALSE-IMPROMPTU IN A FLAT

PAINTING BY HARRY CLARKE (1889-1931)

Created after a Franz Liszt piano recital given by
Tilly Fleischmann in the Abbey Theatre, Dublin in 1923

CHAPTER TWENTY

LISZT

Liszt may be regarded as the founder of modern piano-playing. He extended the range of the instrument's possibilities by inventing new methods of laying out scale passages, arpeggios, broken chords, octave passages and trills, by extending the range of colour procurable by the sustaining pedal, and by using to the full both the extreme depths as well as the extreme heights of the instrument, thereby giving it an orchestral sonority – in fact his inventiveness has since hardly been excelled. Less original, less intensely personal than Schumann or Chopin, his music is more brilliantly effective than theirs; yet it has never attained the popularity which might have been expected, since, among other reasons, it is not easily playable by amateurs, while a fair proportion of the music of any of the other romantic composers makes comparatively small demands on the pianist's technique. There are relatively few works of Liszt (the *Consolations* and some of the *Harmonies poétiques et religieuses* among the exceptions) which do not involve difficult passage work of one kind or another, so that only pianists of professional standard are really competent to attempt his music.

More important still, re-creative ability is needed for its interpretation, since the style is often impressionistic and the structure sketchy, so that the player must be able to piece the various sections together, moulding their outlines so as to give an impression of unity and cohesion. This is probably what Liszt meant when he remarked once to Kellermann that few people could either play or understand his music. Instead of striving to make a continuous line of thought emerge from amidst the oratorical style of argument pianists usually tend to dwell on the asides and interpolations, making the most out of the technical display which those afford. As a result not only is the structure of the whole work impaired, but the *coloratura*, which is meant to serve as an impressionist commentary on the main trend of the music, loses its poetic quality, and is turned into a jingle of meaningless sound or an empty display of jugglery. The once fashionable criticism that Liszt's music is a thing of 'trills, scales and cadenzas' (as a Dublin critic once wrote in connection with a Liszt recital I gave at the Abbey Theatre[116]) may sometimes apply to the transcriptions and pot-pourris, though even here Liszt served a useful purpose in imparting to the piano such powers of delivery as commanded attention even with the largest and most heterogeneous audience. But in his original music, however externalised the idiom may often be, however calculated to achieve a maximum effect in terms of colour and pattern sequence, the display is never cheap or tawdry, for almost always an imaginative quality, an indefinable poetic essence underlies the passage work, raising it to a level consistent with the rest of the context.

As the greater part of Liszt's output is programme music the lore which has become associated with some of the works is almost essential for their interpretation. Again there are traditional emendations and alterations, for when Liszt played his own compositions to his pupils he frequently improved on the published versions. Stavenhagen, who often turned over for Liszt on

---

[116] Tilly Fleischmann's Abbey Theatre Liszt recital was given on 21 Nov 1923; she played *Ballade* in B minor, *Valse impromptu* in A flat, *Nocturne No.3* in A flat, *Two Legends, Two Concert Studies, Rhapsodie Hongroise* No. 2.

such occasions, told us that he once plucked up courage to point out to Liszt that he was not playing a passage as he himself had written it. The work in question happened to be the *Paganini Study* in E major. Liszt looked at the passage closely, then turning to Stavenhagen with a mischievous smile he asked him whether he liked the improvised version better. Stavenhagen confessed that he did, and Liszt suggested to him that he should make a note of the alteration and hand it down.

Unfortunately neither Stavenhagen nor Kellermann seem to have left any detailed records of Liszt's teaching, and in the pages which follow I can only attempt to recall some of the chief points which were impressed upon me by one or other of them in the course of studying Liszt's compositions.

GROSSE PAGANINI-ETÜDEN, BOOK II: *ETÜDE NO. 5* IN E MAJOR

Of the various violin studies by Paganini which Liszt arranged with such masterly ingenuity for the piano the fifth in E major, known as 'La Chasse', is one of the most attractive. In present-day editions the two directions *imitando il flauto* for the beginning and *imitando il corno* for bars 9–16 are often omitted, for no apparent reason, for they indicate graphically the effect intended by the composer.

According to Stavenhagen, in playing this study Liszt used to make the following deviations from the published version. Of the first two four-bar phrases, which imitate the strains of two flutes, he played the first phrase *p*, and the second phrase *pp*, as an echo of the first. In the third phrase, which changes to two answering horns, he played bars 9–10 *forte*, and bars 11–12 *piano*. Throughout the opening section, and again on its recurrence in bars 53–68, the semiquavers should be played *portamento* (i.e. half-*staccato*) with sustaining pedal on the quavers only. All semiquaver chords up to bar 16 should be taken by the right hand, all quaver chords by the left hand.

From bars 37–40 and again from bars 45–48 Liszt arpeggioed the chords in the right hand, and played them *staccato* and *pp*, with *una corda* pedal and without sustaining pedal, thereby obtaining a soft *pizzicato*-like effect. At bar 42 he used to get an amusing result by playing the octaves in the left hand *subito forte* and *marcato*, and treating the corresponding notes in bar 44 in like manner. From bars 49–52 the pedal should be sustained for each crotchet beat, and a big *crescendo* made to bar 52.

At bar 68, where a new theme appears in octaves in both hands, this should be taken broadly and in free tempo, and the first glissando played *pp*, with the sustaining pedal held for the duration of the glissando up to the last three hemidemisemiquavers. The first sixth of this and of the subsequent glissandos should always be accented. Stavenhagen used to insist that the glissandos should not be played too quickly, and added that when Liszt played them they sounded *perlenartig*, like pearly scale-passages. (For glissando-playing see p. 17 above.) The second glissando should be played *pp*, but the third and fourth *p*, without the *una corda* pedal.

From bars 77–84 and again from bars 93–106 the left hand should lie under, not over the right hand. For the demisemiquaver groups in the right hand it is simpler to use fingers 5–1 as against the fingering 4–2 usually prescribed, except where the diminished fifth occurs in bars 81 and 83, where the fingering 4–2 is preferable.

The following is the traditional pedalling for the section commencing at bar 93:

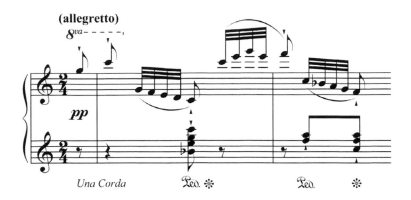

Ex. 269: Liszt *Grandes études de Paganini*, No. 5 in E, bars 93–94

(Release *una corda* pedal before up-beat to bar 99.)

Here is the traditional pedalling for the section commencing at bar 99:

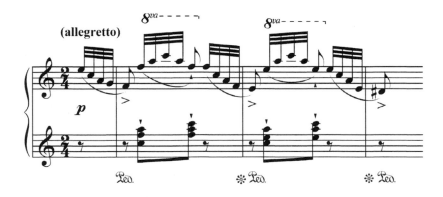

Ex. 270: Liszt *Grandes études de Paganini*, No. 5 in E, bars 99–101

The accentuation and retention of the first quaver of each bar with ever-increasing tone enriches this section of the study appreciably, yet such a method of playing the passage belongs to a tradition which is now apparently lost.

From bar 99 on the tone should gradually increase, reaching to *forte* at bar 106. Instead of the *crescendo* as printed from bars 106–108, however, it is customary to make a *diminuendo* to *pp* at bars 108–109. No sustaining pedal, only *una corda* pedal, should be used for these two bars, but the arpeggio passage in bar 110, rising *crescendo* to the start of bar 111, should be pedalled.

Again, no pedal should be used from bars 112–119 (*un poco animato*). Here the speed is so much faster that the *portamento* previously adopted in the right hand is unobtainable, but *staccato* should be secured in the left hand. Bars 114–115 were emended as follows by Stavenhagen in accordance with Liszt's own practice (the emendation was corroborated by Kellermann):

(un poco animato)

instead of

Ex. 271: Liszt *Grandes études de Paganini,* No. 5 in E, two versions of bars 114–115

After the final *diminuendo* to *ppp* on the first chord of the last bar, a pause is essential before the two *forte* chords are played – to rouse the hearer from his dreams.

VALSE-IMPROMPTU

Kellermann used to tell the following story of the origin of the *Valse-Impromptu.* On one occasion Liszt attended a festive ball in Berlin. Feeling weary and depressed he slipped away from the ball-room, wandered down a corridor into a conservatory, and hidden by ferns and shrubs sat alone, listening to the distant voices and the hum of the merry throng. Suddenly a strain of music reached his ears, a familiar theme which took him back to his boyhood days, to a certain night when he had danced with a golden-haired girl and told her of his love, and then – how she had laughed and mocked at him. The echo of her laughter came back clearly after all those years. Liszt left unobserved, went to his rooms, and wrote the *Waltz-Impromptu.*

The cynic may think such a story serves no purpose, but a knowledge of it would at least serve as a preventative to pianists who have no particular insight into the composer's intentions from playing the introduction *con bravura* – and with how many pianists is this the case! The *Impromptu* should be begun *pp* and with *una corda* pedal, so as to suggest the first, faint awakening of a memory, while the *coloratura* passage of bar 8 should descend from above like a delicate ripple of laughter.

The waltz itself, like the girl of the anecdote, is gay and coquettish. Where the theme commences at bar 14 (*sempre scherzando*) Liszt used to make a little break before the second beat and accent the latter, proceeding similarly at bars 18, 22 and 26, but not at any further point until the recapitulation in bar 140. This break should not be exaggerated, as it sometimes is. The whole section should be played as lightly and daintily as possible, with *una corda* pedal for the first eight bars, after which the theme should be played *p* up to bar 26, where *una corda* pedal should be used again. The next three bars (30–32) should be given rich *mf* tone, with a reduction to *pp* from bars 33–37, after which a *crescendo* should be made to bar 39, which should be played *mf*. Bars 35 and 36 should taper off very slightly, both in tone and pace.

Where the rhythm in the right hand changes to a 2/4 pattern against normal rhythm in the left hand, i.e. from bars 49 to 64, an appreciably quicker tempo should be taken. In bars 65–66 and 75–76 the quavers should not only be played *rinforzando* but *largamente*, and at bars 67 and 77 respectively the full tempo should be resumed. This quickening of the tempo applies to the corresponding section later on. In bars 69–72 the first quaver of each bar in the right hand should be accented and retained with the pedal, thus securing an inner melodic line.

If the first section of the *Waltz-Impromptu* is uniformly light-hearted, like the coquette of the anecdote, the trio which commences at bar 86 (*espressivo*) is earnest, pleading, passionate – as if in the midst of their dance her young admirer were expressing his devotion.

The chords in the left hand on the third beats of bars 86–90 should be played as a joint *arpeggiata* with the right hand, and this procedure should be observed on the repetition of the same passage later. Again, the tenor line in bars 96–101 should be brought out softly but clearly against the melody in the right hand, a procedure which is even still more desirable for the recurrence later on at *Tempo primo*. The section beginning at bar 117 should be played more slowly and with great feeling, but after the *poco ritardando* and the *fermata* of bar 124 the answer seems to be a merry quip, and a ripple of laughter again to bar 129. The pensive, insistent outline of bars 130–136 is answered by a gay cascade of notes, and the waltz begins anew.

The B major section after the second appearance of the trio is the climax of the waltz, and should be played with great passion. Once again there occurs the pleading of the trio, which persists this time when the waltz theme reappears (ninth bar of *Tempo primo*) so that its insistent note becomes fused into the elusive magic of the waltz. All this occurs above a prolonged tonic pedal; a brief coda, commencing after the two pause bars, brings the waltz to an end. The last three *pp* chords should be separated by quite appreciable pauses.

(For the fingering of the last bar see p. 33 above).

LIEBESTRÄUME – NOCTURNE NO. 3

The sickly uses to which the third of the *Liebesträume* has been put in recent years make it imperative to point out that this *Nocturne* in A flat is not essentially or even primarily erotic, as is commonly supposed. 'Dream of Love' can have but one connotation for the thousands of souls who have heard this piece performed by every conceivable combination, and in terms of every shade and variety of sentimentalism. Yet the poem on which the nocturne is based – the three *Liebesträume* were originally written as songs – throws a different light on the real nature of the music and its interpretation. The poem is by Freiligrath, one of Germany's poets of freedom in the early nineteenth century, and invokes man to love, not in the narrow, but in the broadest sense of the word – a love which is all-embracing, which reveals itself in ties of blood, in charity, in a warm deep feeling for all mankind. So well understood is this in Germany that I have heard the poem recited by a young priest after the ceremony of his ordination. The following are the lines from the poem which are inscribed on the original edition:

226

Gedicht von F. Freiligrath:

O Lieb'

O lieb! o lieb so lang du lieben kannst, so lang du lieben magst.
Die Stunde kommt, wo du an Gräbern stehst und klagst
Und sorge, dass dein Herze glüht, und Liebe hegt und Liebe trägt,
So lang ihm noch ein ander Herz in Liebe warm entgegenschlägt.
Und wer dir seine Brust erschliesst, o thu' ihm was du kannst zu lieb,
Und mach' ihm jede Stunde froh, und mach' ihm keine Stunde trüb!
Und hüte deine Zunge wohl; bald ist ein hartes Wort entfloh'n.
O Gott – es war nicht bös gemeint –
Der Andre aber geht und weint.[117]

It is then quite false to limit the application of this *Nocturne* to an erotic concept; both words and music are intended to suggest the universal. Nor is it without significance that an innate warm-heartedness, generosity and a capacity for brother-love were among Liszt's foremost characteristics.

The *Nocturne* should be played with sincerity and depth of feeling, but also with the utmost restraint, and without the insipid exaggerated *rubato* which has come to be associated with its performance. At the same time a virile climax must be achieved in the middle section. Only in this way can the high-minded concept which lies behind the *Nocturne* be properly realised.

Three essentials should be aimed at, namely, a singing melody, a singing bass and a consistently softer accompaniment. The three middle C's in the first two bars are usually played with the same amount of tone. No artistic singer would sing three notes in such a context at the same level. Yet pianists who have no feeling for gradations of tone on the piano usually thump out these C's. The opening theme should be begun *pp* (with *una corda* pedal as far as the recurrence of the theme in bar 7) and each successive C should gain slightly in intensity, the climax of tone being reached on the first C of bar 4, with a slight *rubato* in the latter part of the previous bar. A marked rise and fall of tone occurs in bar 5, with *rubato* in the second half of the bar. From bars 7–12 the same procedure should be adopted, this time at a higher tone level. After a *crescendo* and *diminuendo* in bar 9, however, it is most effective to play the note F of bar 10 *subito pp* and as tenderly as possible. The E major chord of bar 18 might again be played *subito pp*, preceded by a slight *rubato* and followed by a gradual increase in tone. The second half of bar 20 should again be begun *pp*, after which there should be a mounting urgency and intensity up to the beginning of bar 23. The F flat in this bar should be played with a full *f*, and each successive descending note played with a lesser degree of tone and with a *ritardando* until the G natural of bar 24 is reached in *pp*. The arpeggio lead-in to the cadenza should be begun *p* and taken broadly with a *crescendo* to the F flat of bar 25. This note should be held appreciably, and released on to a soft E flat. The cadenza should be played *pp*, with *una corda* pedal, and with a slight *accelerando* and *crescendo* to its apex. This cadenza, a dreamy, delicate maze of sound introducing the middle section, is usually seized upon as an opportunity for showing technical dexterity, and rattled off so that it loses all connection with its context. It should pass virtually unnoticed like a quiet and

[117] Literal translation of Freiligrath's poem 'O Love': O love as long as e'er you can, as long as e'er you may, /The hour will come when by a tomb you stand and mourn. /Then see to it that your heart still glows and nurtures love, /As long as any other heart still beats in answering affection. /Whoever offers you his all, return your utmost for his sake, /And make his every hour a joy, and give no cause for grief, /And guard your tongue! An angry word can soon escape –/Ah me! It was not meant – /But the other, wounded, leaves and weeps.

unobtrusive improvisation interpolated into the main argument, before the reappearance of the theme in B major.

In all editions the B major section commencing at bar 26 is marked *Più animato con passione*. The observation of this marking results in an entirely false and unconvincing presentation of the theme at this particular juncture. After the delicate cadenza it is inconceivable that the theme should start *con passione*; its thread should be taken up again in a tender, dreamy vein, with use of *una corda* pedal, and only from the seventh bar (i.e. bar 33), in approaching the C major section, can the playing become *più animato* and *con passione*. Stavenhagen and other pianists in the Liszt tradition used to play the B major section in this way, and with the following subtle use of dynamic and rhythmic nuance:

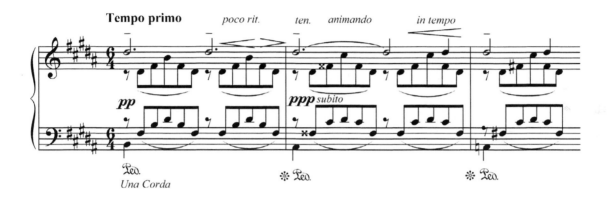

Ex. 272: Liszt *Liebesträume, Nocturne No. 3* in A flat, bars 26–28

The upbeat at the end of bar 31 in the right hand should be a crotchet, not a quaver. There could be no justification for curtailing the rhythmic value of this significant progression involving the interval of the sixth, which is used so extensively throughout the *Nocturne*, and which merely sounds cheap when curtailed. Bars 34–37 should be played broadly, with *allargando* towards the end of bar 36.

It has always been a tradition to begin *mf* at bar 41 and to hold the minims slightly, prolonging their tone, and then to play the quavers of the accompaniment softer and more quickly – in short, *rubato* within each half bar. Again, at bar 46 there should be a slight *ritardando* leading into bar 47, which should begin at a somewhat reduced tone level, otherwise it is not possible to secure a sufficient *rinforzando* in the following bars, which increase in tone until the climax is reached at bar 58. In the preceding bar there should be a slight *rubato*, and the quavers of bar 58 should be begun somewhat more slowly, with a gradual acceleration into the cadenza. The notes of the cadenza (bars 59–60) should be practised in groups of twelve, but in performance they should cascade down smoothly without any accents (for fingering see pp. 31-2). Towards the end of the passage there should be a *diminuendo* to *ppp* and an appreciable *ritardando*, with the pedal sustained for each pair of notes in the last two groups.

The last section, *Tempo primo*, should be played as softly and tenderly as possible, with *una corda* pedal, and with the same dynamic scheme as suggested at the outset. For bar 7, counting from *Tempo primo*, the *una corda* pedal should be released (though the tone should still be kept very soft) and depressed again at bar 8, where the harmonic change calls for added intensity, justifying the use of *rubato* and a reduction of tone to *ppp*. From bar 9 on the melody should sing out again. The tenths which occur in the left hand from bars 9–14 should all be arpeggioed, and their top notes (A natural, G flat, F, F flat, E flat, D, D flat) should be brought out softly but distinctly as a descending line. In bar 15 the pedal should be held for the entire bar so that the low E flat may be retained in the bass, and the whole progression enriched. Bar 17 should be played *pp*, and bar 19 *ppp*, with *una corda* pedal. The latter should be released at bar 21, where the A major chord should sound rich, though soft. In the second half of bar 23 a *crescendo* should be made, with the tenor line prominent and more accent on the G natural than on the E flat in bar 24. From here a *diminuendo* and *ritardando* should be made to the final chord, with the assistance of the *una corda* pedal from the latter part of bar 24. Low A flat is traditionally added to the final chord, with fingering as follows:

Ex. 273: Liszt *Liebesträume, Nocturne No. 3*, bar 85

TWO CONCERT STUDIES

NO. 1. *WALDESRAUSCHEN* (FOREST MURMURINGS)

In this study Liszt shows his ability to capture nature's moods in terms of sensitive tone-painting. We hear the wind rising softly, caressing the leaves as it moves through the forest. The murmuring sounds swell, die away again, then grow stronger and louder until the wind shakes the branches of the mightiest trees and spreads havoc all around. Next it takes to careering wildly, whistling through the leaves; only to die away again at the end to the merest whisper. This in is brief the plan of *Waldesrauschen*. Structurally the study is interesting in that the texture is almost entirely spun from the opening melodic phrase.

One frequently hears the basic figure of accompaniment in this study stressed as follows:

Ex. 274: Liszt *Zwei Konzert-Etüden*, No. 1, *Waldesrauschen*, right hand part, bar 1

This results in the shifting of the metrical accent by half a beat and damages the rhythmic structure. Liszt himself was very particular that the stress should be laid on the first note of each group of six. Every nuance of colour at the pianist's disposal should be utilised to make this opening figure truly *dolcissimo* – the softest zephyr's breath, not a mechanical jingling – while later the beating of the storm-wind should be portrayed with the utmost power and passion.

There is a tradition with regard to the playing of the opening theme in the left hand. Towards the end of bars 3 and 7, and for the cadence of bar 5, a nuance should be effected consisting partly of *rubato* – but not actually a *ritardando* – partly of *diminuendo*, so as to make the contour of the melody more flexible. From bar 8 on there is a continuous though gradual *crescendo*, and an *accelerando* from bars 9–11. At the end of the latter bar a slight *rallentando* and *diminuendo* should be made, and bar 12 then started with rich *mf* tone and more emphasis.

According to Kellermann, Liszt always commenced the theme at bar 15 *pp* and started the corresponding phrase at bar 19 *p*. Bars 22–24 are difficult to play if the quavers in the left hand are held, as they should be, so as to sing out as a *legato* counter-melody against the melody proper in the right hand. It is both careless and ineffective to release the quavers as if they were semiquavers, and to rely on the pedal to sustain them. A *ritardando* should be made on the last two beats of bar 28 (*più rinforzando*) before the delicate *legerissimo*. In bar 33 the nuance again arises already referred to in connection with bars 3–7.

In order to secure clear phrasing in the left-hand part of bars 34 and 35 (*delicatamente*), the second last quaver of each bar should be played *staccato*, in contrast to bar 36 where the quaver G is accented and all the notes played *legato*. At the section marked *tre corde poco a poco più agitato* (bar 45) one should begin *pp*, using the *una corda* pedal for the first two bars, and then work up gradually to the climax of bar 55 (*fff*). In bars 55–58 the chords marked *ten.* in the left hand must be slightly prolonged so that the first half of the bar is somewhat broader, while the second half is played in strict time. In the second half of bar 60 it is wiser to take the top notes of the octaves with the right hand to secure more tone. In bar 70 there should be a slight *allargando* to prepare for the entry of the *stringendo molto* section. The alternative right-hand version printed for this section (bars 71–78) in older editions should of course be disregarded, since it is devised for six-octave pianos on which the top notes of the original version would have been unavailable. Throughout this section the lower line of quavers in the left hand should be brought out forcibly, to secure an adequate foundation for the octave-melody and syncopated chords.

At bar 81 a *subito piano* is necessary in order to secure an adequate *crescendo* to bar 83, which should begin *f* and gradually diminish to *p* at bar 86. The fingering 4–2 is usually prescribed for the left hand in bars 83–85, but it is simpler to use 3–1 throughout. The nuance already referred to arises again in the second half of bars 89 and 91. To secure the maximum delicacy and lightness it is safer to divide each of the two last chords between both hands.

No. 2. *Gnomenreigen* (Dance of the Gnomes)

Out of the novel pointillism of this study there emerges that impish, fantastic streak so characteristic of Liszt, and which may be seen on a grander scale in the 'Mephisto' section of his *Faust Symphony*. Here we have gnomes at play, frisking and capering gaily, even madly, with the lightest of steps. The fun reaches its climax with a whirl of speed and excitement which never, however, exceeds goblin strength.

Kellermann told us of some details in which Liszt's playing differed from the published edition. At the end of the four-bar introduction Liszt used to make a pause on the fourth beat (after the last quaver in the left hand, and before the up-beat) as if to suggest that the gnomes were taking a look-round before beginning the dance. He paused again at the end of the eighth bar, this time after the last quaver, so that the principal theme starts minus the up-beat, thus adding to the humour of the piece. No sustaining pedal should be taken from the fifth to the twelfth bar as marked in all editions, only *una corda* pedal. Most pianists use the sustaining pedal here, so that chords are formed instead of the light *staccato* effect of the quavers preceded by *acciaccaturas*, thus robbing the dance of its nimble, puckish grace. No player conversant with the Liszt tradition would use the sustaining pedal here. This should be used only from bar 13 onwards. The demisemiquavers of bar 20 (after the *rinforzando*) should suddenly be taken *pp* and a shade slower, with a *ritardando* lead-in to the *Ringelreihe* or round-dance section (*un poco più animato*) as Liszt used to call it. For the first four bars of this section *una corda* pedal should be used, and a gradual *crescendo* then made for eight bars to the *rinforzando velocissimo* of bar 33, at which point all the gnomes seem to scatter. Here one pedal should be taken for all three bars (bars 33– 35).

From bars 77–96 (solo dance of a single gnome!) no sustaining pedal and only the *una corda* pedal should be used. Kellermann told us that Liszt used to take this section slightly slower at first to make it sound more droll and puckish, accelerating from bar 85 on. From bars 97–103 one should pedal twice in the bar, and make a slight *ritardando* in bar 102 before the recurrence of the main theme (here all the gnomes seem to join in the dance again).

Although the section marked *vivacissimo*, commencing at bar 121, is the climax of the dance and marked *sempre ff*, it would be inartistic to keep this tone-level throughout. Bars 125, 127 and 131 should be begun at a lower level with an immediate *crescendo* to *ff*. Liszt used to get a magical effect in the section marked *il più presto possibile e ff* by playing the start of bars 134 and 136 suddenly *pp*, with a *crescendo* into the following bar in each case. The sustaining pedal should be held from bars 137–141 (cf. bars 33–35) to add to the sense of general confusion of imps scampering away in all directions.

At bar 143 Liszt used to take a quicker tempo, and a still quicker tempo from bar 157 to bar 162. For the *legato* quavers commencing in the latter half of bar 162 he reduced the tempo somewhat and then accelerated again to the end. He used to pause slightly before playing the last chord, which was so light as to be almost inaudible – a tip … hush … gone.

BALLADE NO. 2 IN B MINOR

The second *Ballade* is one of Liszt's major works for the piano. The programme of the *Ballades* is left to the hearer's imagination, but that Liszt had a definite programme of his own in mind is proved by a remark which he once made to Kellermann. At the beginning of the section marked *dolce placido* (bar 234) Liszt observed: 'Here the knight and his lady cross the river hand in hand.' The whole *Ballade* may then be conceived as a romantic tale, and some of the details readily suggest themselves. The delicate *Allegretto* commencing bar 24 might represent the lady; the boldly rhythmical *Allegro deciso* (commencing bar 70) the call to arms as the knight goes forth to battle on her behalf; the *cantando* theme (bar 135) his pleading with her; while the opening theme of the *Ballade*, sinister and gloomy on its first appearance, increasingly dramatic on its various recurrences, triumphant at last (*grandioso* – bar 284) seems to symbolise the whole love story itself and its development through difficulties and dangers until the knight and his lady have crossed the river of tribulation already referred to, and have set out together into a visionary land to fulfil their destiny.

In this *Ballade* there are opportunities for some striking pedal effects, though Liszt only indicates the pedalling himself at a few points. According to Kellermann he used to pedal twice in the bar in the opening section, accentuating the first note of each group:

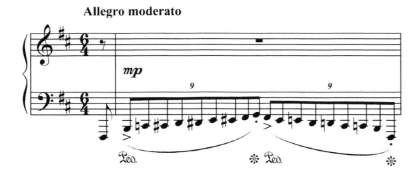

Ex. 275: Liszt *Ballade No. 2* in B minor, bar 1

With accurate pedalling each accented note can be caught and retained, so that tonic and dominant will sound out clearly. Usually this left-hand accompaniment is played as an unrelieved rumble, or mechanically as a five-finger exercise; with the method given above the effect is far more suggestive and colourful, conveying an impression of water, night and gloom.

In several details Liszt's playing of the *Ballade* used to differ from the printed edition. For instance Kellermann used to say that for the *fff* section commencing at bar 207, where minims are sustained at the beginning of six successive bars, instead of a single note in the left hand he would play octaves in both hands (except of course for the low G, which is unavailable), thereby greatly intensifying the tone:

Ex. 276: Liszt *Ballade No. 2* in B minor, bass clef, bars 207–208

In bars 213 and 214 he would accentuate as follows, and retain the interlocked octaves in the left hand two beats after their discontinuance as printed:

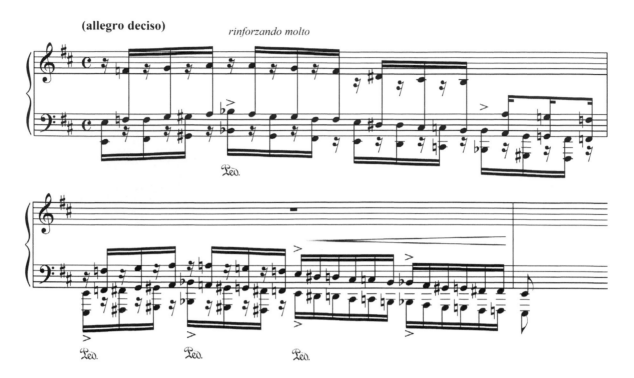

Ex. 277: Liszt *Ballade No. 2* in B minor, bars 213–215

At bar 215 he would play the final octave in the left hand with great force and then retain it with the pedal for six bars, up to the fourth beat of bar 220. By half-pedalling at the beginning of bar 218 the maze of sound is sufficiently thinned down to allow the melody to sing out clearly, while the low octave is still audible. After bar 219 the octave is silently depressed again by the left hand and the pedal released, after which the pedal is again depressed to hold the octave beneath the first three beats of bar 220:

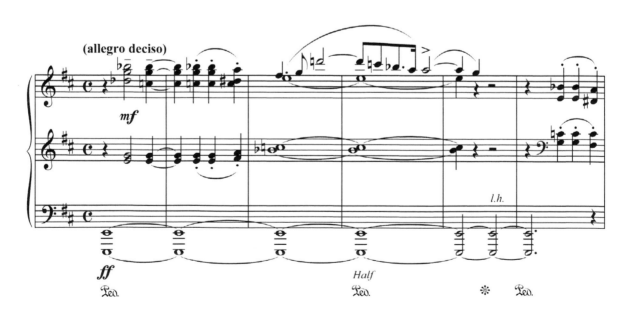

Ex. 278: Liszt *Ballade No. 2* in B minor, bars 215–220

This retention of the low octave into the sixth bar acts as a deep and effective sound-bridge between the two phrases, and creates a tense atmosphere.

At bar 226 (*appassionata* section) the first chord in the right hand should be arpeggioed, as in the preceding and following bars. In bar 230 Liszt used to play the octave instead of the single F sharp in the left hand as printed, and after the third beat depress it silently again and sustain it with the left hand until the second group of bar 232, meanwhile changing the pedal for every group in bars 231–232. This gives a rich substratum of colour to the cascade of notes in the right hand as they ripple down from above:

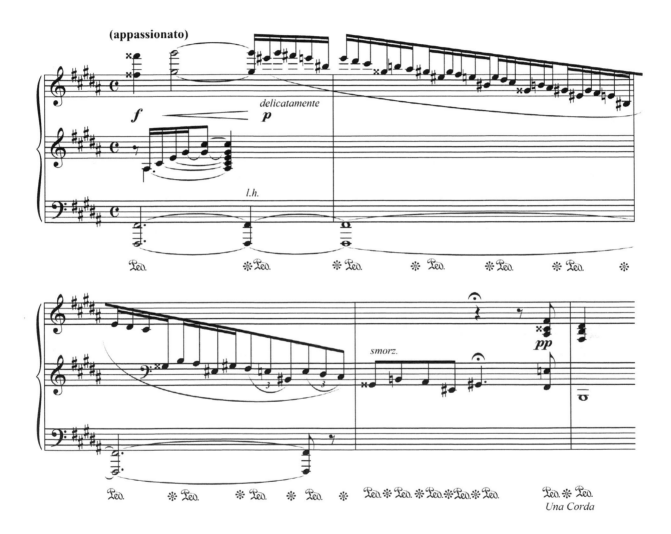

Ex. 279: Liszt *Ballade No. 2* in B minor, bars 230–234

In bar 234 (*dolce placido*) the left hand interchanges with the right hand, and this interchange should continue in bar 235, but with the proviso that each hand may pass under as well as over the other hand, where this is more advantageous. On playing the *Ballade* for Kellermann on one occasion, when I came to this passage and kept passing my right hand above the left with the pawing movement which this entails, Kellermann called out: 'Is this the knight and his lady crossing the river? It sound more like a poodle paddling across!' And it is true that by keeping the relative position of the hands unchanged as far as possible, all disturbing and unnecessary movement is avoided. The following illustration will make this clear, together with the pedalling necessary to ensure both *legato* playing and soft, rich colour:

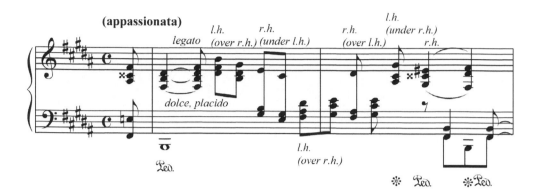

Ex. 280: Liszt *Ballade No. 2* in B minor, bars 234–235

In bars 238–240, the left hand should still interchange with the right as follows:

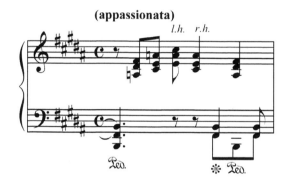

Ex. 281: Liszt *Ballade No. 2* in B minor, bar 238

A *ritardando* is essential towards the end of bars 241 and 249, though not indicated in any edition. In bars 242–3 the right hand, in alternating with the left, should be kept under the left hand throughout. An interesting instance of *rubato* occurs in the section covering bars 234–253, where for the sake of rhythmic balance it is necessary to play the quaver figure in the left hand, at the end of the bars in which it occurs, at a somewhat slower speed, so that the persistent figure in the bass offsets the lighter movement of the floating chords above.

In bar 254 (*Allegro moderato*) Liszt used to begin *pp*, with *una corda* pedal to the end of bar 257. From bar 262–265 the melody should be played *mf* with the accompaniment *pp*. Again bars 269–274 (*un poco più mosso*) should be played *pp*, with a gradual *crescendo* from this point onwards.

The grace-notes in bars 270, 271, 274, 275 are but conventionally written as such, and should actually be played as groups of three semiquavers (as in bar 225) against two in the left hand. A cheap effect is produced by crowding these notes as a group-*acciaccatura* above the topmost note of the accompanying pattern in the left hand. The first chord in the right hand of bars 273 and 274 should be arpeggioed. From bars 284–289 (*grandioso*) the last octave after the semiquaver groups in each bar should be taken over by the left hand and forcibly accented, thus securing maximum tone while releasing the right hand for the coming chords.

The upper alternative version given from bars 292–299 is invariably played, being far more effective than the conventional chord repetitions of the lower version. For this great point of climax the theme should be played *fff* while the scale-passages are played lightly.

Reference has been made above (see p. 76) to a point of timing in bars 310–311. *Legato* pedalling should be employed for the transition from one melody note to the other in the two last bars, so that the pedal is lifted precisely at the point at which the final F sharp begins to sound, and is then depressed again.

ANNEES DE PELERINAGE *III*, NO. 4: *LES JEUX D'EAU DE LA VILLA D'ESTE* (THE FOUNTAINS OF THE VILLA D'ESTE)

This work belongs to the third set of *Années de pèlerinage*, a collection of twenty-eight piano pieces which form a musical diary of the outstanding impressions made on Liszt during his wanderings over a long period in Switzerland and Italy. In 1869 Cardinal Hohenlohe placed the Villa d'Este with its gardens, reputed to be amongst the most beautiful in Europe, at Liszt's disposal. Some three centuries before, Palestrina had conducted performances in this villa as music master to Cardinal Ippolito d'Este, the wealthy prince who had built the villa and maintained there a private orchestra and choir. Just as Palestrina must have been inspired by the beauties of the place, and probably wrote there some of his last madrigals, so too Liszt was moved to write three pieces of music descriptive of the gardens, the two *Aux cyprès de la Villa d'Este*, and *Les jeux d'eau de la Villa d'Este*, which sets out to capture the shimmering, rhythmic movement of the gardens' innumerable fountains.

The introductory section of the latter work consists of sheer colour-weaving in the upper register of the piano, as if to suggest light breaking through the scintillating waters. Presently a motif based on the chord of F sharp major (bar 41) appears, followed by a limpid melody in the left hand which is then repeated and developed at some length. Later motif and melody reappear above an arpeggio accompaniment (D major section) and in a footnote, now usually omitted, Liszt quotes the fourteenth verse of the fourth chapter of the Gospel according to St. John: 'Sed aqua quam ego dabo ei, fiet in eo fons aquae salutis in vitam aeternam.' (But the water that I will give him shall become in him a fountain of water springing up into life everlasting). This conception of the fountain as a symbol of life, and of life-giving faith, is worked out in the emphatically resurgent passages which follow, until the main theme reappears, and the work ends with a delicate modulatory passage based on the motif alluded to.

Both the main theme and the motif seem to have some affinity with phrases from the antiphons for Vespers on the feast of Pentecost, as the following comparison will show:

Ex. 282a: Liszt *Années de pèlerinage, No. 4, Les jeux d'eau de la Villa d'Este*, main theme bars 48–52; motif theme bars 40–44

Ex. 282b: *Vespers for Pentecost*, 1st Antiphon, 5th Antiphon: final Alleluia
[*Liber Usualis* 884, 889]

In view of the texts of the fourth and fifth antiphons for this feast – 'Fontes, et omnia quae moventur in aquis, hymnum decite Deo, alleluia' [Let you fountains and all that move in the water sing a hymn to God] and 'Loquebantur variis linguis Apostoli magnalia Dei, alleluia' [the apostles spoke in different tongues of the great works of God] – it seems unlikely that the resemblance could be a mere coincidence, and Liszt probably borrowed the Gregorian phrases to link the liturgical ideology with that of Pentecost; the play of the waters symbolising the spreading of the light of the Word.

Liszt liked to think of himself as the modern Palestrina, an epithet bestowed on him on one occasion by Pope Pius IX, and however inapplicable the epithet may seem, it is true that in his last period he devoted himself chiefly to religious music with the ambition of revitalising such music with his own peculiar style. And in such works as *Les jeux d'eau* and the *Légendes* he was the first composer of distinction to interpret religious subjects in terms of major works for the piano.

The above considerations should be sufficient warning to pianists who make a mere technical exercise out of *Les jeux d'eau de la Villa d'Este*, for not only are delicacy and sensitiveness required to portray the evanescent beauty of the waters, but fervour is also needed to reveal the spiritual background which underlies the superficial attractiveness of the music.

In the opening passages, which should be played with *una corda* pedal to bar 6, the accent should be on the *staccato* quavers which constitute the melody. (For Liszt's own pedalling of bars 15–31 see p. 89 above.) There should be a slight *ritardando* before bar 15 (*pp, leggierissimo non legato*). In bars 46–48 pianists usually fail to perceive the motif in the tremolo in the right hand, and it does in fact require some effort to make the notes of the motif stand out clearly while continuing the demisemiquaver tremolo. There should be an appreciable *ritardando* towards the end of bars 64, 68, 88 and 108. It would be well to pedal twice in bars 101–104, and to take the *una corda* pedal from bars 109–121, releasing it at the start of the latter bar and making a gradual *crescendo* to the *rinforzando* of bar 129. At bar 131 a *decrescendo* should begin, reaching *pianissimo* at bar 133.

Counting now from the D major section, bars 29 (*rinforzando*) to 31 should be played slower, with rich full tone and intense expression. The octave melody in the left hand in bar 39 should be begun *pp* with *una corda* pedal, but singing out clearly in spite of the softer tone level, the *una corda* pedal being only released at bar 46. Bar 47 should begin *p*, bar 51 *mf*, with a *crescendo* and *diminuendo* for each four-bar phrase. Again, from bar 55 (*poco a poco accelerando*) the *una corda* pedal should be used for four bars and then released, after which a gradual *crescendo* should be made to the climax in bar 98 (*ff brioso*).

LEGENDS

LEGEND NO. 1 – ST. FRANÇOIS D'ASSISE LA PREDICATION AUX OISEAUX (ST. FRANCIS PREACHING TO THE BIRDS)

This work is based on the following legend taken from the *Fioretti di St. Francesco*:

When St. Francis came to the country between Cannaio and Bevagno, preaching as he went, he saw myriads of birds filling the trees by the wayside and the fields beyond. St. Francis was astonished at this, and spoke to his disciples, saying: 'Wait for me here on the highway, whilst I go to preach to my brothers, the birds.' He went into the fields, and soon the birds that were perched on the trees came down to him, and each and all remained motionless before him as he spoke thus: 'You, my little brothers, ought to be deeply grateful to God, your creator, and praise and magnify His name always and in all places; for He has given you the power to fly whithersoever you please. He has given you warmth and light and has preserved your seed in Noah's ark, so that your race has not become extinct. You should be thankful too for the kingdom of the skies, which he has assigned to you. Again, you neither sow nor reap, and yet your heavenly Father feeds you and gives you the rivers and the springs to quench your thirst. He gives you the mountains and valleys as places of refuge, and the lofty trees whereon to build your nests; and though you neither spin nor sew, He clothes you and your children. Your creator loves you dearly, since He has done so much for you; beware, therefore, of the sin of ingratitude, my little brothers, and be ever zealous in singing God's praises.' At these words all the birds began to open their beaks and stretch forth their necks. Then they spread their wings and bent their heads in reverence, and so manifested by song and gesture that the holy man had brought them great joy. St. Francis was enraptured with them and wondered at their numbers, their beauty, their earnestness and their confiding air. When his sermon had come to a close, St. Francis made the sign of the cross over them, and all the birds sprang from the earth, soaring into the sky and giving utterance to the most exquisite song. They followed the sign which St. Francis had made, and ranging themselves in four flocks, one soared towards the rising, another towards the setting sun, a third towards the south and a fourth towards the north, winging their flight to a tune of wondrous melody.[118]

Liszt's tone poem follows the above narrative closely. After an opening section in which the chirping of the songsters is brilliantly reproduced in the treble of the instrument, St. Francis'

---

[118] Fra Ugolino da Monte Giorgio (attrib.), *Fioretti di San Francesco d'Assisi,* Chapter XVI, early 14th century.

sermon (bar 52–) takes shape in the form of a recitative which is at first interrupted by the cries of the birds. But gradually the chirping ceases (bar 68–) and all are silent (bar 71–). Then St. Francis solemnly tells them of the glory and greatness of God. The birds at first listen in awe, and then start to twitter quietly (bar 86–) to indicate their assent, while some glide around the saint (bar 89–). Their song has now become an integral part of the Saint's monologue; they understand his words and respond even when he speaks with the deepest weight and gravity.

After the prayer (bars 132–141) St. Francis adds a few final words and then blesses the birds, making the sign of the cross towards north, south, east and west, each stage being interrupted by renewed twitterings on the part of the birds, after which they soar into the sky and the sound of their song grows ever fainter in the distance.

Liszt's pedalling for the first four bars has already been given (see p. 88 above). In bars 3 and 7 the thirds on the first and third beats should also be played by the left hand. This ensures a lighter touch and a more even trill. Again in bars 13–16 all three notes of each *staccato* chord should be played by the left hand. In bars 18–30 (*dolce graziosamente*) the fingering 3 2 1 2 as marked in all editions might well be changed to 2 1 2 1, which gives a smoother and surer result.

Kellermann showed us a special way in which Liszt used to play the passage marked *un poco stringendo* commencing at the end of bar 45. He accented the last note of each group of eight demisemiquavers on the first and third beats, and sustained it with the pedal so as to get the line B–C sharp–C natural–B–A sharp–A natural, underneath. The A natural of bar 48 should be sustained by the pedal to the end of bar 50:

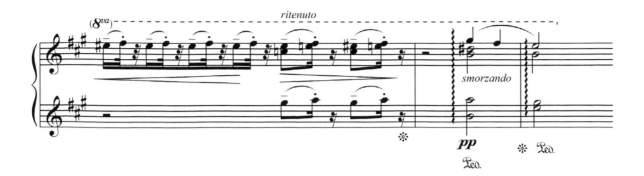

Ex. 283: Liszt *2 Légendes*, No. 1 *St François d'Assise: 'La prédication aux oiseaux*, bars 46–52

This considerably enhances the effect of the passage, while the pedalling imparts a rich haze of colour such as Liszt so frequently evokes, foreshadowing Debussy.

The sermon commencing at bar 52 should be begun *pp* with *una corda* pedal; with the start of each new phrase more tone should be given until a climax is reached at bar 65. The interpolated twittering of the birds, however, should each time be played *pp* with *una corda* pedal.

In bars 119 and 122 a slight *ritardando* should be made on the last three quavers (descending octaves in the left hand). Again in the fourth and third-last bars, instead of a tremolo in each hand the passage should be executed as a series of alternating chords between both hands which allows for a more even and delicate effect:

Ex. 284: Liszt *2 Légendes, No. 1* 'St François d'Assise: La prédication aux oiseaux', bar 156

LEGEND NO. 2 – ST. FRANÇOIS DE PAULE MARCHANT SUR LES FLOTS (ST. FRANCIS DE PAUL WALKING OVER THE WAVES)

The second legend concerns St Francis de Paul, Liszt's patron saint. In the Rozsavölgyi edition the origin of the work is given in detail. It appears that Princess zu Sayn-Wittgenstein showed Liszt a picture by a contemporary painter of religious subjects named Steinle,[119] depicting a miracle which St. Francis wrought in crossing the straits of Messina.[120] When the saint asked to be ferried across one stormy day the boatmen refused to take a person of such mean appearance on board; but he, undaunted, walked with firm step across the sea. In the picture St. Francis stands

[119] Eduard Jakob von Steinle, an Austrain painter, born 1810 in Vienna, died 1886 in Frankfurt am Main.

[120] According to Julius Kapp, drawings by Doré of St. Francis walking over the waves, and of St. Francis preaching to the birds, hung in the rooms which Liszt occupied in Pest in 1881, *Franz Liszt*, 2nd revised ed. (Berlin 1911), p. 272.

erect upon the seething waters which carry him to his goal by the power of faith, before which all natural laws give way. His mantle is spread beneath his feet; he raises one hand as if to command the elements, in the other he holds a burning coal, a symbol of that inner flame which kindles the disciples of Christ. His eyes are tranquilly fixed on the heavens where the motto of St. Francis, the divine word 'Caritas', shines in perpetual splendour.

The *Legend* opens with a theme which can be associated with St. Francis himself. Underneath this theme as it develops, the bass, depicting the surging waves, gradually grows louder and more menacing until their fury seems to shatter the very fabric of the music in an orgy of violence. The pinnacle of the storm is reached, and now St. Francis' theme resounds triumphantly (*Allegro maestoso e animato*), passing undaunted on its course above the turmoil – the sea has been safely crossed.

Then follows (*Lento*) a prayer of thanksgiving, in no vein of exultant joy, but humbly and deeply felt. For the coda the St. Francis theme now appears softly in the bass, rising in the final bars with ever greater majesty to the accompaniment of the surging waters. Few works move so steadily and clearly to a single great climax, and having reached it end with so complete a sense of fulfilment.

It may be well to note here that dynamics played a vital part in Liszt's performance both of his own and of other composers' works. Unfortunately, however, the dynamics which he used in performance do not appear with any fidelity in the published edition of his works, and players conversant with tradition make many changes from the printed score.

In *St. Francis de Paul*, for instance, each of the first two phrases should be begun with rich full tone and rounded off with a *diminuendo* (bars 2 and 5), while the *non troppo lento* should be begun *pp* and with *una corda* pedal. The latter should only be released at the upbeat to bar 10, which should be begun *p*, and depressed again for bars 16–20. From bar 24 (*legato*) the tempo should be very slightly slower, as if to suggest the quietly undulating movement of St. Francis' mantle on the waters – with *una corda* pedal from here until the end of bar 27. At bar 32 there should be a *subito pp*, with a gradual working up to *ff* at bar 36. Having played an *ff* chord at the beginning of bar 36, however, the demisemiquaver passage in the left hand should again be begun *pp* with *una corda* pedal, but continued with a *molto crescendo*, the *una corda* pedal being released on the third beat of the bar. From the second beat of bar 37 to the end of bar 41 the first note of each group of eight demisemiquavers should be accented. The dark, swirling sounds of bars 39–41 might be dealt with as follows:

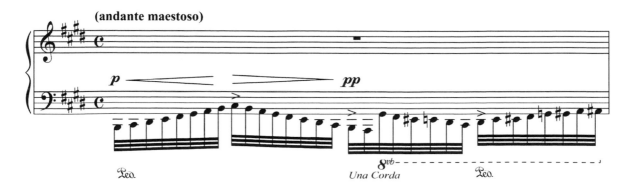

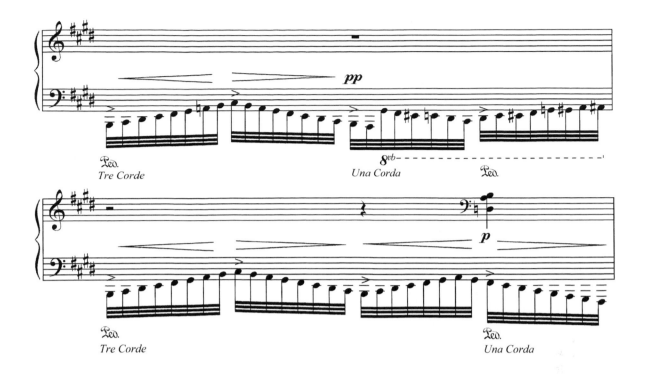

Ex. 285: Liszt *2 Légendes, No. 2 St François de Paule marchant sur les flots*, bars 39–41

Una corda pedal should be used from the end of bar 41 to 46 from which bar a gradual increase in tone should be made. In bar 52 the accented D sharp in the bass (third beat) should be taken by the thumb in the right hand and held for the beat, and a similar procedure should be adopted in bars 53, 58 and 59. From bar 64 the top note of each *arpeggiata* chord in the left hand should be emphasised and prolonged, i.e. played as a crotchet instead of a quaver.

The pairs of bars commencing with bar 64–65 seem to suggest the rearing of the waves to a peak-point, and breaking again. No pedal should be taken for the second and third chords in the left hand of bars 65, 67, 69 and 71 to give clarity to the peak points. From bar 72 the real fury of the waves begins to mount to a climax – the ineffective alternative version given here in every second bar (bars 72–78) is of course never played. From bar 79–84 the pedal should be depressed on each of the second, third and fourth beats of the bar, and released on the accented chord at the beginning of each ensuing bar.

In the section marked *Allegro maestoso e animato*, where St. Francis seems to walk triumphant and majestic above the waves, the theme should not be played *staccato*, but *legato* and broadly. Pianists usually take this section too fast, and when played *staccato* the theme sounds trivial and commonplace. From bar 113 the tempo and rhythmic intensity should gradually increase, as if a multitude of people on the shore were watching the approach of the saint with growing astonishment and excitement. This reaches its peak at the commencement of bar 127, after which the ascending octaves should be begun *pp*, with *una corda* pedal for two bars, so as to secure a mysterious and threatening effect. From here a continuous *crescendo* should be built up as far as bar 137.

The recitative (*Lento*), St. Francis' prayer of thanksgiving, should be begun *f*, without pedal on the arpeggioed chords but with a *diminuendo* in bars 3–4. The second phrase, starting at bar 5, should, however, be begun tenderly, with *una corda* pedal, but again without sustaining pedal on the arpeggioed chords. The third phrase, starting at bar 9, should be given somewhat warmer tone, and the chord in this and in the next bar should be played *legato* with sustaining pedal, not *staccato* as marked. From here a considerable *crescendo* should be made to bar 13, the chord of which should be played with maximum expression. The ensuing quaver passage should be played freely, with the pedal depressed and released for each note from bar 14 on, and with a marked *crescendo* and *diminuendo* within this bar. The crotchets of bar 15 should be played *portamento* and *crescendo*, the minim G sharp of bar 16 being given a *fermata* and the arpeggioed chord played softly and with *una corda* pedal. The coda should be begun quietly, the octaves in the bass gradually gaining in tone until once more a great climax is built up. For the octaves of bars 27–29 (counting from the *Lento*) a slight *accelerando* should lead to an *allargando* on the last three octaves in each of these bars, the most marked *allargando* and fullest tone being reserved for bar 29. In the second half of bars 27–29 the two groups of six semiquavers in the right hand should be played, not as such, but as a tremolo and as near to two groups of twelve demisemiquavers as possible (semiquaver movement at this juncture sounds thin and feeble). For the playing of the last chord see p. 39 above.

CONCLUSION

In the earlier chapters we have been dealing with either the general orientation of the works discussed, or with details of interpretation traditionally handed down. Taking interpretation now in its broadest aspect, it is the pianist's prime obligation to sink himself wholly into the spirit and meaning of the music he is attempting to reproduce, to make himself a mere instrument for the proper expression of the composer's intention. This presupposes more humility and sincerity than many performers possess, but it is this very virtue which distinguishes the artist from the showman. Having first submitted his own individuality to that of the composer, amid the gradual working out of the details of interpretation his personal outlook will gradually assert itself, so that the music will ultimately be produced in terms of his particular emotional and intellectual background.

This, however, cannot be achieved where the pianist is accustomed to mass-produce works for inclusion in his repertoire. Some pianists are content to regard a work as finished when its technical difficulties have been overcome, when it can be reproduced without a fault as far as notes and accuracy of finger work are concerned. But it is only here that the real work of interpretation begins, the work of planning the different variations of speed, the balance of the parts, the minute details of phrasing, dynamics and pedalling, so that after careful experiment with various methods of procedure the most appropriate method is selected. In this respect the work of interpretation resembles the minute work of some Chinese craftsman who will labour over the smallest detail with infinite patience and love, knowing that the more perfect his creation the more easily will it reveal the slightest blemish, just as the polished mirror reveals every speck of dust. It is the artist's high mission to make the moment imperishable, however perishable the means.

APPENDIX A
MUSICAL EXAMPLES PER CHAPTER

CHAPTER 1: TECHNICAL EXERCISES

Ex. 1:   Scales in thirds, p. 8

Ex. 2a: Scales – right hand, major keys, pp. 8-9

Ex. 2b: Scales – right hand, minor keys, p. 9

Ex. 3a: Scales – left hand, major keys, p. 9

Ex. 3b: Scales – left hand, minor keys, p. 10

Ex. 4:   Right hand, alternative fingering, p. 10

Ex. 5:   Topmost third, right hand, left hand, p. 10

Ex.6a: Right hand thumb-stretching exercise, p. 11

Ex.6b: Left hand thumb-stretching exercise, p. 12

Ex. 7:   Finger-stretching exercise, p. 12

Ex. 8:   Octave playing, p. 14

Ex. 9:   Skipping in two octaves, p. 14

Ex. 10a: Chromatic variant 1, p. 14

Ex. 10b: Chromatic variant 2, p. 14

Ex. 11:   Moeran *Toccata*, bars 36–38, p. 15

Ex. 12:   Schumann *Toccata*, Op. 7, bars 116–132, p. 15

Ex. 13:   Rhythmical variant, p. 16

Ex. 14:   Liszt *Hungarian Rhapsody No. 2*, bars 219–220, p. 16

Ex. 15:   Liszt *Grandes études de Paganini, No. 5* in E, bars 70–71, p. 17

Ex. 16:   Weber *Konzertstück* in F minor, Op. 79, bars 260–261, p. 17

Ex. 17:   Trills, p. 18

Ex. 18:   Two-hand trills, p. 18

Ex. 19:   Trills in thirds, p. 18

CHAPTER 2: TONE AND TOUCH

Ex. 20:   Liszt *Isoldens Liebestod* from Wagner's *Tristan und Isolde*, bars 1–2, p. 19

CHAPTER 3: PRACTICE

Ex. 21:   Chopin *Trois nouvelles études*, Op. posth., No. 2, bar 1, p. 24

Ex. 22:   Chopin *Trois nouvelles études*, Op. posth., No. 2, bar 1, coordination of hands, p. 24

Ex. 23:   Chopin *Études*, No. 14 in F minor, Op. 25, No. 2, bar 1, p. 25

Ex. 24a: Scriabin *Five Preludes*, No. 2, Op. 16, bars 1–2, p. 25

Ex. 24b: Scriabin *Five Preludes*, No. 2, Op. 16, bars 1–2, coordination of hands, p. 25

Ex. 25:   Liszt *Five-finger exercise*, adapted from Clementi's *Gradus ad Parnassum*, p. 29

CHAPTER 9: DYNAMICS

CHAPTER 10: RUBATO

248

CHAPTER 13: TEXTUAL ACCURACY

CHAPTER 14: BACKGROUND INFORMATION

CHAPTER 15: ORNAMENTS

251

CHAPTER 16: CHALLENGE TO TRADITION

CHAPTER 17: BEETHOVEN

CHAPTER 18: SCHUMANN

CHAPTER 19: CHOPIN

CHAPTER 20: LISZT

APPENDIX B
MUSICAL EXAMPLES PER COMPOSER

Technical Exercises

LITERATURE CITED

Music editions cited

Beethoven Piano Sonatas, Ed. Giuseppe Buonamici (London 1903, Augener)

Sämtliche Klaviersonaten von Ludwig van Beethoven, Ed. Frederic Lamond, (Leipzig 1918)

Klaviersonaten von Ludwig van Beethoven, Ed. Sigmund Lebert (Stuttgart n. d.)

Chopin, *Complete Works*, Ed. Ignace Jan Paderewski (Warsaw 1949)

Chopin, *Oeuvres Complètes*, 6 Vols., Ed. Charles Klindworth (Moscow 1873-6)

Chopin *Nocturnes*, Imperial Edition, Ed. Louis Arensky (Melbourne 1924)

Chopin *Préludes*, Associated Board Edition, Ed. Donald F. Tovey (London 1924)

The Oxford Original Edition of Frédéric Chopin, Ed. Édouard Ganche (London 1932)

Mozart Sonatas, Associated Board of the Royal Schools of Music Edition (London n. d.)

Literature cited

Abraham, Gerard, *Chopin's Musical Style* (London 1939)

Ashton Jonson, George Charles, *A Handbook to Chopin's Works* (London 1905; revised edition 1908)

Barra, Séamas de, *Aloys Fleischmann* (Dublin 2006)

Boissier, Auguste, *Franz Liszt als Lehrer* (Vienna 1930)

Cohen, Harriet, *Music's Handmaid* (London 1936)

Cortot, Alfred, *Studies in Musical Interpretation,* Collected and edited by Jeanne Thieffry, translated by Robert Jacques (London 1937).

Cunningham, Joseph P., Fleischmann, Ruth, Barra, Séamas de, *Aloys Fleischmann (1880-1964): Immigrant Musicians in Ireland* (Cork 2010)

Dannreuther, Edward, *Musical Ornamentation* (London 1923)

Dunn, J. P., *Ornamentation in Chopin's Music* (London 1921)

Emery, Walter, 'An Introduction to the Textual History of Bach's *Clavierübung*, Part II', *The Musical Times (*May and June 1951)

Emery, Walter, 'New Methods in Bach-Editing', *The Musical Times* (August 1950)

Fay, Amy, *Music-Study in Germany* (Chicago 1880)

Fleischmann, Aloys, Ed., *Music in Ireland: A Symposium* (Cork and Oxford 1952)

Fleischmann, Tilly, 'Some Reminiscences of Arnold Bax', *British Music Society Newsletter* No. 86 (2000)

Focht, Josef, 'München leuchtete – Das Münchner Musikleben der Prinzregentenzeit', Ursula K. Nauderer, Ed., *Aloys Georg Fleischmann: Von Bayern nach Irland – Ein Musikerleben zwischen Inspiration und Sehnsucht*, Catalogue for the Fleischmann exhibition, District Museum, Dachau 2010, pp. 9-22

Friedheim, Arthur, 'Life and Liszt', *Remembering Franz Liszt* (New York 1987)

Göllerich, August, *Beethoven* (Berlin 1903)

Hilmes, Oliver *Franz Liszt: Biographie eines Superstars* (Munich 2011)

Hummel, Johann Nepomuk, *Ausführliche theoretisch-practische Anweisung zum Piano-forte-Spiel* (Vienna 1828); *A Complete Theoretical and Practical Course of Instruction on the Art of Playing the Pianoforte* (London 1828)

Huneker, James, *Chopin the Man and His Music* (New York 1900; London 1903 / 1921)

Kapp, Julius, *Franz Liszt* (Berlin 1909; 2nd revised ed. 1911)

Kellermann, Berthold, *Erinnerungen: Ein Künstlerleben*, Eds. Sebastian Hausmann and Hellmut Kellermann (Zürich and Leipzig 1932)

Kleczynski, Jan, *Chopin's Greater Works*, Translated by Natalie Janotha (London 1896)

Köhler, Louis, *Theorie der musikalischen Verzierungen* (Leipzig 1887)

Lamond, Frederic, *The Memoirs of Frederic Lamond* (Glasgow 1949)

Leimer, Karl, *Modernes Klavierspiel nach Leimer-Gieseking* (Mainz 1931)

Lenz, Wilhelm von, *Berliner Musik-Zeitung Echo*, Vol. XXVI (Berlin 1876)

Liszt, Franz, *Aus den Annalen des Fortschritts*, Ed. Lina Ramann (Leipzig 1882)

Liszt, Franz, *Friedrich Chopin, Gesammelte Schriften* Vol. 1 (Leipzig 1896)

Lowery, Harry, 'On Reading Music', *The Dioptric Review and The British Journal of Physiological Optics, New Series,* Vol. 1, No. 2 (July 1940)

Mackworth, Cecily, Ed., *A Mirror for French Poetry 1840-1940: French poems with translations by English poets* (London 1947)

Mickiewicz, Adam, *Poems,* Ed. G.R. Noyes (New York 1944)

Mickiewicz, Adam, *Gems of Polish Poetry – Selections from Mickievicz,* Translated by Frank H. Fortey (Warsaw 1923)

Nauderer, Ursula K., 'Die Dachauer Weihnachtsspiele 1903-1906 und ihr Schöpfer Alois Georg Fleischmann', *Auf Weihnachten zu: Altdachauer Weihnachtszeit*, District Museum Dachau 2003, pp. 69-86

Newman, Ernest, 'Are Autographs Authoritative?', *The Sunday Time,* (23 June 1946)

Niecks, Frederick, *Frederick Chopin as a Man and as Musician* (2nd edition, London, 1890; the 3rd edition of 1902 rpt. 1921 is the edition quoted)

Niecks, Frederick, *Robert Schumann* (London 1925)

Pachmann, Vladimir de, 'My New Method of Piano-Playing', *The Music Lovers' Portfolio,* Ed. Landon Ronald, Vol. IV (London 1922)

Paderewski, Ignace Jan and Lawton, Mary, Eds., *The Paderewski Memoirs* (London 1938)

O'Brien, Grace, *The Golden Age of Italian Music* (London 1950)

O'Brien, Grace, *The Golden Age of German Music and its Origins* (London 1953)

Ramann, Lina, *Franz Liszt als Künstler und Mensch*, Vol. 2 Section 7 (Leipzig 1894)

Rehberg, Paul, *Liszt: Die Geschichte seines Lebens, Schaffens und Wirkens* (Zürich 1961)

Sand, George, *Histoire de ma vie* (Paris 1855)

Sauer, Emil, *Meine Welt: Bilder aus dem Geheimfache meiner Kunst und meines Lebens* (Stuttgart 1901)

Schindler, Anton, *Biographie von Ludwig van Beethoven* (Münster 1840)

Schumann, Robert, *Essays and Criticisms: Music and Musicians,* First series, Translated, edited, annotated by Fanny Raymond Ritter (London 1876)

Siloti, Alexander, 'Meine Erinnerungen an Franz Liszt', *Zeitschrift für der Internationalen Musikgesellschaft* 12, (1912/1913)

Stockhammer, Robert, *Franz Liszt: Im Triumphzug durch Europa* (Vienna 1986)

Strub-Ronayne, Elgin 'Bernhard Stavenhagen: Pianist, Dirigent, Komponist und letzter Schüler von Franz Liszt', *Das Orchester*, No. 3 (1987)

Strub-Ronayne, Elgin, *Skizze einer Künstlerfamilie in Weimar* (London 1999)

Ugolino da Monte Giorgio (attrib.), *Fioretti di San Francesco d'Assisi,* early fourteenth century

Wagner, Richard, 'Über das Dirigieren', *Gesammelte Schriften und Dichtungen,* Vol. 7, (Leipzig 1898)

Walker, Alan, *Franz Liszt, The Final Years 1861-1886* (London 1997)

Wegeler, Franz Gerhard und Ries, Ferdinand, *Biographische Notizen über Ludwig van Beethoven* (Koblenz 1838)

Weingartner, Felix, *Lebenserinnerungen* (Zürich 1929)

TILLY FLEISCHMANN 1882-1967
PIANIST, ORGANIST, TEACHER

Personal:

02.04.1882	Born in Cork to Hans Conrad Swertz and Walburga Rössler as second of nine children
13.09.1905	Marriage in Dachau to Aloys Fleischmann
07 1906	Return to Cork with her husband
13.04.1910	Birth in Munich of their only child, Aloys
1916-1920	Husband interned as civilian prisoner of war
04.06.1941	Marriage of son to Anne Madden
1942-1952	Births of five grandchildren
03.01.1964	Death of husband after two years in a hospice
17.10.1967	Death

Education:

1887-1899	Schooling in St Angela's Ursuline College Cork
1889-1901	Tuition in organ from Hans Conrad Swertz (Cathedral organist)
1889-1901	Tuition in piano Cork Municipal School of Music
1901-1905	Royal Academy of Music in Munich: Piano (Stavenhagen, Kellermann) and organ studies (Becht)
June 1905	Graduation with 1st honours in both subjects

Professional work:

1905-1906	Private piano teacher in Munich and Dachau
1906-1919	Private piano teacher in Cork
1916-1920	Acting organist and choir director at Cathedral of St Mary and St Anne, Cork
1919-1937	Professor of piano at the Cork Municipal School of Music
1937-1967	Tilly Fleischmann School of Piano Playing

Professional activities:

1903-1905	Organ and piano performances at Academy concerts in Munich
1904-1905	Performances in Dachau with her husband
1906-1950	Recitals in Cork and Dublin
1927-1947	Broadcasts
1958	Radio talk: Interpretation and Tradition

Publications

'Liszt's Ancestry', *Liszt Society Newsletter* Sep. 1967, London

'Liszt and Stavenhagen in London 1886', *Liszt Society Newsletter,* Sep. 1967 *London*

'Album d'un voyageur and Années de pèlerinage' *Liszt Society Newsletter,* Sep. 1967 London

Aspects of the Liszt Tradition ed. Michael O'Neill, Cork 1986; re-published by: Roberton Publications, Aylesbury and Theodore Presser Co. Pennsylvania 1991

Some Reminiscences of Arnold Bax, The British Music Society Newsletter 86, editor Rob Barnett June 2000, thereafter placed on the Bax website by Richard Adams, on the Fleischmann website by Cork City Libraries in 2010

http://www.corkcitylibraries.ie/music/aloysfleischmann/aloysfleischmann-thelife/familyandfriends/arnoldbax/somereminiscencesoftillyfleischmann/

Recordings

4 LPs recorded in the BBC studios, privately distributed

Unpublished writings

Diary: Munich September 1901–March 1902

The Story of Aloys Fleischmann's Gravestone (31 Dec 1965), distributed to friends

Anecdotes (mid 1960s)

LITERATURE ON TILLY FLEISCHMANN

Cork Examiner, 'In Grateful Appreciation', May 1963: Gerald Y. Goldberg's Lunchtime Concerts in the Crawford School of Art to be dedicated to Aloys and Tilly Fleischmann

Cork Examiner, Obituary 18 Oct. 1967

Neeson, Geraldine, 'Meeting the Fleischmanns' *Cork Examiner* 29 March 1977

Acton, Charles, review of *Aspects of the Liszt Tradition* by Tilly Fleischmann, *Irish Times* 8° August 1986

Strub-Ronayne, Elgin, Review of *Aspects of the Liszt Tradition* by Tilly Fleischmann, *Piano Journal of the European Piano Teachers Association*, (EPTA) Vol. 8 No. 22 Feb 1987

O'Dea, Jane W., 'Turning the Soul: A personal memoir of a great piano teacher', *The Spirit of Teaching Excellence*, ed. David Jones, Calgary, Alberta 1995

O'Dea, Jane W., *Virtue or Virtuosity? Explorations in the Ethics of Musical Performance*, Westport CT/London 2000 (See Chapter 2: 'Turning the Soul towards Excellence')

Neeson, Geraldine, *In My Mind's Eye*, Dublin 2001 pp. 54-8

de Barra, Séamas, 'Bax, the Fleischmanns and Cork', *Journal of Music in Ireland*, June 2005

Cunningham, Joseph and Fleischmann, Ruth, 'Dachau und Cork: Drei Musiker-generationen verbinden beide Städte', *Amperland*, Heft 41, Dachau 2005

Zuk, Patrick, 'Tilly Fleischmann's *Tradition and Craft in Piano Playing*', Paper given at the Royal Musical Association Conference, April 2005

de Barra, Séamas, *Aloys Fleischmann*, Field Day Publications, Dublin 2006

Cunningham, Joseph P., Fleischmann, Ruth, de Barra, Séamas, *Aloys Fleischmann (1880-1964) Immigrant Musician in Ireland*, Cork University Press 2010

Nauderer, Ursula Katharina, Ed., *Aloys Georg Fleischmann: Von Bayern nach Irland – Ein Musikerleben zwischen Inspiration und Sehnsucht*, Exhibition Catalogue, Bezirksmuseum Dachau 2010

Zuk, Patrick, 'Tilly Fleischmann', *The Fleischmanns – A Remarkable Cork Family: A Companion to the Fleischmann Centenary Celebration*, Cork Public Libraries 2010

Motherway, Nicholas, 'Tilly Fleischmann – Renowned Cork Musician and Teacher', *Africa – St Patrick's Missions*, Kiltegan, July 2011

de Barra, Séamas, 'Tilly Fleischmann', *The Encyclopaedia of Music in Ireland*, Gen. Eds. Harry White, Barra Boydell, Dublin 2013

Pernpeintner, Andreas, *Aloys Georg Fleischmann (1880-1964) Musikalische Mikrogeschichte zwischen Deutschland und Irland*, Tutzing 2014

Internet articles:

Fleischmann website, hosted by Cork City Libraries:
http://www.corkcitylibraries.ie/music/aloysfleischmann/

http://en.wikipedia.org/wiki/Tilly_Fleischmann

Fleischmann, Ruth, 'Tilly Fleischmann', 2010:
http://www.corkcitylibraries.ie/music/aloysfleischmann/aloysfleischmann-thelife/familyandfriends/tillyfleischmann/

Pernpeintner, Andreas, 'Tilly Fleischmann', *Bavarian Musicians Lexicon Online*, 2010:
http://www.bmlo.lmu.de/s2941/A1#S7

Fleischmann, Ruth, 'Continental Cathedral Musicians in Cork', 2008:
http://www.corkcathedral.ie/Choir/HansConradSwertz.html

Fleischmann, Ruth, 'Hans Conrad Swertz', 2010:
http://www.corkcitylibraries.ie/music/aloysfleischmann/aloysfleischmann-thelife/familyandfriends/hansconradswertz

BIOGRAPHICAL NOTES

Dr Ruth Fleischmann

Ruth Fleischmann is Tilly Fleischmann's eldest grandchild. She was born in Cork in 1942, graduated from University College Cork in 1963 and, having won a Travelling Studentship from the National University of Ireland, continued her studies at the University of Tübingen, Germany. In 1968 she began to teach English at third level. From 1981 until her retirement in 2007 she held a lectureship in the English Department of the University of Bielefeld in Germany; during her last years there she was Dean of Studies of her faculty. Her field of research is Irish Studies. She has produced about 40 articles and eight books.

Dr John Buckley

Born in Templeglantine, Co. Limerick in 1951, John Buckley is a composer and lecturer. His catalogue of compositions extends to over 100 works, which have been performed and broadcast in more than fifty countries worldwide. In 1984 he was elected a member of Aosdána, Ireland's state sponsored academy of creative artists. He has been awarded both a PhD and a DMus by the National University of Ireland and is on the staff of St Patrick's College, Drumcondra, Dublin, a college of Dublin City University. A monograph on his work *Constellations: The Life and Music of John Buckley* by Benjamin Dwyer was published in May 2011 by Carysfort Press.

Dr Patrick Zuk

Dr Zuk is an Irish composer and pianist; he lectures in the Music Department of Durham University. He has published extensively on Irish and on Russian music and has received major funding for research in both fields. In 2010 he organised an International Conference on Irish music; in 2011 one on music in Russia and the Soviet Union. He edits, with Séamas de Barra, a series of monographs on Irish composers issued by Field Day Publications in conjunction with the Keough-Naughton Institute for Irish Studies, University of Notre Dame. In 2011 he received a Durham University Excellence in Teaching Awards.

Dr Gabriela Mayer

Dr Mayer is Head of the Keyboard Studies Department at the CIT Cork School of Music. Her early training was in her native Romania, Italy and the USA, where she won numerous awards and scholarships. As a recipient of a Fulbright Graduate Fellowship, she studied at the Hochschule für Musik 'Hanns Eisler' in Berlin. She completed a doctorate in Musical Arts at the University of Maryland, USA, graduating with highest honours. Her dissertation was entitled: 'Rhetoric, Drama and Singing in Solo Piano Music from Mozart to Liszt.' Since moving to Ireland, she has engaged in teaching, performing, and giving presentations at conferences on pedagogical and performance topics. She is involved in the Association of European Conservatoires (AEC) and European Piano Teachers Association (EPTA) and an international representative of the AEC on institutional review panels.

INDEX